IAIN D CAMPBELL

D1471470

On the first day
of the week

God, the Christian and the Sabbath

DayOne

© Day One Publications 2005
First printed 2005

ISBN 1-903087-95-3

ISBN 1 903087 95 3

Published by Day One Publications
Ryelands Road, Leominster, HR6 8NZ
☎ 01568 613 740 FAX 01568 611 473
email—sales@dayone.co.uk
web site—www.dayone.co.uk
North American—e-mail—sales@dayonebookstore.com
North American—web site—www.dayonebookstore.com

Designed by Steve Devane and printed by Gutenberg Press, Malta

Dedication

Dedicated to the memory of
John Macdonald (1924–2003)
Ivor Mackay (1922–2004)
Kenneth Stewart (1923–2004)
of Upper Coll, Isle of Lewis,
friends of the Lord, of his Day, and of one another.

Contents

Acknowledgements

I would like to thank John G. Roberts and Jim Holmes of Day One Publications for the initial invitation to write this book, and for guiding the book through the editorial process. Their support and enthusiasm for the project has been invaluable.

So, too, has the support of Professors Joel Beeke of Puritan Reformed Theological Seminary, Grand Rapids, Michigan, and O. Palmer Robertson of Africa Bible College, Uganda. Their contributions and endorsements are both humbling and uplifting.

I have lived and worked all my life within a matrix of church and community life which has had a high view of the Lord's Day. I ought, therefore, to acknowledge here my debt to the Free Church of Scotland, whose fellowship, ministry and people helped open my eyes to the blessings of 'a Sabbath well kept', and whose rich theological tradition helped to shape my conviction that the Lord's Day is indeed the Christian Sabbath, given for the good of the church and the world.

For that reason I have dedicated the book to the memory of three office-bearers from my congregation of Back Free Church who passed away within months of one another, and whose lives were fragrant with love to the Lord and his Day. They have entered into their eternal Sabbath rest.

Finally, my wife and family, as always, provide me with the emotional stability and encouragement needed for all my work. They are God's great gift to me, and I thank them for always being there.

May this book educate and encourage the church, and stimulate our society to the blessings of the God who governs our time, so that we might all come at last into the eternal Sabbath rest.

Iain D. Campbell
August 2005

Foreword

On the first day of the week is a courageous book on a difficult subject. Dr Iain D. Campbell makes a good case for using the entire Bible to understand the doctrine of the Sabbath. He says 'the Sabbath principle is as much an element of New Testament religion as of Old Testament worship, and that the change of day from the last to the first day of the week does not change our obligation to the fourth commandment.' His conclusions are based on solid exegesis. Behind his exegesis is a wealth of pastoral experience and godly practice. The author not only loves the doctrine of the Sabbath but obviously loves remembering the Sabbath and keeping it holy.

The book is well organized. It commences with God as the author of Sabbath, then uses a progressive redemptive approach (Moses, the prophets, Jesus, and the apostles), followed by an historical overview that focuses on the Puritans. All of that leads to how we should apply the Sabbath principle today and how that principle will culminate perfectly in heaven.

The chapter on the twenty-first century Christian's relation to the Sabbath is alone worth the price of the book. It steers clearly between legalism and laxity so that we don't grieve the Spirit by our disrespect for God and his Sabbath or become frustrated by unbiblical restrictions. Some people will not agree with every detail of this chapter, but Campbell does a masterful job of avoiding the contemporary pitfalls of the doctrine of the Sabbath, without avoiding the issues.

The concluding chapter on the relation of heaven and Sabbath deserves special mention. What a fitting, unifying, spiritually enriching conclusion to a potentially controversial issue! As I read this chapter, I found myself longing for the eternal Sabbath even as I felt a deeper appreciation for the present-day Sabbath.

Dr Campbell's book is a joy to read. It is well written and easy to understand. Its chapter introductions are attention grabbers, yet the book is packed with substance. It is suitable for both the young and the mature Christian. Readers will find in this book theological and practical direction for Sabbath-keeping in our contemporary world. Whatever is one's view of the Sabbath, this book deserves a careful reading. Use your Sunday afternoons to read it and pass it on to your friends.

I pray that God will use this book to restore Christians to a lost heritage of Sabbath observance and obedience to biblical standards. May God's pleasure, not our fleshly desires, reign in our Sabbath-keeping (Isaiah 58:13–14). Only when the Christian church reclaims the joy of Sabbath observance will her mind be renewed and her adherence to this world be broken.

Joel R. Beeke
Puritan Reformed Theological Seminary
Grand Rapids, Michigan

Appreciation

J ust as the person who respects God's law will get more out of life, so the person who digests Iain D. Campbell's work on the Sabbath will get more than just an excellent, exegetically based treatment of the Lord's Day. This book provides a comprehensive understanding of the relevance of the Sabbath. But it offers far more. If you are wrestling with the question of how the Christian should relate to the civil and ceremonial laws of the Old Testament, you can find a solid answer here. If you want guidance concerning the way to interpret Israel's prophets for today, begin here.

Yet the author continually shows his ability to communicate effectively to a popular audience. He alludes to the problem of playing football without rules, to abbreviated 'text messages' on cellular phones, and to young people's coded wrist bands—all designed to introduce the reader to the more significant subject of the Sabbath.

Campbell carefully explores the significance of the Sabbath from creation to consummation, from Eden to Heaven. The Sabbath at creation is 'full of grace and truth.' As one of the Ten Commandments, it stands apart from Israel's other laws. Jesus set the example by worshipping on the Sabbath day 'as was his custom' (Luke 4:16). He also lived by its positive implications, since he was known as 'the carpenter' and not merely as 'the carpenter's son' (*cf.* Mark 6:3).

Campbell provides a good service to the Church by interacting with false views of the Sabbath. This Day was never meant exclusively for Israelites, and so it cannot be argued that it was repealed when the new covenant emphasized the availability of the gospel to all nations.

This book offers the basis for an enriched lifestyle for the twenty-first century Christian. It calls for a new respect for the blessings that come from God's holy day.

O. Palmer Robertson
Vice Chancellor, African Bible College of Uganda

Introduction: the Christian Sabbath

I gave them my Sabbaths, as a sign between me and them, that they might know that I am the LORD who sanctifies them. Ezekiel 20:12

An interesting thing happened to me as I was preparing this book for publication. I wrote the manuscript on my laptop computer, saving it to my hard drive every so often. Every computer user knows, however, that saving a manuscript to the hard disk is no guarantee against loss; it is always wise policy to back up your file to another disk, so periodically I would save the manuscript on to a floppy disk too.

Of course, in my case, the manuscript, which kept the name 'Sabbath' for a while, grew and grew. So I was actually replacing the file on my floppy disk with the lengthening file on my hard drive. Just in case you are saving something by mistake, the computer will ask you whether you are sure of what you are doing. So every time I wanted to save the new file to my floppy disk, the message on the computer would read:

DO YOU WANT TO REPLACE THE EXISTING 'SABBATH'?

Computers, of course, ask very logical and very sensible questions. In this case, what was being asked was, 'Do you want to replace the file already on the floppy disk entitled "Sabbath" with the new file entitled "Sabbath"'? But when I read it first—*Do you want to replace the existing Sabbath?*—I thought, 'Isn't that the nub of the issue?'

What I mean is simply this. Not all that long ago, evangelical Christians in the United Kingdom were probably united in the view that the fourth commandment, which required of Israel that a Sabbath day be observed on a weekly basis, is still binding. The argument was that its requirement was as applicable to the Lord's Day, the first day of the week, in the New Testament era, as the commandment was to the seventh day of the week in the Old. Society reflected that view, and the first day of the week was generally observed in society as a day of rest and worship.

Consider the words of historian Tom Smout as he describes the Scottish Victorian Sabbath:

A universal stillness fell over Glasgow and Edinburgh (except in the unredeemed slums) at the time of divine service and pervaded small towns and villages from dawn to dusk … on Sundays the churches held the country in thrall for Christ.[1]

But the turn of the twentieth century brought a discernible change. Half a century later things were very different. Not only had the existing Sabbath been replaced by a secular one, but the churches themselves had acquiesced in the change. Sabbath observance was not the burning issue it had once been. As early as 1940, according to Smout,

even in the remotest and sternest corners things had changed somewhat. Thus a visitor to Lewis in the Second World war found an army hut used by the island youth for monthly dances.[2]

I find Smout's reference to the Isle of Lewis interesting. It is the island of my childhood and youth, and now it is the island where I have been called to preach the gospel. Even now, on the cusp of the twenty-first century, there is still a remarkable degree of social sabbatarianism, but nonetheless a marked change has been taking place. In the course of my lifetime, the Sabbath that existed a generation ago, in which there was little travel on the Lord's Day, and no shops open, has been replaced with a Sabbath entirely different. It is now possible to buy groceries and petrol on the Lord's Day, and to leave from and arrive at our island as commercial aircraft operate routes in and out of Stornoway each Sunday.

There are some people, of course, who want to replace the existing Sabbath, for various motives of financial, personal, or social gain. To witness such a social change in the way of life of a small community is one thing. But the interesting thing is the mixed reaction of the churches to all of this. Some denominations were vociferous in their opposition to the secularization of the Lord's Day on Lewis. Others were not.

And that reaction is typical of modern evangelicalism. Even within the evangelical world, there is a wish to replace the old Sabbath with something different. It is argued on exegetical grounds that the church was wrong to regard the Lord's Day as the New Testament equivalent of the Old Testament Sabbath; indeed, it was wrong to argue for the abiding validity of any of the Old Testament legislation.

This position was adopted in an important symposium on the issue of the Sabbath, which appeared in 1982. In it, New Testament scholar A.T. Lincoln stated that 'It cannot be argued that the New Testament itself provides warrant for the belief that since the resurrection God appointed the first day to be observed as the Sabbath'.[3] Much the same position was adopted by the prominent evangelical pastor-scholar, James Montgomery Boice, in his influential and helpful book, *Foundations of the Christian Faith*:

[Exodus 31:12–17] portray the sabbath as a covenant sign between God and Israel ... It is hard to see, therefore, how the observance of the sabbath can legitimately be said to be applied to other nations ... Sunday is another day established by God, but for the church rather than for Israel and with quite different characteristics.[4]

One result of this is that many Christians see nothing wrong with working or taking part in other activities on the Lord's Day. Can we say that one position is right and the other wrong? Ought we to make this kind of judgement at all? Are we not counselled by Paul to judge no one in respect of a Sabbath day (Colossians 2:16)? Is it not time that we replaced the old Sabbath with the new realization that Sabbath laws are part of the old covenant which is now abolished in Christ?

This book has been written with the conviction that the Puritans did, in fact, have it right: that there are good Scriptural grounds for believing that the Lord's Day is the Christian Sabbath, and that the fourth commandment applies still. Like much else in the Old Testament, the essence remains, while the structure changes. It was neither to the benefit of the church nor of society that we replaced the old Sabbath with the modern free-for-all that has seen increasing pressures and demands on individual and family life.

But I am not going to argue that the traditional view was right simply because it was a *traditional* view: I am arguing that it was essentially right because it was a *scriptural* view. I hope that these short chapters will demonstrate that the principle of the Sabbath runs throughout the Bible from beginning to end, and that its loss has impoverished the church.

The confessional position of the Scottish church was reflected in the teachings of the Westminster Confession of Faith. According to that document, God has set apart one day in seven as a day of rest and worship. God, we are told, commands us to set apart one seventh of our week as a day in which we rest from our 'worldly employment and recreation', and spend time in private and public worship.

But the Confession of Faith goes further: it says that this commandment is 'positive, moral and perpetual'; which means at least three things. First, it means that observing a weekly holy day is not just a matter of not doing certain things, but engaging positively in the worship of God. Secondly, it is saying that keeping the Sabbath holy is a matter of morality, just as much as other moral principles. Thirdly, it is saying that the commandment is enduring, and not to be confined to the Old Testament age. We are taught here that the Sabbath principle is as much an element of New Testament religion as of Old Testament worship, and that the change of day from the last to the first day of the week does not change our obligation to the fourth commandment.

There is an increasing desire to move away from this theological position in today's church. Many who would claim to be Christians would argue that Sabbath-keeping is a feature of Old Testament religion, which is not required of us now. After all, while Jesus endorsed most of the Ten Commandments, he says nothing about observing a weekly New Testament Sabbath, and reserves some of his greatest criticisms for those who were failing to keep the Sabbath as it was meant to be kept. How does the Westminster Confession of Faith arrive at the position it adopts?

To answer that question will require us to look at various elements of the Bible's teaching: the fourth commandment itself, its origins in the story of the creation of the world, its outworking in the Old Testament, Jesus' teaching concerning Sabbath-keeping, the place of a special day of worship in the New Testament, and the church's traditional view of the place of the Sabbath in her life and worship. I hope we will discover at the end of our study that the Confession of Faith is right: God, in his wisdom, grace and kindness, has structured our week so that we will have space for him in our lives. When we give him that space, we will benefit physically and emotionally, but, above all, we will benefit spiritually.

Let's look at what the Bible tells us about the Sabbath, and about how we can apply the Bible's teaching to our lives. The paragraphs in the different typeface, such as the two at the end of this page, are 'meaty' quotations from theologians who have thought long and hard about the issues involved. I trust you will stop at them and think about them seriously.

Perhaps more than ever before, in this mad, rushing world of ours, we need to find a place of rest and of quiet. One of the blood-bought treasures of Calvary is a weekly holy-day, in which we may—and ought to—turn aside from other things to live before the face of God. How much we need to delight in God's provision, and rejoice in the good things of God's grace!

As it is of the law of nature, that, in general, a due proportion of time be set apart for the worship of God; so, in his word, by a positive, moral, and perpetual commandment, binding all men in all ages, he hath particularly appointed one day in seven for a sabbath, to be kept holy unto him; which, from the beginning of the world to the resurrection of Christ, was the last day of the week; and, from the resurrection of Christ, was changed into the first day of the week, which in Scripture is called the Lord's Day, and is to be continued to the end of the world, as the Christian Sabbath.

This sabbath is then kept holy unto the Lord, when men, after a due preparing of their hearts, and ordering of their common affairs beforehand, do not only observe an holy rest all the day from their own works, words and thoughts about their worldly employments and recreations; but also are taken up the whole time in the public and private exercises of his worship, and in the duties of necessity and mercy.

Westminster Confession of Faith, Chapter 21, Paragraphs 7–8

Notes

1. **T.C. Smout,** *A Century of the Scottish People 1830–1950* (London, Fontana Press, 1987), p. 183.
2. **Smout,** *Scottish People*, p. 184.
3. **A.T. Lincoln,** 'From Sabbath to Lord's Day: A Biblical and Theological Perspective', in **D.A. Carson** (ed.), *From Sabbath to Lord's Day: A Biblical, Historical and Theological Investigation,* (Grand Rapids: Zondervan, 1982), p.386.
4. **J.M. Boice,** *Foundations of the Christian Faith* (Downers Grove: IVP, 1986), p.235.

God and the Sabbath

God blessed the seventh day and made it holy, because on it God rested from all his work that he had done in creation. Genesis 2:3

You shall love the LORD your God with all your heart and with all your soul and with all your might. And these words that I command you today shall be on your heart. Deuteronomy 6:5–6

Like many other ministers, I live with my family in a house that does not belong to me. It is a house provided by my church—their house, my home. What goes on in our manse is typical of what goes on in any home populated by two parents and three teenage children, who leave their mark—often literally!—on every room in the house.

Except one. We have always found it necessary to keep at least one room free from the normal routines of family life, so that it can be pretty much dedicated to congregational and church business. So our lounge is rarely used by us in the normal course of the week. Its usage is generally dictated by church business. After church services, perhaps people will be there. Any special gatherings or discussion of business take place there. It is a special place, kept for special purposes.

At the same time, given the public nature of my work, and the public function of the house in which we live, we have found it necessary to designate other rooms as private and personal. When we moved in, we called a small room off the kitchen our 'family room'. That's private for us. Family business gets conducted there. Getting into it is sometimes a luxury, but times in it are precious. That, too, is a special place, kept for special times.

The focus of our study in this book is on special times and places which God gives to his people as they live and work in his world. I'm glad to have the Lord's Day as long as I'm living in the Lord's world. In someone else's house, I observe someone else's time.

Israel's worship of God in the Old Testament was very much focused on special places and special times. There was no place in which Israel was found which was not special: when God covenanted to Abraham that 'I will give to you and to your offspring after you the land of your sojournings, all the land of Canaan, for an everlasting possession and I will be their God' (Genesis 17:8), he was pronouncing the places of Israel's pilgrimage as special places.

Yet it was necessary for God to designate one particular locality as sacred and holy. When God gave Moses the regulations for the construction of the tabernacle in Exodus 25ff, the purpose was stated as follows: 'let them make me a sanctuary [literally, a 'holy place'], that I may dwell in their midst' (Exodus 25:8). God was with his people wherever they went, but in a unique way his presence was localized. The tabernacle was a special place, where special business was transacted between God and his people.

Similarly, while every moment of their pilgrimage was a special moment, God appointed special times for his family, in which they could give attention to things of particular importance and value. The Sabbath was one such time. So too were other feasts and festivals throughout the Jewish year. God's people, dedicated to him in holiness and called to please him at every moment, were given special places and special times for the benefit of their lives and their faith.

It is in that context that we begin our discussion of the Sabbath principle in the Old Testament. And at the outset I want to say that we need the whole Bible if we are to know God's will for our lives and for the way in which our lives ought to be patterned. The New Testament church lived by the Old Testament Scriptures, recognizing that with the coming of Jesus Christ, there were continuities and discontinuities from Old Testament to New, from Old Covenant to New.

Using the whole Bible

The reason we must begin with the Old Testament is simply that the story of God's salvation in the world does not begin with Jesus. It focuses on the historical Jesus, centres on him, and is nothing without him: but it does not begin with his historical appearance. In fact, Paul uses a magnificent phrase in Galatians 3:8 when he says that 'God preached the gospel *beforehand* to Abraham'. That means that when God spoke and made promises to Abraham, way back in the book of Genesis—he was actually proclaiming the gospel, the same gospel in which eternal life is now offered to us in Jesus Christ.

So we need to use the Old Testament, as well as the New, if we are to appreciate the wonder of God's grace in the lives of men and women. We need to go back to Genesis, to the creation of the world, with its explanation of how things came into being. There, we are told, God created a beautiful world—beautiful to live in, and beautiful to look at. And it took him six days to do it.

Days and Ordinances

Or did it? It has become standard practice now in discussion of the opening chapter of Genesis to point out that the word 'day' can mean a longer time-span than a twenty-four hour period. Indeed, in Genesis 2:4, it is used in the following statement:

These are the generations of the heavens and the earth when they were created, in the *day* that the LORD God made the earth and the heavens.

Without going into questions of style and literary form here, it is clear that Genesis 2:4 is using the word 'day' to refer to the whole period of the creation. So there may well be some merit in the argument that the days of creation were long periods of time; and some have used this to accommodate theories of evolution and development over many millions of years into the statements of Genesis 1.

But there are even stronger and more pressing reasons to believe that the days were—well—days! God did not just create a world; he did not just fill a space. He created time, too. Why should he not have created the world just in an instant? Everything brought into being in the twinkling of an eye—would that not have been possible for God? Of course it would; but instead, he imposed a chronological pattern by which the world would be regulated. Why do we not have eight-day weeks, with each day measuring twenty-five hours instead of twenty-four? Because the time patterns were established right at the outset.

This is brought out in at least two ways in Genesis 1. First there is the repeated formula, 'there was evening and there was morning ...' (1:5, 8, 13,

19, 23, 31). This is a standard way of referring to an ordinary day. While the word 'day' could refer to a long period of time, the words 'morning' and 'evening' can hardly be used in that way. Instead, we have language used here which both defines the duration of the day, and makes us realize that time is God's invention!

Secondly, there is the strong argument that the phrase 'the first day' (1:5), should actually be translated 'one day'.[1] Basing his reasoning on the use of numbers in the Hebrew Bible, Andrew Steinmann suggests that Genesis 1:5 is simply stating that 'evening + morning = one day … by a most unusual grammatical construction, Genesis 1 is defining what a day is'.[2] So the grammar changes as we go through the chapter, and we read that 'there was an evening and a morning, a second day', and a third, and a fourth, and so on.

The importance of this for our discussion is that what happens on the seventh of these days is foundational for our whole discussion of the Sabbath principle. The fourth commandment, as we shall see, is grounded in the fact that 'in six days the LORD made heaven and earth, the sea, and all that is in them, and rested the seventh day' (Exodus 20:11). The example of God becomes the basis for the commandment.

This is an extremely important point. If the Sabbath principle is merely part of the law of Moses, it could be argued that it is no longer binding. However, it is not grounded in the Mosaic law, but in the creation narrative. The Sabbath principle is of ancient origin—as old as creation itself. For this reason, too, it was not merely a gift to Israel—it is something binding on all of humankind, simply because it is part of the fabric of the world which we inhabit.

William J. Dumbrell draws our attention to the care with which the narrative of Genesis 2 is written. In particular, he highlights the importance attached to the number seven, not only as the day on which God rested, but also in the way in which the story is told with great care and subtlety. From Genesis 1:1–2:3, he says, the words 'create' and 'make' are both used seven times; in addition, he says:

Genesis 2:1–3 presents a pattern of seven lines rising to a crescendo in the first part of Genesis 2:3, with the second part of the verse emphasizing by way of conclusion the matter of Genesis 2:2, namely that God had ceased from his work. The seventh day is mentioned three times (Genesis 2:2, twice; 2:3), each time in a sequence of seven words. In this way, Genesis 2:2–3 combines the creation account of Genesis 1 with a sabbath in a seven-day scheme.[3]

The account of God's Sabbath-keeping, therefore, is of a piece with the whole narrative; this is the point to which it has been moving: the point of completion and consummation.

So what did God do on the seventh day of the creation week? Genesis 2:2–3 uses several words to describe God's activity—or lack of it—on this day. First, he did no more work; second, he rested; third, he blessed the day; fourth, he made it holy. The activity that had characterized the other six days was now over. Obviously the work of *providence*, by which God superintends and maintains his creation, was never suspended; but there was no new creative activity. God rested; but not because he was exhausted and needed to rest! He rested simply in the sense that on this day he was engaged in a different form of existence, which involved no new work.

Furthermore, precisely because of this, God highlighted the importance of this seventh day by *blessing* it and by making it *holy*. Both of these words are crucial in Scripture. We sometimes carelessly define the word 'blessed' as 'happy'; but how do you make a day happy? The meaning of the word 'blessed' can be determined from its opposite, which is 'cursed'. To be cursed by God is to be out of his favour, outside his friendship, and subject to his judgement. To be blessed, on the other hand, is to be in a special relationship with him, and to be the object of his unique favour. In this sense, God, who had invented time, placed the seventh day in a unique position relative to himself.

That, in turn, becomes the foundation for the next thing: God makes the day holy. Holy is what God himself is (Isaiah 6:3). Consequently, it is what everything that belongs to him is. In one sense, every day is holy, and all of creation is holy. But in another sense, in the sense that he demarcates the seventh day for himself, he makes it holy. As Bruce Waltke puts it, 'in the first six days space is subdued: on the seventh, time is sanctified'.[4]

From the very outset, therefore, God makes one day in seven to be different, to be unique. For whose benefit? For his own? Surely not! What need does God have to rest or to sanctify part of a perfect creation? No; his purpose is to establish a chronological pattern, to call the attention of man, whom he has already created, to the fact that in his world there are special places and special times for drawing close to God and for honouring him.

The older theologians used to talk about 'creation ordinances'. Before any laws were given or enacted, God ordained certain patterns for his world, which were to remain absolutely fundamental to man's needs and condition and situation in the world. Supposing no change had come on the world as a result of sin, these ordinances would have remained necessary for the good of the human race.

The first was the ordinance of *marriage*. The one thing that was not good, according to Genesis, in an otherwise good world, was man's loneliness. In all of animate creation, there was no being to whom man could relate in the way which his emotional, psychological and physiological constitution required. So God 'built' a wife for him (Genesis 2:22). In the New Testament, in teaching about divorce, Jesus takes his point of departure from the fact that God created man, with a differentiation of sexes, with the intention that the two should be one flesh (Matthew 19:4–5). That provision is normative for all mankind everywhere: 'the original ordering of the Creator presumes that one man shall be united to one woman'.5

A second 'ordinance' was that of *labour*. God gave Adam a specific commission to 'be fruitful, and multiply and fill the earth and subdue it and have dominion over the fish of the sea and over the birds of the heavens and over every living thing that moves on the earth' (Genesis 1:28). Adam was to act with responsibility over God's world, harnessing its resources and governing it, all for the glory of the Creator. As Donald Macleod memorably puts it: 'we remember with gladness that God put the first human pair into a garden, not into an academic institution, and that they were to express their divine image-bearing by digging and delving, by the great conjoint operations of conservation and improvement'.6

But is it right to talk about the *Sabbath* as a third 'ordinance'? Did God communicate to man the principle of Sabbath observance in the same way as the communication regarding marriage and labour was made to him? John Bunyan certainly had difficulty with this idea; he argues at one point that 'the seventh day sabbath … was not from paradise, nor from nature, nor from the fathers, but from the wilderness, and from Sinai'.[7] For Bunyan, therefore, the Sabbath law is grounded in Genesis 2, but was not enjoined on man until God gave the commandment to Moses.

But Richard Gaffin is still correct to argue that 'Genesis 2:2 is *prescriptive* as well as *descriptive*',[8] basing this on the usage of Hebrews 4:3–4. The writer to the Hebrews has no argument unless the Sabbath principle is ordained at creation, since it was precisely God's rest that showed man what the goal of created life was meant to be. By resting on the seventh day, God showed that he had made the world in general, and man in particular, to enjoy his blessing and share in his life. Creation was made with that specific purpose in mind. And as God gave man sacred space in Paradise, and sacred time in his weekly cycle, he gave him a constant reminder of what he had made him for.

Now, there is still, it has to be admitted, a recognition of the silence of Genesis on how the Sabbath principle was communicated to man. But, as John Murray puts it,

it is contrary to analogy and sound reason to suppose that Adam, if he had retained his integrity, would not have known the pivotal data of Genesis 1 and 2 … it is inconceivable that Adam would have been ignorant of the fact that in six days God made heaven and earth and on the seventh day rested.[9]

Adam knew what had taken place, and knew the pattern after which his life was to be lived. 'Creation ordinances' simply means that, even if the world had continued in integrity and righteousness, without sin or fall or corruption or death, it would have required three basic, fundamental things: it would have required marriage, work and the Sabbath in order to allow it to fulfil the Creator's objective.

In a recent book on *God's Pattern for Creation*, Robert Godfrey sets all of this in a covenant context. He reminds us that the days of creation 'are actual for us but figurative for God. They are not a timetable of God's actions but a model timetable for us to follow'.[10] And in giving this timetable, God, he suggests, is laying down principles that are at the heart of our bond with him. For this reason, 'Genesis 1 is the foundation of our covenantal relationship with God'.[11] It not only summarizes events which brought the world into being, but actually sets the scene for a world with which God wishes to enjoy a personal relationship.

Since that is the case, Dr Godfrey argues, the silence of Genesis regarding a specific command to keep Sabbath is not a problem: 'a covenantal reading of Genesis 1 shows us that a command is implicit in the description of the seventh day'.[12] The conclusion is unmistakable: 'the Sabbath is part of the created order and a perpetual obligation for humankind'.[13]

But ...

Clearly, however, the world is now not the good world that God made. Sin exists, not because of any flaw in creation, but because Adam and Eve deliberately and wilfully broke covenant with God. What the Bible says to us is devastatingly clear and simple: 'one trespass led to condemnation for all men' (Romans 5:18). What other explanation is there for the fact that is acknowledged by Christians and atheists alike: 'no-one's perfect'?

The beauty of the good news of God's salvation is that God did not leave mankind to perish and engage in self-destruction. The objective of creation—that man should enjoy God's blessing and enter into God's rest—still remained. The remainder of the Bible is all about God's gracious salvation. What man lost by his sin and rebellion, God has restored by his grace and mercy. Although the early chapters of Genesis tell us about various attempts to get back to God in a world that drifted further and further from him, they also tell us of God's salvation promise-plan, which was woven into the history of the world from the outset. The first sign that there was good news for a fallen world came in Genesis 3:15, where God promised an eventual deliverer and saviour. He said to the serpent, the devil, who had orchestrated man's fall into sin, 'I will put enmity between you and the woman, and between your offspring and her offspring; he shall bruise your head, and you shall bruise his heel.'

I doubt whether Adam and Eve (or even the devil himself!) realized the enormity of this promise. God was actually saying that the sin, condemnation, death and corruption that man had brought into God's good universe, would be dealt with and removed by himself. He would ensure that ultimately, from Eve's offspring, one would come to deliver man by destroying the devil. According to the New Testament, that is the only way for us to understand the meaning of Christ's appearance and death in the world: 'the reason the Son of God appeared was to destroy the works of the devil' (1 John 3:8). Hebrews 2:14–15 tells us that Jesus did this by his death on the cross:

Since therefore the children share in flesh and blood, he himself likewise partook of the same things, that through death he might destroy the one who has the power of death, that is, the devil, and deliver all those who through fear of death were subject to lifelong slavery.

That is not just good news—that is the best news that sinful man could possibly hear! And the Sabbath principle cannot be understood apart from that gracious move to redeem and recreate a world in which righteousness dwells (2 Peter 3:13).

So how did God prepare the world for this unique, wonderful, saving event in the coming and the dying of the Lord Jesus Christ? He did it by making promises to Abraham, by calling him to follow him, and by undertaking to have a people for himself, who would serve the Lord in a land which he would give them. These promises set a pattern and programme of salvation in motion, which saw God's saving grace worked out in the history of ancient Israel.

It is important for us to realize what God was doing through the Old Testament. He deliberately confined the story of his redemption to one favoured nation, to Israel:

… ask now of the days that are past, which were before you, since the day that God created man on the earth, and ask from one end of heaven to the other, whether such a great thing as this has ever happened or was ever heard of. Did any people ever hear the voice of a god speaking out of the midst of the fire, as you have heard, and still live? Or has any god ever attempted to go and take a nation for himself from the midst of another nation, by trials, by signs, by wonders, and by war, by a mighty hand and an outstretched arm, and by great deeds of terror, all of which the LORD your God did for you in Egypt before your eyes? To you it was shown, that you might know that the LORD is God; there is no other besides him ... (Deuteronomy 4:32–35)

These words were spoken by Moses, God's servant, to the people of Israel, as they were about to take possession of the promised land of Canaan. God had blessed the sons of Abraham, the descendants of Jacob, through all the circumstances that had befallen them; and eventually he had intervened to save them (to 'redeem' them) out of the land of Egypt, where they were held in slavery. That one act of redemptive salvation was to characterize the people of God throughout the Old Testament, and Moses is here telling Israel that no god ever did this for his followers.

The reason is not hard to find: the gods of the nations are idols of silver and gold, 'the work of human hands' (Psalm 115:4); whereas the God of Israel is the only living and true God. He intervened powerfully and supernaturally to free his people. Through Moses he preached the good news beforehand in a lost and fallen world!

The New Testament makes it clear that all that God did for Israel was by way of preparing the world for the coming of Jesus. But more than that: his great, redemptive acts were a picture of what Jesus himself was to do, not just for one nation, but also for all those who believe in him. When John sees the church in heaven, in the book of Revelation, he hears the saints of God singing 'the song of Moses, the servant of God, and the song of the Lamb' (Revelation 15:3), a song which picks up on the theme of Deuteronomy:

Great and amazing are your deeds, O Lord God the Almighty! Just and true are your ways, O King of the nations! Who will not fear, O Lord, and glorify your name? For you alone are holy. All nations will come and worship you, for your righteous acts have been revealed. (Revelation 15:3–4)

Indeed, it is interesting to go through the book of Revelation, and see these parallels between God's redeeming work in saving Israel out of Egypt, and his saving work in bringing his people safely to heaven. Let me just pick up on one theme. When God brought his people out of Egypt, saving them from destruction by commanding that a lamb (another parallel theme) be put to death in place of the families of his people (see Exodus 12:1–13), he led them across the Red Sea, and through the wilderness of Sinai, to a place where God would meet with them (and give them his commandments). There, at the holy mount of God, Moses commanded the people to make themselves holy, in preparation for a meeting with their Saviour God. This is what God said to Moses:

> You yourselves have seen what I did to the Egyptians, and how I bore you on eagles' wings and brought you to myself. Now therefore, if you will indeed obey my voice and keep my covenant, you shall be my treasured possession among all peoples, for all the earth is mine; and you shall be to me a kingdom of priests and a holy nation. (Exodus 19:4–6)

Now compare this with what John saw in the book of Revelation, particularly in chapters 4 and 5. He saw the scroll of God's sovereign purposes, and only one person in the whole universe fitted to unwrap the scroll: one who is described as 'the Lion of the tribe of Judah, the Root of David' (Revelation 5:5). But the Lion is a Lamb! Listen: 'I saw a Lamb standing, as though it had been slain ...' (Revelation 5:6). When the Lamb took the scroll, those who were around the throne burst into song:

> Worthy are you to take the scroll and to open its seals, for you were slain, and by your blood you ransomed people for God from every tribe and language and people and nation, and you have made them a kingdom and priests to our God and they shall reign on the earth. (Revelation 5:9–10)

Do you see what John is telling us? The saving work of God, originating in God's eternal plan, and proclaimed before the coming of Jesus Christ into the world, was revealed among the shadows of Old Testament history by the redemption of Israel out of Egypt. Just as the sons of Jacob were to be a kingdom of priests for God, consecrated to him by the death of the Passover lamb, so we, redeemed by the Lamb of God who takes away the sin of the world, are to be a kingdom and priests to God. Or, as Peter puts it, taking up the same Old Testament language, having been redeemed 'with the precious blood of Christ, like that of a lamb without blemish or spot'

(1 Peter 1:19), God has made us 'a chosen race, a royal priesthood, a holy nation, a people for his own possession, that you may proclaim the excellencies of him who called you out of darkness into his marvellous light' (1 Peter 2:9).

In other words, if we are to understand the meaning of the gospel, and the meaning of the lamb who redeemed us by dying in our place, the change that Christ makes in our lives, and the way to live the Christian life, we need the Old Testament as well as the New. The acts of God in the Old Testament, as well as the words of the prophets, shed light for us on the wonderful salvation that God has provided.

And this is relevant because ...

As I have said, it is impossible to consider the Bible's teaching on the Sabbath apart from God's original purpose in creation, and his subsequent purpose of redemption. So by the time we come to the giving of the fourth commandment, which we shall consider in the next chapter, the great act of redemption from Egypt has taken place. God now brings them to a point where he will give laws to his people. As we approach this part of Old Testament revelation, let's always bear in mind the connection between what is going on in the experience of the Israelites, and what God is going to do in Jesus Christ. That connection is brought out in Paul's description of the children of Israel, as he expresses his longing for them to come to trust in the Messiah:

They are Israelites, and to them belong the adoption, the glory, the covenants, the giving of the law, the worship, and the promises. To them belong the patriarchs, and from their race, according to the flesh, is the Christ, who is God over all, blessed for ever. Amen (Romans 9:4–5).

We need, therefore, to understand the Sabbath commandment in the context of the Old Testament law, and we cannot understand the law apart from God's saving work for the redemption of mankind. God redeemed his people from Egypt, brought them to Sinai, and gave them the commandments, one of which has to do explicitly with the Sabbath day.

So we have to ask: what was the function of these laws? Much has been written on this subject, and on the place of the law in Israel, and the extent to which the laws given to Israel are binding on Christians in the New Testament. But before we come to look at the place of the Sabbath commandment in the law, let's remind ourselves of several important points.

First, from the moment Adam and Eve were created, they were under obligation to serve and obey God. As Old Testament Professor O. Palmer Robertson puts it:

By the very act of creating man in his own likeness and image, God established a unique relationship between himself and creation. In addition to his sovereign creation-act, God spoke to man, thus determining precisely the role of man in creation.[14]

It is the combination of God's *action* and God's *speech* that defines what man is, and what his role in the world is. The very fact that God *created* Adam showed that Adam was dependent on God for his life, and that he required God's care of him every moment—'in him we live and move and have our being' (Acts 17:28). And the fact that God *spoke* to him showed the extraordinary care God took for man and for his welfare. In Genesis 1:28–30, we find God extending to Adam and Eve the bounty of the garden of Eden; and in Genesis 2:16–17, we find him intimating the special provision he had made for them: 'You shall surely eat of every tree of the garden, but of the tree of the knowledge of good and evil you shall not eat, for in the day that you eat of it you shall surely die'. By obeying God, Adam and Eve could continue in their fellowship with God, enjoying both him and the bounty of his gifts and provisions. Obedience would lead to life; but disobedience would lead to death.

In their innocence, Adam and Eve enjoyed pleasing God. They were not forced into obedience, but were willing to devote their whole lives to the purpose of honouring and serving their Creator. His gracious relationship to them was manifested, intimated and channelled through the word of law and covenant obligation.

Second, it was because of Adam's failure to obey God that he lost his innocence and became subject to guilt and death. When Adam and Eve were expelled from the paradise of the Garden of Eden, they could not blame God for treating them too harshly. What he was doing was simply what he had threatened. Could God say, 'in the day you eat of it you shall die', and then be faithful to his covenant word by ignoring their rebellion and sin? Of course not; which is why there is no appeal against God's sentence.

But something else, equally important, comes before us here: Adam and Eve *die*—yet they are still alive! How can this be? We need to understand that when the Bible talks about dying, it does not necessarily mean ceasing to exist (in any sense). The Bible defines death as *separation*. Adam and Eve died as a result of their disobedience in the sense that they separated themselves from the life that it is in God. And God confirmed them in that position. 'Sin came into the world through one man, and death through sin' (Romans 5:12). Adam's law-breaking was also his covenant-breaking, and it led to God constituting the whole of mankind in a state of enmity and hostility against him. It spelt the outbreak of war. The moment man sinned, God declared that hostilities existed where once there had been friendship and peace.

But there is another side to this. How do we define sin? How do we know what sin is? For many people, right and wrong are matters of personal choice, no different from deciding what to have for breakfast. Why shouldn't Adam eat whatever he wanted in the Garden of Eden? Who is to say that what he did was wrong? As Paul explains to us, however, commenting on his own spiritual struggles, 'if it had not been for the law, I would not have known sin. I would not have known what it is to covet if the law had not said "You shall not covet"' (Romans 7:8). Or, as he puts it earlier, 'through the law comes knowledge of sin' (Romans 3:20).

In other words, the law helps us to understand why an action of eating fruit has such dire consequences. God was not over-reacting when he expelled Adam and Eve from Paradise. What they did was an affront to his holiness, his righteousness, and his moral standards. Until we realize what sin is, and what sin has done, we can never appreciate the glorious work of redemption for us in Jesus Christ. It was in grace, therefore, that God gave the law, to act as a 'guardian until Christ came, in order that we might be justified by faith' (Galatians 3:24).

Law and grace are not absolute opposites; law and life are not either. God imposed a law on Adam so that he would know what the limits of life were; to move outside these limits was to turn his back on God. When God gives us commandments, it is not because he acts as a joyless despot, but because he speaks words of grace and love to us, in order that we might know the blessings of life in its fullness. The giving of his law to mankind was a *gracious* act on the part of God, and the work of his grace in the lives of men and women is never lawless.

Third, God's promises of salvation to Adam, Noah and Abraham were all related to his sovereign lordship in the lives of his people. God gave Adam the promise of an ultimate deliverer (Genesis 3:15); that was not unrelated to the command to work in the sweat of his face (Genesis 3:19). Noah was preserved when God's judgement fell on an ungodly world; but his salvation and preservation by grace was not unrelated to the commandments God gave him: 'be fruitful and multiply' (Genesis 9:1); 'you shall not eat flesh with its life, that is, its blood' (Genesis 9:4); 'whoever sheds the blood of man, by man shall his blood be shed' (Genesis 9:6). These were commands that were for the good of Noah and his seed, and, indeed, for the good of the whole world. They were to be kept because of gratitude for God's saving work.

Again, there is the combination of God's *action* and God's *speech*. The great drama of salvation had been worked out in the building of the ark, which subsequently was the means of preserving the lives of Noah and his family. Now, there was to be the action of the placing of the rainbow in the sky (or at least giving it special significance), explained by God's word of gracious promise:

I establish my covenant with you, that never again shall all flesh be cut off by the waters of the flood, and never again shall there be a flood to destroy the earth ... this is the sign of the covenant that I make between me and you and every living creature that is with you, for future generations: I have set my bow in the cloud ... (Genesis 9:11–13)

This is significant for us, because later in the Old Testament God will call the Sabbath itself a sign of the covenant, functioning in a manner similar to the rainbow. It is also important to note the emphasis in Genesis 17 on *keeping* the covenant. In that chapter, God renewed his promise with

Abraham, taking up the themes of Genesis 12, with the promise of a people, an inheritance and a blessing. Then he gave Abraham a specific command:

As for you, you shall keep my covenant, you and your offspring after you throughout their generations. This is my covenant, which you shall keep, between me and you and your offspring after you: every male among you shall be circumcised … so shall my covenant be in your flesh an everlasting covenant. Any uncircumcised male who is not circumcised in the flesh of his foreskin shall be cut off from his people; he has broken my covenant. (Genesis 17:9–10, 13–14)

God's covenant is gracious and loving: it is a further demonstration of his determination to deliver and save man from the ruin and condemnation of sin. But that grace and that love are channelled to Abraham through a specific command. The covenant is to be cut into the flesh of Abraham's male descendants. Circumcision is commanded. It is a sign of the covenant; and both covenant and sign are so closely related to one another that God can say it is actually his covenant which is *in* their flesh! Abraham knows that obeying God is not the foundation of his relationship with God; his relationship with God is grounded in his faith in God's covenant promise (Genesis 15:6). In order to enjoy that relationship, and God's continued blessing on his life, Abraham is obligated to 'keep' the covenant. God relates to Abraham as Saviour and Lord.

By the time we come to Exodus 20, therefore, with the giving of the Ten Commandments, we are already prepared for the fact that God is both Saviour and Lawgiver, Redeemer and King of his people. To know his saving power is to serve him gladly as King.

How much we need to discover the wonder of this message in the modern world and the contemporary Christian church! Christ is Saviour *and* Lord! Those who know his power and grace have become his servants. Is that not where Paul's great teaching on law, sin, grace and justification takes him: 'you who were once slaves of sin have become obedient from the heart to the standard of teaching to which you were committed' (Romans 6:17). The New Testament does not separate faith in God from obedience to God, any more than the Old Testament does. Faith and obedience feed into each other constantly. Look at the following Scriptures:

I hate the double-minded, but I love your law. You are my hiding-place and my shield; I hope in your word. Depart from me, you evil-doers, that I may keep the commandments of my God. Uphold me, according to your promise, that I may live, and let me not be put to shame in my hope! (Psalm 119:113–16)

By this we know that we love the children of God, when we love God and obey his commandments. For this is the love of God, that we keep his commandments. And his commandments are not burdensome. (1 John 5:2–3)

The Psalmist in the Old Testament and the apostle in the New, both discovered the joy of trusting and obeying. The hymn-writer was correct:

Trust and obey,
For there's no other way
To be happy in Jesus,
But to trust and obey!

Fourth, when God gave his people the Ten Commandments, he gave them within the context of his gracious, covenant salvation. We come to Sinai, and we discover that the twin themes of God as Saviour and Lawgiver merge. That is why the commandments are introduced with the words, 'I am the LORD your God, who brought you out of the land of Egypt, out of the house of slavery' (Exodus 20:2). The commandments were a response to God's saving action, and were to determine how God should consequently be worshipped and served by his people.

So here is the recurring principle: grace and law intermingle within God's covenant salvation. We will deal later with the meaning of New Testament texts which seem to set grace and law over against each other (texts like John 1:17, 'the law was given through Moses; grace and truth came through Jesus Christ'; or Romans 6:14, 'you are not under law but under grace'). But for now, we will simply observe this principle in the experience of God's people in the Old Testament. When God says, 'I have talked with you from heaven' (Exodus 20:22), he is reminding us that his words are saving, covenant words; the fact that God talked with sinful men and women at all is a register of grace; the fact that he talked *commands* is a register of law.

We need to hear again what Exodus says about the law: it is 'the Book of the Covenant' (Exodus 24:7), to which the people responded by saying 'All that the LORD has spoken we will do, and we will be obedient'. Interestingly, Exodus 24 is a chapter all about the covenant between God and his people. There is a covenant *bond*, which binds God and the seed of Abraham in a saving relationship. There is covenant *blood*, which is sprinkled on the people (24:8) in order to symbolize the provision made by God for the forgiveness of their sins and their consecration to him. Finally, there is the covenant *book*, which gives God's people a revelation of his mind and will, in obedience to which they will be recognized as the covenant people of God.

So what makes the Ten Commandments special?

One argument that is often raised against the permanent obligation to keep one day holy to the Lord is that the Ten Commandments are a small fraction of the total number of laws and regulations which Moses gave to Israel. What makes these Ten Commandments special? Surely if we have moved on from the Old Testament system, we have left all its laws behind?

But our Lord himself makes a distinction between the ten words of Mount Sinai and the other regulations of the Old Testament. When he meets a ruler who asks him about the way to eternal life, Jesus says, 'You know the commandments: "Do not commit adultery, do not murder, Do not steal, Do not bear false witness, Honour your father and mother"' (Luke 18:20). The ruler had a lot to learn about the way to heaven, and about the meaning of eternal life and of following Jesus. But the important point is that Jesus homes in on the Ten Commandments by quoting five of them and by saying, 'you know *the* commandments', so as 'to make it clear even to persistent misunderstanding what commandments he had in mind'.[15] For Jesus, these commandments were not simply local to Israel, but, as theologian B.B. Warfield put it, 'he treats them as the law of the universal and eternal kingdom which he came to establish'.[16]

The same point is made by Jesus in the Sermon on the Mount. There he tells us that the law is permanent and binding: 'until heaven and earth pass away, not an iota, not a dot, will pass from the Law until all is accomplished' (Matthew 5:18). But what does he mean when he talks of 'law' in this passage from the Sermon on the Mount? Well, the examples he chooses clarify this for us, as he cites the sixth commandment (Matthew 5:21) and the seventh (Matthew 5:27). Far from telling us that we are now free to steal or to commit adultery, Jesus reminds us that the force of these commandments go far deeper than the religious teachers of his day were suggesting. Again, B.B. Warfield is correct: 'It is with the Ten Commandments clearly in his mind, therefore, that [Jesus] declares that no jot or tittle of the law shall ever pass away, but it all must be fulfilled.'[17]

But the Old Testament itself draws a distinction between the law given at Mount Sinai and the other laws. For one thing, the Ten Commandments were written down on two stone tablets. So we read that God 'gave to Moses, when he had finished speaking with him on Mount Sinai, the two tablets of the testimony, tablets of stone, written with the finger of God' (Exodus 31:18). The traditional understanding of this has been that half the commandments were written on one stone and half on the other; but more recently it has been suggested that one stone was a copy of the other. In the ancient world, it was common practice for a conquering king to impose obligations on other nations he had conquered, to have these written down (in what is often called a 'vassal treaty'), and to have one copy placed in the temple of the conqueror's god and another in the temple of the vassal's god. The two tablets of stone, therefore, may have been two copies of the covenant treaty, one of which was a witness to God, and the other a witness to the people.

Interestingly, too, these stone tablets were to be deposited in the Ark of the Covenant, and kept in the presence of God in tabernacle and Temple. The covenant renewal ceremony of Exodus 34 resulted in the giving of various laws to Israel, regarding their relationship with neighbouring cultures, feasts, festivals and harvest laws. But the Ten Commandments have a unique place:

And the LORD said to Moses, 'Write these words, for in accordance with these words I have made a covenant with you and with Israel. So he was there with the LORD for forty days and forty nights. He neither ate bread nor drank water. And he wrote on the tablets the words of the covenant, the Ten Commandments. (Exodus 34:27–28)

Only the Ten Commandments were written down—not the laws governing slaves, harvests, feasts or sacrifices. And these commandments, which are described as 'the testimony', were to be placed in a specially constructed box, and were kept in the presence of God (Exodus 25:16; 40:20), as a perpetual reminder of the authority of the 'ten words' and the obligation of the covenant people of God to keep them.

The importance of these Ten Commandments is emphasized throughout the Old Testament. In his call to Israel to obey God, Moses says:

[God] declared to you his covenant, which he commanded you to perform, that is, the Ten Commandments, and he wrote them on two tablets of stone. And the LORD commanded me at that time to teach you statutes and rules that you might do them in the land that you are going over to possess. (Deuteronomy 4:13–14)

Here, Moses makes a distinction between the covenant, written in the ten words of the Sinai commandments, and the rules and regulations which were specifically for governing the life and experience of Israel in the land of Canaan. The Ten Commandments were specifically the laws of the covenant-making God, as Moses makes clear in the version of the commandments we have in Deuteronomy 5. The preface to this chapter states:

Hear, O Israel, the statutes and the rules that I speak in your hearing today, and you shall learn them and be careful to do them. The LORD our God made a covenant with us in Horeb. Not with our fathers did the LORD make this covenant, but with us, who are all of us here alive today. The LORD spoke with you face to face at the mountain, out of the midst of the fire… (Deuteronomy 5:1–4)

The uniqueness of these ten laws is also brought home to us in the closing words of the Old Testament, when the prophet Malachi says to us to 'Remember the law of my servant Moses, the statutes and rules that I commanded him at Horeb for all Israel' (Malachi 4:4). This is not a suggestion that we carry with us every individual piece of Old Testament legislation, but that we remember particularly the ten words of the covenant which God gave to his people at Mount Sinai.

God gave to Adam a law, as a covenant of works, by which he bound him, and all his posterity, to personal, entire, exact and perpetual obedience; promised life upon the fulfilling, and threatened death upon the breach of it; and endued him with power and ability to keep it.

This law, after his fall, continued to be a perfect rule of righteousness; and, as such, was delivered by God upon mount Sinai in ten commandments, and written in two tables; the first four commandments containing our duty towards God, and the other six our duty to man.

Besides this law, commonly called moral, God was pleased to give to the people of Israel, as a church under age, ceremonial laws containing several typical ordinances; partly of worship, prefiguring Christ, his graces, actions, sufferings and benefits; and partly holding forth divers instructions of moral duties. All which ceremonial laws are now abrogated under the New Testament.

To them also, as a body politic, he gave sundry judicial laws, which expired together with the state of that people, not obliging any other now, further than the general equity thereof may require.

Westminster Confession of Faith, Chapter 19, Paragraphs 1–4

We must distinguish, therefore, between the Ten Commandments and the other laws of the Old Testament. The old classification has much to commend it: the Ten Commandments were described as the *moral* law, laws governing Israel's worship described as the *ceremonial* law, and laws governing Israel as a theocratic nation under God described as *judicial* or *civil* law. Now that the church has 'come of age' in the New Testament, much of the ceremony is obsolete; Christ has ended all sacrifices with his last, definitive, unrepeatable sacrifice. And now that the church is no longer identified with one particular nation, many of the civil laws are no longer binding, except insofar as they set before us general rules of justice and equity.

But what has never been repealed, and what, in fact, Jesus reminds us is perpetual in its force, is the *moral* law of the Ten Commandments. These moral principles go as far back as Adam, and reflect God's right to govern our behaviour and our lives, and extend to the end of time.

Let's conclude this chapter with two further observations about God's law.

First, the primary emphasis and aim of the Ten Commandments is that God will be worshipped. The essence of sin is self-worship; as Paul puts it in Romans 1, men have defiled God's image by worshipping created idols instead of the Creator God. In consequence, God has handed men over to their own lusts, thus giving them room to deface God's image as it appears in themselves. God deserves our worship; it is the only fitting response to such a great God as he is in himself.

Jonathan Edwards, the famous American theologian-pastor, discusses the fourth commandment in three sermons printed under the title 'The Perpetuity and Change of the Sabbath'. In the first of these, he discusses objections to the position that the fourth commandment is still authoritative for all men, including the argument that the weekly day of rest in the Old Testament prefigured and foreshadowed the spiritual rest which Christ has obtained for us in the New. But, says Edwards,

this is an absurd way of interpreting the command, as it refers to Christians. For if the command be so far abolished, it is entirely abolished. For it is the very design of the command to fix the time of worship. The first command fixes the object, the second the means, the third the manner, the fourth, the time.[18]

In other words, God's purpose in giving the law was to evoke the response of worship, by making it clear in the opening commandments that he alone is the true object of our worship and devotion, that he is honoured when we worship him in the way he commands, in the spirit of reverence, and on the weekly day he has set apart for that purpose. The community which takes seriously the law of God is a worshipping community.

And that takes us back to the point made at the outset. God still makes provision for special times and special places in which and at which his people may know his special blessing. The Sabbath law is part of a moral code which will modify behaviour and provide an opportunity for a deepening understanding of the God who is holy.

But there is a second emphasis we must make: it is the relationship between law and love. On one occasion, one of the learned men of his time asked Jesus a question in order to test him: 'Teacher, which is the great commandment in the Law?'. Jesus replied, 'You shall love the Lord your God with all your heart and with all your soul and with all your mind. This is the great and first commandment. And a second is like it: You shall love your neighbour as yourself. On these two commandments depend all the Law and the Prophets' (Matthew 22:36–40).

If the man who asked the question hoped to trip up Jesus by getting him to elevate one of the commandments above the others, he was sadly mistaken. Jesus turned the issue round, by highlighting the command which summarizes all the commands: 'love God' and 'love your neighbour'. Jesus is not here reducing the Ten Commandments to love, as if the particularity of the commandments was of no consequence; on the contrary, he tells us that the keeping of the law requires us to devote our hearts to God in the first instance, and subsequently to others. As B.B. Warfield puts it,

all the precepts of the law are but the development in detail, in the form of announced obligations, of the natural workings of love towards God and man. The two tables of the Decalogue are clearly in mind as respectively summed up in these two great commandments. And the meaning is, again, not that love to God and man supersedes the duties enumerated in these two tables, but that it urges prevailingly to their punctual and complete fulfilment.[19]

In other words, duty and love are not incompatible—they are not mutually exclusive. If I love my wife, I will fulfil the obligations and responsibilities of a husband to her—love will motivate me to be dutiful towards her. Duty without love will dishonour her, and love without duty will disgrace her. But flowing into each other, they will bring life and dynamic into our relationship. So it is with the people of God. They are to obey God; but they are to do it with loving and glad hearts:

You shall therefore love the LORD your God and keep his charge, his statutes, his rules and his commandments always ... and if you will indeed obey my commandments that I command you today, to love the LORD your God and to serve him with all your heart, and with all your soul, he will give the rain for your land in its season, the early rain and the later rain, that you may gather in your grain and your wine and your oil. (Deuteronomy 11:1; 13–14)

Summary
The Ten Commandments must be understood in their proper, biblical context. They are given to Israel as God's way of revealing his purpose to save men and women, who were created for him and who have drifted far from him. They are not given as ten easy steps to heaven; they are given as part of the covenant, the bond which binds God to his people, and in which he undertakes to be their Saviour. They reveal God's character, God's holiness, God's righteousness. They show how far from him we have gone, and by what standard we are to live. They are designed to provoke and produce love for him, and the worship of his name. They are different from all the other Old Testament regulations, and set before us the absolute moral standards by which we are to live, and by which we can once again discover the original intention of God in making the world. After all, as the commentator John Walton puts it, as long as we are in this world, 'we are in Someone Else's house.'[20]

The *obligations* under which man is to yield that obedience which God requires are these:

Man is bound to obey God, because he is his creator, preserver and benefactor.

Man is bound to obey God, because he is the supreme sovereign Lord, king and lawgiver. As he is the one lawgiver of all, and ours in particular, having committed to us his law, we are bound to receive it in the love of it, and to make it appear that we have not received it in vain.

Man is bound to obey God, because this is the chief end for which man was made.

Man is bound to obey God, because of his glorious excellencies. Surely they must be blinded to the excellencies of the Divine nature, who see nothing in God why he should be loved. And how can love to him be manifested but by obedience?

Man is bound to obey God in a special manner, from a sense of his love to sinners in Jesus Christ. If this love, which passeth all understanding, has no effect in producing an unfeigned obedience, nothing whatever will. This is the peculiar motive by which the friends of Jesus are actuated.

Alexander S. Paterson, *A Concise System of Theology on the Basis of the Shorter Catechism* (London: T. Nelson, 1884), p. 154.

Notes

1 This is forcefully argued in **Andrew E. Steinmann's** article '… as an ordinal number and the meaning of Genesis 1:5', *Journal of the Evangelical Theological Society*, 45.4 (December 2002), pp. 577–84.
2 **Steinmann,** 'meaning of Genesis 1:5', p. 583.
3 **W.J. Dumbrell,** 'Genesis 2:1–17 A Foreshadowing of the New Creation', in **S.J. Hafemann** (ed.), *Biblical Theology, Retrospect and Prospect*, (Leicester: Apollos, 2002), pp. 53–54.
4 **Bruce K. Waltke,** *Genesis: A Commentary* (Grand Rapids: Zondervan, 2001), p. 67.
5 **O. Palmer Robertson,** *The Genesis of Sex* (Phillipsburg: P&R, 2002), p. 6.
6 **D. Macleod,** *A Faith to Live By* (Fearn, Tain: Mentor, 1998), p. 77.
7 **John Bunyan,** 'Questions about the nature and perpetuity of the seventh-day Sabbath', in *The Whole Works of John Bunyan*, Vol II, (Grand Rapids: Baker, 1977), p. 365.
8 **Richard B. Gaffin jr.,** 'Westminster and the Sabbath', in **J.Ligon Duncan III** (ed.), *The Westminster Confession into the Twenty-First Century*, Volume One (Fearn, Tain: Mentor, 2003), p. 136.
9 **J. Murray,** *Principles of Conduct* (London: Tyndale Press, 1957), pp. 32–33.
10 **W.R. Godfrey,** *God's Pattern for Creation: A Covenantal Reading of Genesis 1* (Phillipsburg: P&R, 2003), p. 90.
11 **Godfrey,** *God's Pattern*, p. 89.
12 **Godfrey,** *God's Pattern*, p. 59.

13 **Godfrey,** *God's Pattern,* p. 60.

14 **O. Palmer Robertson,** *The Christ of the Covenants*, (New Jersey: Presbyterian and Reformed, 1980), p. 67.

15 **B.B. Warfield,** 'The Foundations of the Sabbath in the Word of God', in *Selected Shorter Writings* Vol. I (ed. **J.Meeter**) (New Jersey: Presbyterian and Reformed, 1980), p. 313.

16 **Warfield,** 'The Sabbath in the Word of God', p. 313.

17 **Warfield,** 'The Sabbath in the Word of God', p. 314.

18 **Jonathan Edwards,** 'The Perpetuity and Change of the Sabbath', *Works*, Vol. 2 (London, 1840), p. 95.

19 **Warfield,** 'The Sabbath in the Word of God', p. 316.

20 **John H. Walton,** *Genesis*, The NIV Application Commentary (Grand Rapids: Zondervan, 2001), p. 161.

Moses and the Sabbath

Remember the Sabbath day to keep it holy. Six days you shall labour, and do all your work, but the seventh day is a Sabbath to the LORD your God. On it you shall not do any work, you, or your son, or your daughter, your male servant, or your female servant, or your livestock, or the sojourner who is within your gates. For in six days the LORD made heaven and earth, the sea, and all that is in them, and rested the seventh day. Therefore the LORD blessed the Sabbath day and made it holy. Exodus 20:8–11

You know the commandments … Luke 18:20

I was never a footballer. In fact, I was never a sportsman of any description. If God gave me any gifts, they were deposited in my head, rather than in my feet. I have memories of embarrassing moments on school playing fields, with me running in the opposite direction of play. I was never top choice for the team.

My teenage sons, however, inherited the sports gene which was prevalent in their mother's side of the family. Through careful coaching and discipline, they have become accomplished sportsmen. What a joy it gives parents to see healthy children enjoying their lives and making progress in growth and physical development! And how important it is to channel that exuberance and energy in worthwhile and valuable directions.

I have learned enough to know, however, that nothing can be enjoyed without rules. Sometimes, if I am addressing young people in our school or in the football club, I ask them whether they think football would be more enjoyable or less enjoyable without rules. Their instinct—as with all totally depraved youngsters!—is to say 'NO RULES!', until they think about it and realize that it is the rules that make the game enjoyable.

I then apply the same test to driving along the road. What is the purpose of the rules governing traffic and its movement? To enable us to progress, in safety, from our point of origin to our destination. Without the rules, our safety could never be guaranteed.

So, for the purpose of safe journeying and of enjoyable passage, God gave laws to his people. We have noted in the previous chapter that God relates to men and women as Creator and Sovereign Lord. Our lives depend on him, and are subject to him. We are called to live the way he wants us to live, and to be a people committed to him in a covenant relationship. The tragedy is that we have strayed from God; to use Isaiah's expression, 'all we like sheep have gone astray' (Isaiah 53:6). Yet God appears as a great Saviour, a shepherd who will bring his straying sheep back on to the path of truth and righteousness.

He does this by establishing a covenant relationship, founded on his grace, and flowing from his mercy, between himself and lost, unworthy sinners. In the Old Testament, that covenant relationship was established with Israel, the physical descendants of Abraham, to whom God gave an external summary of his mind and will in the Book of the Covenant, the Ten Commandments. We saw in the previous chapter that these commandments are full of grace, as they are full of truth. We now want to focus on the fourth commandment in particular, the commandment concerning the Sabbath day. The version of the commandment given in Exodus 20 is cited at the top of this chapter. This is how it is recorded in Deuteronomy 5:12–15:

Observe the Sabbath day, to keep it holy, as the LORD your God commanded you. For six days you shall labour and do all your work, but the seventh day is a Sabbath to the LORD your God. On it you shall not do any work, you or your son or your daughter or your male servant or your female servant or your ox or your donkey or any of your livestock, or the sojourner who is within your gates, that your male servant and your female servant may rest as well as you. You shall remember that you were a slave in the land of Egypt, and the LORD your God brought you out from there with a mighty hand and an outstretched arm. Therefore the LORD your God commanded you to keep the Sabbath day.

Both Exodus and Deuteronomy record the commandment governing the Sabbath *day*. But the Sabbath principle was applied in other ways too, as we shall see later in this chapter.

What are the elements of this commandment?

- First, there is a positive command regarding the *Sabbath day*.
- Second, the Sabbath day is to be kept *holy*.
- Third, the Sabbath day is different from the other days, in which *work* is required.
- Fourth, the keeping of the Sabbath day extends to *all* who are in our household.
- Fifth, the Sabbath day is identified with the day on which *God rested*.
- Sixth, the Sabbath day is a day which God has uniquely *blessed*.

First, there is a positive command here regarding the Sabbath day

The way in which the fourth commandment is written immediately sets it off against the other nine commandments, most of which are simple prohibitions, beginning with 'You shall not...' This command, however, begins with a positive injunction to 'Remember' (Exodus 20:8) or to 'Take care' (Deuteronomy 5:12) to keep the Sabbath day holy. That is not to say that there are no negatives in it; balancing the command to sanctify the Sabbath is the prohibition 'on it you shall not do any work' (Exodus 20:10).

The opening of the fourth commandment is itself very instructive, and looks in two directions. On the one hand, it looks back, since it assumes that the Sabbath already exists. On the other hand, it looks forward, since the covenant people of God are commanded to ensure, by remembering and by taking care, that they will observe this day in a particular manner each week.

The backward (or retrospective) element is very important. It reminds us of the fact that *the Sabbath did not begin with the Ten Commandments*. Moses did not invent the Sabbath day, nor did the law at Sinai create it. What the law did was to enshrine within the law-code an already existing provision. How could anyone 'Remember the Sabbath day to keep it holy' if the Sabbath day did not already exist?

In fact, the Sabbath principle is clear in Exodus 16, when God fed his people in the wilderness with bread from heaven. The bread, or manna, which covered the wilderness floor, was to be gathered each day, in order to feed the families of Israel. But on the sixth day of the week, they were to gather enough for two days:

On the sixth day they gathered twice as much bread, two omers each. And when all the leaders of the congregation came and told Moses, he said to them, 'Tomorrow is a day of solemn rest, a holy Sabbath to the LORD: bake what you will bake and boil what you will boil, and all that is left over lay aside to be kept till the morning'. So they laid it aside till the morning, as Moses commanded them, and it did not stink, and there were no worms in it. Moses said, 'Eat it today, for today is a Sabbath to the LORD; today you will not find it in the field. For six days you shall gather it, but on the seventh day, which is a Sabbath, there will be none'. (Exodus 16:22–26)

This was an explanation of the principle which God had already explained to Moses in verse 5: 'on the sixth day, when they prepare what they bring in, it will be twice as much as they gather daily'. But where did this principle come from? It was obviously known to Moses, and thus pre-dated Sinai. In fact, it goes back to creation itself, as we have seen. The fourth commandment is simply building on what is already part of God's order for his world.

But there is a forward (or prospective) aspect to this too. The Sabbath is to be sanctified continuously. The commandment is asking God's people to find room for this holy day in their weekly cycle and routine. There is no doubt about this: the commandment lays down the principle that the Sabbath is a permanent and perpetual ordinance. This is how Jonathan Edwards puts it:

The mind of God in this matter is clearly revealed in the fourth commandment. The will of God is there revealed, not only that the Israelitish nation, but that all nations, should keep every seventh day holy; or, which is as well as the rest, is doubtless everlasting and of perpetual obligation, at least, as to the substance of it, as is intimated by its being engraven on the tables of stone. Nor is it to be thought that Christ ever abolished any command of the ten; but that there is the complete number ten yet, and will be to the end of the world.[1]

In other words, the principle of one day of rest and worship is placed by God himself on the same footing as the exclusive worship of the Creator, the sanctity of his name, the sanctity of life, the sanctity of marriage and the sanctity of truth. If we believe that God's law absolutizes the moral

44 On the first day of the week

principles that govern our behaviour in these areas, then we have to accept that there is an absolute moral principle governing our use of our time, so that God commands us to give one day of the week to himself.

Second, the Sabbath day is to be kept *holy*

In the context of Sinai, this is a tremendous and awesome requirement. Everything about the law, about Sinai, spoke of holiness. The command to keep one day a week holy was given in the context of a situation in which the holiness of God was everywhere evident.

When Moses came to 'Horeb, the mountain of God' (Exodus 3:1), and stood on the site where God would later speak to him face to face, he was told, 'Do not come near; take your sandals off your feet, for the place on which you are standing is holy ground' (Exodus 3:5). God continued: 'I am the God of your father, the God of Abraham, the God of Isaac and the God of Jacob. And Moses hid his face, for he was afraid to look at God' (Exodus 3:6). The meeting with God on this occasion was significant as the point at which God revealed to Moses his covenant name 'I AM WHO I AM' (Exodus 3:14), which gives us the name LORD, or 'Jehovah'. The presence of God, the revelation of his name, and the identification of his purpose to honour covenant promises and save his people, all combined to create a sense of the 'otherness' of God, the weighty, sinless purity which remind us of the sacred nature of God's being: he is a holy God.

The song of Moses in chapter 15, following the defeat of Pharaoh's armies, also registers the fact of God's greatness and holiness. There is the same emphasis on the divine name: 'The LORD is a man of war, the LORD is his name' (15:4). There is an emphasis on his work: 'You have led in your steadfast love the people whom you have redeemed' (15:6), and there is the end for which God has shown his saving power: 'you have guided them by your strength to your holy abode' (15:6). For this reason, Moses can say, 'Who is like you, O LORD, among the gods?' (15:11).

But it is particularly at Sinai itself that the awe-inspiring holiness of God presses home on the consciousness of the people. The Lord descended on Mount Sinai (Exodus 19:18), with the result that the ground shook, and the place was convulsed. To prepare for a meeting with God, the people were commanded to consecrate themselves, to wash their garments, and to abstain from sexual activity (19:10–15). Above all, they were to be careful to keep their distance; Moses set limits round the mountain, so that neither person nor animal would touch the mountain, for fear of dying. The point is that it is impossible for sinful men to encounter the holiness of God and live.

The writer to the Hebrews in the New Testament takes up the same theme, of the mountain that was 'a blazing fire and darkness and gloom and a tempest', a sight so terrifying that Moses said, 'I tremble with fear' (Hebrews 12:18, 21). And although the purpose of the writer is to draw a contrast between the Israelites' coming to Mount Sinai and our coming to Christ, it is significant that the words with which the chapter ends remind us that God has not changed his nature across the Testaments: 'our God is a consuming fire' (Hebrews 12:29). The God whom we may approach in Christ is no less holy than the God from whom the Israelites had to distance themselves for fear that they might be put to death.

But in this context, the holy God of Israel also sets his people apart to be like him. They are to be a holy nation (Exodus 19:6), consecrated (made holy) to the Lord (Exodus 22:31). Then, in the closing chapters of Exodus, with the regulations for the construction of the Tabernacle and the service to be rendered to God in it, we find the holiness of God stamped on every element of the worship. There is to be a holy place for the ark of the covenant (Exodus 26:33–34), the priests' garments are to be holy (Exodus 29:29), the consecrating oil is to be holy (Exodus 30:25). Only a holy place could be fitting for a holy God, and the result was that God's presence could fill the tabernacle. Thus Exodus concludes with the great statement that 'the glory of the LORD filled the tabernacle' (40:34), and God, in his grace, has made provision for the restoring of a covenant relationship with mankind, following the breaking of that relationship through Adam's disobedience.

Thus the giving of the law which reveals the searing, burning holiness of the God of Israel, also makes provision for God to dwell among his people. What Sinai could not hold without shaking, the tabernacle can contain. God's presence has to be delimited at Horeb, or else the people will die; but God's grace finds a way for him to dwell among his people, and they may live. Law and grace are not antithetical; it is in the giving of the law that grace is channelled to a sinful people.

It is against this background that we need to understand the force of the fourth commandment. When God says 'keep the Sabbath day HOLY', he is making a powerful statement. God is a holy God, who dwells in a holy place, who demands holy service, who consecrates holy people to himself: and who asks that holy TIME be given to him. In a recent book on Christ in the Old Testament, Professor Tremper Longman III looks at the three main elements of Israel's worship: sacred space (paradise, altars, the tabernacle, the temple), sacred acts (the sacrifices), sacred people (priests and Levites), and sacred time (the Sabbath, feasts and festivals).[2] This is exactly the correct approach to Israel's worship: 'God is our heavenly King who establishes his rulership in the midst of his people. As King he consecrates space, people, certain acts, and times that are especially dedicated to his service'.[3]

The Sabbath is an indication of *sacred time* which is to be devoted to the service of the Lord, just as the mountain is an example of sacred space, and the nation of Israel an example of sacred people. As we have seen, the foundation of the Sabbath principle is in the fact that God *created* time, just as he created space, and people, and things. His work of creation was in order to display his glory, and the majesty of his sovereign holiness. The Sabbath principle reflects God's claim on his creation, and his right to rule over time. We hear a lot today about *time management*; the whole point of the fourth commandment is that God is our time manager, who consecrates one day in particular to be his.

It is interesting, in this connection, to note the importance of Exodus 31:12–18, which is an extended discussion on the place of the Sabbath, and its importance for God's people. Of all the commandments, the fourth receives this additional commentary and explanation, as God calls Moses to remind the people of God of the importance of this sacred time. This is a passage to which we will return again later; but we need to underline the relationship which, according to this passage, exists between the Sabbath principle and the holiness principle. The following verses highlight this point:

31:13: 'you shall keep my Sabbaths ... that you may know that *I, the* LORD, *sanctify you*.

31:14: 'you shall keep the Sabbath, because *it is holy for you*.

31:15: 'the seventh day is a Sabbath of *solemn rest, holy to the* LORD.

This weekly, sacred day is important as a reminder that God makes his people holy. It is not a day for ordinary rest, but for solemn rest. And the day derives its holiness from the holiness of God himself.

Let us view this true holiness, as it shines in the holy and spiritual law of God; for Adam being now fallen, and so that image extinguished, and never a patter left by which to see what this image was, God therefore set forth a copy of it in his word, which now is the means of sanctifying of us; and sanctification itself is but a writing of that law in the heart, and a confirmation of the heart thereunto ... that is holiness which is a conformity to the first table, the duties whereof are called 'the great things of the law' (Hosea 8:12); and which indeed are especially called holiness, as being immediately for God, when the other are for man; and the duties of the second table are called 'righteousness', of the first 'holiness' (Ephesians 6:24) and so distinguished (Luke 1:75) ... all you that do boast of God's image, and yet the duties of the first table are in a great part left out, or slighted by you, in comparison of the second, you may say truly, this heart never came under the broad seal of heaven.

Thomas Goodwin, 'An Unregenerate Man's Guiltiness before God', *The Works of Thomas Goodwin,* Vol. 10 (Edinburgh, 1865 reprint), pp. 419–420

Third, the Sabbath day is to be different from all other days, on which we are required to work.

The fourth commandment is not just about the Sabbath day; it has something important to tell us about the other six days of the week too. 'Six days you shall labour and do all your work' (Exodus 20:9; Deuteronomy 5:13). Often the fourth commandment is cited as if its total concern was with one day and with what we are not allowed to do on that one day. But in fact its concern is with the weekly cycle of our lives, and the way we are to use our time.

Underlying this commandment, therefore, is the principle that biblical faith is a whole-life faith. If our faith and our Christianity are only a matter of one-day-a-week religion, then whatever we have is not biblical. There is no area of our lives over which our covenant God is not sovereign. Once we are in that covenant, we are in it one hundred per cent!

We could approach the work requirement in this commandment from several different perspectives. We could remind ourselves, first, that *God is a worker*. Indeed, the force of the commandment is derived from the fact that God was active in creation over a period of six days. As John Murray describes it, 'in the realm of God's activity in creating the heavens and the earth there were six days of creative action and one day of rest'.4 That is what sets the pattern for our weekly routine.

We then have to remind ourselves that *God made Adam a worker*. It stands to reason that if God said, 'Let us make man in our image' (Genesis 1:26), then that image must include the ability to say 'Let us make...'. If man's creation somehow reflects God, then creative ability—ability to engage in work—is part of that image, and part of man's function. But the work element in the story of Adam is not simply derived from his being made in God's image, but from the specific command given to Adam and Eve in the Garden of Eden: 'Be fruitful and multiply and fill the earth and subdue it and have dominion over the fish of the sea and over the birds of the heavens and over every living thing that moves on the earth' (Genesis 1:28). Adam was to rule over God's world, harnessing its resources and making use of its opportunities to live a God-centred and God-glorifying life.

That work ethic was not revoked after man sinned. As John Murray says, we might have expected that the new situation which was the result of sin's entrance into the world might have altered and changed the relationship of man to marriage, the Sabbath and labour. But, says Murray,

this, however, is precisely what we do not find. The creation ordinances of procreation, replenishing the earth, subduing the earth, dominion over the creatures, labour, marriage, and the sabbath are not abrogated. It is of paramount interest and significance to observe the ways in which the continuance of these ordinances is intimated and their sanctity preserved.5

God ordained marriage as the fundamental building block of human society, and did not alter this when man sinned. In speaking to Eve after the fall, God says, 'I will surely multiply your pain in childbearing; in pain you shall bring forth children. Your desire shall be for your husband, and he shall rule over you' (Genesis 3:16). Marriage is not disannulled, revoked or set aside: it still remains God's appointed and ordained means for the expression of sexual relationships and the procreation of children. But sin has brought an element of frustration, tension and pain into marriage. In a fallen world, marriage will not remain unaffected.

But it does remain guarded and defended by God, which is why one of the commandments is devoted to it. When the seventh commandment forbids adultery, it is simply reiterating the ideals of man's original creation, highlighting the importance of this exclusive relationship of commitment, love and trust. The original creation ordinance is now made a Sinai ordinance.

Similarly, God says to Adam concerning his work and labour:

Cursed is the ground because of you; in pain you shall eat of it all the days of your life; thorns and thistles it shall bring forth for you; and you shall eat the plants of the field. By the sweat of your face you shall eat bread, till you return to the ground, for out of it you were taken; for you are dust, and to dust you shall return. (Genesis 3:17–19)

This is at one and the same time a word of grace and a word of curse. The curse aspect is to be seen in the way in which work and labour will produce pain and sweat. Work will have its frustrating aspects, as well as its rewarding aspects. The difference between Adam before the fall and after the fall is that what was formerly a pleasure is now to be a necessary chore. Sinclair Ferguson describes it in this way:

[Adam] grasped for independence by making himself the centre of the universe; he sought satisfaction in the fruit of the garden and the relationships of this world. Instead he found himself under a curse. His work became frustrating and hard, rather than fruitful and enjoyable. The final enigma was that he was told that, eventually, he would disintegrate into the raw materials of his own labour and become dust: 'dust you are and to dust you will return'. Adam who looked after the animals was eventually trodden upon by the very beasts he nurtured![6]

Yet there is grace here; man is still able to enjoy God's good gifts, and God promises to meet man's needs. God does not destroy man immediately; he undertakes to provide for his life and to nourish it. Sin is checked by grace, so that there are limits of mercy set around the consequences of sin. The curse reflected itself in Adam's being driven out of Paradise; grace reflected itself in his being spared at all.

The Old Testament registers for us the toil and the pain of work in a fallen world:

Vanity of vanities, says the Preacher, vanity of vanities! All is vanity. What does a man gain by all the toil at which he toils under the sun? ... All things are full of weariness; a man cannot utter it; the eye is not satisfied with seeing, nor the ear filled with hearing. (Ecclesiastes 1:2;8)

Yet work we must, and the lesson of the Old Testament is inescapable: when Adam put God first, work was a pleasure. When Adam put himself first, work became a chore. The work ethic, so much part of our experience in the world, is itself enshrined in the fourth commandment. As John Murray says, 'the day of rest has no meaning apart from the background of labour'[7]. We appreciate the rest for body and mind which the Sabbath offers, precisely because of the toil and labour of working the other six days of the week. The fourth commandment, therefore, was a magnificent law which showed the Creator's concern for the well-being and welfare of his world and his creatures. In managing our time in this way, he has the most simple recipe for avoiding burnout and being swamped with overwork, with the consequent dangers of depression and exhaustion: after the work of the week, rest!

There are two other considerations which bear on the relationship between the Sabbath principle and the work ethic of the fourth commandment. One is the example of Jesus himself. He is the Messiah, the Servant of the Lord, who would magnify God's law and make it glorious (Isaiah 42:21). It is of him that Peter, one of those who knew him best, says that 'he committed no sin' (1 Peter 2:22). If we want to see the law in action and fulfilment in a human life, we need look no further than the example of Jesus Christ himself. B.B. Warfield is correct to say that 'we have no ... formal commentary from our Lord's lips on the Fourth Commandment. But we have the commentary of his life'.[8]

And it is not merely in respect of the sanctifying of the Sabbath that

Christ leaves us an example. His life is also a commentary on what it means to use six days to do our work. As he grew up in the home of Joseph and Mary in Nazareth, he learned a noble trade as a carpenter. So involved and dedicated in his work was he, that when he preached his first public sermon in the synagogue (on the Sabbath), his contemporaries asked, 'Where did this man get these things? What is the wisdom given to him? How are such mighty works done by his hands? Is not this the carpenter …?' (Mark 6:2–3). The passage not only demonstrates to us Christ's zeal to keep the Sabbath in a way that would honour and glorify God; it also shows us that he had not overlooked the work clause either.

Indeed, his public ministry, for which we have a record in the gospel, is a record of work and worship. This Jesus 'went about doing good' (Acts 10:38), not wasting a moment or a day, if he could help others and extend the love of God to them. Transferring from manual labour to the work of an itinerant preacher did not lead Jesus to compromise one bit on the principle enshrined in the fourth commandment: 'six days you shall labour'.

It is also worth noting that the New Testament is also concerned to remind us of the importance of time and the importance of work. We are reminded, for example, that in Christ, all our lives can be restored to their proper orientation—we can fulfil the purpose for which we were originally created—to give glory to God: 'whether you eat or drink, or whatever you do, do all to the glory of God' (1 Corinthians 10:31). That means that we can restore time, and use it wisely and well, 'making the best use of the time, because the days are evil' (Ephesians 5:16). Actually, that translation is a paraphrase of Paul's original counsel, which was to 'redeem', or 'buy back' the time. It was Jesus who said that 'we must work the works of him who sent me while it is day; night is coming, when no one can work' (John 9:4), and set a pattern for his people to follow. Throughout the New Testament, we are reminded that one of the goals of Christ's redemptive activity was 'to redeem us from all lawlessness and to purify for himself a people for his own possession who are zealous for good *works*' (Titus 2:14, italics mine). The work that he has begun in his people is to issue in their work for him (Ephesians 2:10).

So when the fourth commandment talks about working, it is talking about something that characterizes Christ and his people. He was a worker, and so are they. The Sabbath rest contrasts with all other work. The force of the commandment is to set the work of the six days over against the rest of the seventh. And again the principle is clear: the original creation mandate to work and labour is now enshrined within the moral code that must govern our behaviour in this world.

Fourth, the command to observe the Sabbath and keep it holy was to extend to the whole Israelite household, in the widest possible sense

This is clear in the terms of the commandment: 'on it you shall not do any work, you, or your son, or your daughter, your male servant, or your female servant, or your livestock, or the sojourner who is within your gates' (Exodus 20:10). It seems to me that this commandment is placing a particular responsibility on the head of the household, since it directs the prohibition in the first instance to 'you'. It envisages a situation where rule and government within the family unit falls particularly upon the father. That was God's way from the very beginning: although Adam and Eve were created in the image of God, with a distinction and a complementarity of gender, headship was vested in Adam. It is a principle which appears in the New Testament in the following way: 'the head of every man is Christ, the head of a wife is her husband, and the head of Christ is God' (1 Corinthians 11:3). The meaning of 'head' (Greek *kephale*) in this verse has caused much discussion of late, with commentators divided between whether it means 'origin' or 'authority'. There does appear, however, to be overwhelming evidence to show that when Paul uses the word 'head' he means 'authority over'.[9]

Yet society has lost sight of the important concept of male headship and authority in family life. Quite apart from the fact that many children are growing up in single-parent situations, in many homes parental control has turned into parental compromise. Social breakdown may be traced to family breakdown.

So one of the implications of the fourth commandment is that just as God devolved authority to Adam in the world he created, he also devolves authority in the household to the husband and father. Also implied is the fact that our children will learn much by our example. When God says, 'you, or your son or your daughter', he seems to be suggesting that if the father sets a good example, the sons and daughters will learn from it and will be inclined to follow it. It is precisely for this reason that those of us who are privileged to be parents, and entrusted with the onerous task of childrearing, need to take care that what our children see us doing is what we would wish them to follow and to do in their own lives.

So here is the application of the prohibition: the head of the household is to observe the Sabbath, and his children are to follow his lead. But so too are the servants. While we cannot use the fourth commandment to justify slavery, we can apply its implications to the whole area of employment law. Employers ought not to expect their employees to break the Sabbath. This is a brilliant example of employment protection legislation. Indeed, it is interesting to note that the Mosaic law insists on the fair treatment of slaves, and, in Exodus 21, the giving of the Ten Commandments is followed by a detailed account of how slaves are to be offered their freedom in the seventh year (an interesting application of the Sabbath principle, as we shall see).

What is more intriguing is the fact that the account of the fourth commandment in Deuteronomy 5 differs from Exodus 20 precisely on this point. Whereas in Exodus 20 the reason for keeping a Sabbath day holy to the Lord is the fact that God himself has left us an example by resting from the work of creation, Deuteronomy argues that because God's people were once slaves, now set free by God, they should look after their own servants. There is no contradiction between the form of the commandments in Exodus, and the form given in Deuteronomy. Both draw attention to the protection to be given to servants, but while the Exodus version points back to the original giving of the Sabbath commandment, the Deuteronomy version re-casts it in a form more suited to future settlement in the land of Canaan.

But more than that, the version in Deuteronomy has the effect of reminding us that the Sabbath commandment is directly related to the theme of *redemption* as well as to the theme of creation. It is not simply that Israel is asked to observe the Sabbath because God said so; it is that, having come into bondage because of her law-breaking, Israel's release, liberation and freedom are the consequences of grace: God has stepped in to save when no other salvation was possible.

Commentator Peter Craigie is correct, therefore, to highlight the interest that the Christian believer must have in the Sabbath commandment. He says:

We are participators in that tradition which goes back in history to the Exodus, when God revealed to his people his activity in human history by liberating his chosen people.[10]

The commandment is for us, because it is for those who have been redeemed.

The other element of this is that there is a new life for God's people. The argument is that they were slaves in Egypt, but now they are redeemed; 'therefore the LORD your God *commanded* you to keep the Sabbath day' (Deuteronomy 5:15). They have been liberated from their previous masters in order to serve the Lord, from one state of death-bondage to a state of life-service. That is precisely the kind of language we find Paul using in Romans 6:17–18:

But thanks be to God, that you who were once slaves of sin have become obedient from the heart to the standard of teaching to which you were committed, and, having been set free from sin, have become slaves of righteousness.

We have not been set free in Christ from a state of servitude to a state of anarchy or lawlessness. But we have been liberated from being slaves, with only the prospect of death in view, to become willing servants of Jesus Christ, who long to serve and please him.

The Sabbath command, therefore, combines the themes of creation and redemption in a way that makes it supremely relevant for the people of God in every age and in every place. It focuses our attention on the unity of God's purpose and the continuity of God's work over every stage of human history.

Fifth, the Sabbath day is identified with the day on which *God rested*

We have already noted the significance of God's 'resting' in the previous chapter. It was not that he needed to rest because of being exhausted after his work; it was that he entered into a new kind of day, in which the activity of the previous six days ceased.

The commandment applies that with consummate logic: 'on [the Sabbath day] you shall not do any work'. By the time of Jesus, the Jewish rabbis had set so many hedges around this prohibition that even plucking grains of corn was regarded as work (see Matthew 12:1–8 and the discussion of this passage in chapter 4). By 'working', Jesus was regarded as breaking the Sabbath and sinning against God.

But John Murray is right to remind us that the fourth commandment does not prohibit all kinds of work; it prohibits only a certain kind of work which could be done on other days: 'the sabbath in man's week is not to be defined in terms of cessation from activity, but cessation from that kind of activity involved in the labours of the other six days'.[11] It's not that certain things *became* sins on the Sabbath day. It is that, just as God turned aside from the business of creation on the seventh day, so we are to devote the Sabbath to other, and different kinds of, activity.

Exodus 31:17 puts it like this: 'in six days the LORD made heaven and earth, and on the seventh day he rested and was refreshed'. John L. Mackay is right to describe this as 'a bold anthropomorphism',[12] in which God applies to himself an idea that could never be true of God. The image, says Professor Mackay, is 'the refreshment that comes to an individual who stops from a physically demanding task to catch his breath'.[13] So while it remains true that 'the Creator of the ends of the earth ... does not faint or grow weary' (Isaiah 40:28), it is also true that he conveys to us a truth about himself best described in terms of a 'refreshment'.

Can we pour any content into this idea of God resting? John Frame describes it this way: 'God *celebrates* his creative work in a sabbath of rest'.[14] It is a rest of satisfaction, of enjoyment, of contemplation, of engagement with all that he is and has done. And that is precisely what establishes the pattern of our Sabbath-rest. We do turn aside from secular labour, from all unnecessary labour. But we do not become idle in our Sabbath keeping. God's people were told to keep the day holy as they ceased from other activities, entering into God's celebration of his work of creation and redemption.

Glen Knecht is right, therefore, to suggest that 'the design of the Sabbath calls for a ceasing from our secular labours and our turning to the works that we shall be engaged in throughout eternity'.[15] For God's people, eternity will be an endless worship of God, in which we will marvel at all that God is. God's people will join with the elders to sing of the Lamb:

Worthy are you, our Lord and God, to receive glory and honour and power, for you created all things, and by your will they existed and were created (Revelation 4:11).

The things, therefore, that we expect to do in heaven, are the things which ought to characterize our Sabbath rest. We cannot simply draw up a list of proscribed activities, as the Jewish leaders did, and expect to please God by not shaving on Sunday, or not brushing our jacket, or not polishing our shoes. That approach is precisely what Jesus condemns. But we will please God, and we will enjoy his blessing, if we use our Sabbath to rejoice in God, in all that he is and in all that he has done. That will be for us a following of his own example at creation.

Sixth, the Sabbath day is a day which God has uniquely *blessed*

We saw in the previous chapter that the word 'blessed' is a relational word, a word that means that something, or someone, is in a unique and privileged position with respect to God. God blessed this day by claiming it as his own, and doing something different on the Sabbath day.

But in the Bible, what is blessed is a channel of good to others. That is certainly the import of the covenant which God established with Abram, saying to him, 'I will bless you and make your name great, so that you will be a blessing' (Genesis 12:3). The Sabbath is a blessed day, which will be a blessing to those who observe it, since God pronounces a blessing on all those who keep his law (Deuteronomy 11:27). By setting apart the Sabbath, God was not so much thinking of himself, as of his people. They, in the normal course of life, require physical rest. And as the covenant people of God, they are privileged to enjoy something of the blessing that is in God himself.

This, then, is the meaning of the fourth commandment. Grounding the Sabbath law in the example of God in creation, and anticipating the fullness of spiritual redemption and liberation, God builds the Sabbath ordinance of creation into the Decalogue, as he does the ordinances of marriage and labour. Man has broken covenant with God, and has left himself exposed to the restlessness sin brings. He has lost what was promised to him in the covenant of works which God made with him at the outset. And what was the promise? It was that of continued life, light and rest in God: 'the so-called "covenant of works" was nothing but an embodiment of the Sabbathic principle', says Geerhardus Vos.[16] In his grace, God has come into the experience of his redeemed people, maintaining for them in the weekly pattern of their lives a reminder of what it is they have lost, and what it is that grace restores for them.

THE SABBATH SIGN

It is in the light of the fourth commandment and its provision that we must look at Exodus 31:12–17, a passage to which we have already alluded, and one which adds its own expansive commentary on the Sabbath principle:

> And the LORD said to Moses, 'You are to speak to the people of Israel and say, Above all you shall keep my Sabbaths for this is a sign between me and you throughout your generations, that you may know that I the LORD sanctify you. You shall keep the Sabbath, because it is holy for you. Everyone who profanes it shall be put to death. Whoever does any work on it, that soul shall be cut off from among his people. For six days shall work be done, but the seventh day is a Sabbath of solemn rest, holy to the LORD. Whoever does any work on the Sabbath day shall be put to death. Therefore the people of Israel shall keep the Sabbath, observing the Sabbath throughout their generations, as a covenant for ever. It is a sign for ever between me and the people of Israel that in six days the Lord made heaven and earth, and on the seventh day he rested and was refreshed.

For some bible scholars and commentators, this passage proves that the Sabbath principle is no longer valid, since it was a sign between God and the people of Israel. So James Montgomery Boice argues that since the Sabbath sign revealed the unique covenant relationship between God and *Israel*, it had a very limited reference, and could not in any sense apply to the other nations of the world:

On the contrary, it was the observance of the sabbath that was to distinguish Israel from the nations, much as circumcision also set them apart.[17]

But this is surely to miss the big picture. God's covenant was made with Israel, as a means of bringing salvation into a lost world. And much that was given to Israel by way of revealing that covenant salvation was, indeed, temporary and 'shadowy'. If there were no reference to the Sabbath prior to Moses, we might conclude, as Boice does, that the Sabbath day was one of these temporary measures which was to be done away with when Christ came. Yet the Sabbath existed prior to any covenant being made with Israel! Therefore we must conclude that the 'sign' was not the creation of a new day, but the consecrating of an existing day for a spiritual purpose.

In Exodus 31, it is clear that God is adding a new dimension to the Sabbath observance which was evident in Exodus 16, before the law was given, and which was evident in the creation ordinance itself. He is now making the already existing Sabbath specifically covenantal: the day will be observed in the light of the covenant. To that extent, it is still the case that the Sabbath day is a sign of God's covenant with Israel, although in the New Testament, all the elements of that statement are to be nuanced differently. The day is now the first day of the week, the Israel is all of God's people (a spiritual, not an ethnic, Israel), and the covenant is now the new covenant, which has no need of ritual and ceremony.

And Exodus 31 feeds another element into the Sabbath doctrine too: the fact that the day signifies that the people of God themselves are to be made holy (31:13). Just as the day is sanctified, so the people are to be sanctified. Just as the day is to be set apart, so are the people. The sanctification principle is central to the Gospel: Christ loved the church and died for her to make her holy (Ephesians 5:25–7). And it is that principle that comes to our attention with each Lord's Day Sabbath, as we are reminded that God is bringing his creation to its consummation and goal.

HOW MANY SABBATHS ...?

Another element of the Mosaic law which many people ignore is the fact that the Sabbath principle is not just about one day in seven. In the

Exodus 31 passage, God talks about 'my Sabbaths' (plural). Does he simply mean the regular and repeated weekly Sabbath observance? Or does he mean to include other instances and expressions of the Sabbath principle? There are other passages which have an important bearing on this whole theme.

Exodus 21: release for the slave

Immediately following the Ten Commandments in Exodus is the concrete example and application of the moral principles of the Decalogue to the situation of the Israelites. The law here is stated like this: 'When you buy a Hebrew slave, he shall serve for six years, and in the seventh he shall go out free, for nothing' (Exodus 21:2). It is interesting that, following the Ten Commandments, with their interest in the welfare of servants, this particular law should be given. In it, Moses provides for an amnesty every seven years, so that the seventh year will be a year of release.

According to the terms of this legislation, it is possible that a Hebrew slave may not desire release from the service of his master, in which case he has the choice between freedom and life-service. If he chooses the latter, he is to have a mark placed in his ear, a point given significant moment in Psalm 40:6 and its subsequent citation in Hebrews 10:5–7.

These provisions do not mention the Sabbath specifically, but are clearly related to the principle of the Sabbath commandment. One year in seven is to be a year of special opportunity for the slaves of the Hebrews. God's interest in the release of the oppressed and the captive comes to the fore here, as the Israelites are commanded to do for their own slaves what God did for them. It is impossible to read these laws without catching the sabbatarian principle in them.

Exodus 23:10–12—work on the land

For six years you shall sow your land and gather in its yield, but the seventh year you shall let it rest and lie fallow, that the poor of your people may eat; and what they leave the beasts of the field may eat. You shall do likewise with your vineyard and with your olive orchard. For six days you shall do your work, but on the seventh day you shall rest, that your ox and your donkey may have rest, and the son of your servant woman, and the alien, may be refreshed.

The Sabbath principle is again implicit in this regulation governing the working of the land. This principle is more clearly enunciated in Leviticus 25, which we shall consider soon. But it is clearly important here also: the land needs its rest, just as we do ourselves.

It is important to note that 'land' is a major theme in the Old Testament. God placed Adam and Eve in a garden. He promised Abraham and his descendants a land of their own. God is the God of the land; and land, as Elmer Martens reminds us, 'is the fourth most frequent noun or substantive in the Old Testament: it occurs 2,504 times. Statistically, land is a more dominant theme than covenant'.[18] As such, Martens goes on to argue, 'land' functions as a major theological motif, as God's promise, God's gift and God's blessing to his people.

Against this background, then, obedience to the God of the covenant shows itself in the way in which the land is used. God does not want his people to be materialistic, to pay attention to the land at the expense of the spiritual issues it represents. But he does teach his people spiritual truths through material things.

Here, one of the major spiritual realities is that of the Sabbath principle. The land is to enjoy rest, and the poor are to benefit from the yield. Again, God's bias is towards the poor and the needy, reinforced by the demands he makes of his own people. They honour him by the way they apply the principle of rest, one year in seven, to the part of the creation he has given them to inherit.

Exodus 35:1–3—Sabbath principles and tent-building

Moses assembled all the congregation of the people of Israel and said to them, 'These are the things that the LORD has commanded you to do. For six days work shall be done, but on the seventh day you shall have a Sabbath of solemn rest, holy to the LORD. Whoever does any work on it shall be put to death. You shall kindle no fire in all your dwelling places on the Sabbath day.'

At first sight, this seems to be just another reference to the Sabbath law; but its position is significant. It appears in the middle of the section of Exodus dealing with the construction of the tabernacle. The description of the sacred tent in which God's presence resided among his people is told in two parts: first, in chapters 25–27, the description of the tabernacle is given, and in chapters 35–40 we have an account of its construction. In between, the story is told of the rebellious 'worship' which God's people give to the golden calf, disobeying his law, and the gracious renewal of the covenant.

The Sabbath principle is so significant in all this, that it is reiterated by Moses at the point at which he has come down from Sinai, and before the construction of the tabernacle begins. That fact reinforces the role of the tabernacle not only as a place of revelation, and a tent of meeting; it also highlights that the tabernacle was a symbol of a new creation. That comes across in a variety of ways. The two accounts of the tabernacle parallel the two accounts of creation. In Genesis 1, we find the phrase 'and God said' used seven times (1:3, 6, 9, 14, 20, 24, 26); similarly in the construction of the Tabernacle we have the phrase 'And the LORD said' used seven times (25:1; 30:11, 17, 22, 34; 31:1,12). Just as the Spirit hovered over the first creation, so the Spirit was given to Bezaleel for the purpose of tabernacle construction (Exodus 25:30). Similarly, just as God blessed the Sabbath day at the close of the creation, so Exodus 49:43 says that 'Moses saw all the work, and behold, they had done it; as the LORD had commanded, so had they done it. Then Moses blessed them'.

The structure of the tabernacle, too, was clearly a 're-creation'. Just as God had dwelt with man in the paradise of the Garden of Eden, so he was to dwell among his people in the tabernacle. For that reason, Hebrews 8:5 describes the Tabernacle as a 'shadow of the heavenly things', and Hebrews 9:24 calls the holy places of the Tabernacle 'copies of the true things'.

Within the tabernacle there were many things that were reminiscent of Paradise and of Redemption. There was a golden lampstand shaped like a tree with leaves and buds, reminiscent of the tree of life. There was a golden table, with twelve loaves of bread which had to be renewed each Sabbath day, reminiscent of the manna gathering in the desert. Important redemptive and theological principles were interwoven into the design and construction of this holy place where God dwelt.

It is in this context that God appoints the Sabbaths as signs of the covenant (Exodus 31), at the conclusion of the first account of the tabernacle, and now reiterates the Sabbath regulations at the beginning of the second. The symbolism of creation is evident, therefore, as much in the

Sabbath principle as in the tabernacle construction and its account. The cumulative evidence of these early passages of Genesis and Exodus points to the intimate relationship between creation and redemption, with the Sabbath principle of creation binding these motifs and themes together.

No doubt the command had the effect of regulating the actual construction of the tent, which would not be built on the Sabbath. But it also had the effect of reminding the people of what the tabernacle was for, as a gracious provision by which the end of creation would be realized, in spite of what sin had done in human experience. In the last chapter, we saw the importance of special places and times—the Sabbath was given to man as a dweller in the world, in God's house. That idea is now localized and focused on the tabernacle as the special house which God inhabits and into which 'the people are received ... as His guests'.[19] This is the grace that brings salvation, enabling man to enjoy God's presence in spite of the expulsion from Eden. In the tabernacle there is hope, as 'man appears as admitted into, adjusted to, and subordinated to, the life of God.[20]

It is significant, therefore, that Genesis should begin with the creation account, and Exodus should conclude with the creation of the tabernacle, this new creation, this new place of God's dwelling, this new provision for fallen man. God is en route to recover a lost humanity, so that the purpose of rest and blessing, signified by the seventh day of the creation week, will be realized. It is no accident that the Sabbath day should feature so vividly as part of the tabernacle story. What John Frame says about the temple— the later, permanent structure which replaced the temporary tabernacle of the wilderness—is applicable to our study: 'The Sabbath is God's dwelling in time; the temple is his dwelling in space'.[21] We have seen God claim sacred time and sacred space among his people. In doing so, he is graciously restoring to the life of man that which he did not take away (Psalm 69:4).

Leviticus 23—the Sabbath in Israel's feasts

For six days shall work be done, but on the seventh day is a Sabbath of solemn rest, a holy convocation. You shall do no work. It is a Sabbath to the LORD in all your dwelling places (Leviticus 23:3).

Chapter 2

Leviticus 23 is one of the most important passages in the Old Testament, for it outlines the annual programme of religious festivals which God asks his people to observe. Interestingly, these begin with the Sabbath regulation of verse 3, which is almost as if God is reminding them that they have a weekly festival to enjoy, in addition to which he is going to sprinkle their year with holy festivals and sacred times. This is full of theological significance.

Andrew Bonar, in his dated but insightful commentary on Leviticus, says that

> This Sabbath-feast is to be ever repeated, each week, as a testimony of the Lord's good will to have men restored to their original rest. And it is to be kept when all other feasts have finished—a type of the deep rest yet to come when earth's sins are swept away, and creation itself is restored to holiness, and the liberty of the sons of God.[22]

No less significant is the fact that there are seven feasts mentioned in this chapter. The first month of the year marked the Feast of Passover (vv 4–5), Unleavened Bread (vv 6–8) and the Firstfruits (vv 9–14). In the third month, Pentecost was to be celebrated (vv 15–22). In the seventh month, the people were to observe the feast of Trumpets (vv 23–5), the Day of Atonement (vv 16–32) and Tabernacles (vv 33–44). Thus there were seven feasts spread over seven months.

And, in a sense, they provided the people with additional Sabbaths. The weekly Sabbath is referred to in verses 3, 11,15,16 and 38. But the same stipulations regarding holy rest are applied in other places. So, for example, the Day of Atonement, which was to be marked on the tenth day of the seventh month, is described as 'a Sabbath of solemn rest ... On the ninth day of the month beginning at evening, from evening to evening shall you keep your Sababth' (v32). Just as no work was to be done on the weekly Sabbath, so no work was to be done on the festival days either. And just as special sacrifices were appointed for the weekly Sabbath (Numbers 28:9–10), so special sacrifices were appointed for the festival days. Bible scholar Kevin Connor brings out the significance of this: 'sometimes there would be two Sabbaths in the same week; that is, the weekly Sabbath and the Festival Sabbath'.[23] That is a point we often overlook, but one which serves to highlight the important theological symbolism running through the Old Testament.

Passover was the first feast of the year, and had as its function the commemoration of the redemption moment from Egypt. It was followed by seven days of eating unleavened bread, and the seventh day was holy. Jesus himself uses the concept of leaven, or yeast, as a picture of sin (see Mark 8:15, Matthew 16:6–12). The third element of the feast, the waving of the sheaf of the firstfruits of the harvest was to be done 'on the day after the Sabbath', on the first day of the week. The calendar of God, therefore, not only brings out the important turning points of redemptive history, but also anticipates the special place of the first day of the week in the New Testament. It is not without reason that Christ's resurrection, for example, is described in terms drawn from this religious calendar: 'Christ has been raised from the dead, the *firstfruits* of those who have fallen asleep' (1 Corinthians 15:20).

The importance and significance of the first day of the week is also brought out in the feast of the third month, the feast of Pentecost, so called because of the 'fifty days' (the meaning of Pentecost) which separated it from the feast of firstfruits:

You shall count seven full weeks from the day after the Sabbath, from the day that you brought the sheaf of the wave offering. You shall count fifty days to the day after the seventh Sabbath. Then you shall present a grain offering of new grain to the LORD ... You shall not do any ordinary work (Leviticus 23:15–16, 21).

These carefully marked holy times serve to draw a clear connection for us between the Old Testament Sabbath and the New Testament Lord's Day. Warren Wiersbe puts it like this:

Firstfruits and Pentecost both occurred on the first day of the week. For Christians, this is the Lord's Day. The Feast of Firstfruits commemorates our Lord's resurrection from the dead, and the Feast of Pentecost commemorates the coming of the Holy Spirit. By His resurrection and by His sending of the Holy Spirit, our Lord has consecrated the first day of the week in a very special way.[24]

My conviction remains, therefore: not only is there a Sabbath for us in the New Testament: there is also a Lord's Day for us in the Old! Woven into the regulations for Jewish festivals and holy times, things which were to pass away with the coming of Christ, were the elements of permanence and substance which would never pass away. Without knowing it, Israel, each year, kept Sabbath AND anticipated the Lord's Day!

The feasts of the seventh month—Trumpets, Atonement and Booths (or Tabernacles)—bring us to the most solemn of all days in Israel's year. On the Day of Atonement, blood was sprinkled in the presence of God (see Leviticus 16) by the High Priest, and the sins of the people were confessed in God's presence. It was a day of intricate ceremony and particular solemnity. Its importance for us is highlighted in the epistle to the Hebrews, where we are told that Jesus 'entered once for all into the holy places, not by means of the blood of goats and calves but by means of his own blood, thus securing an eternal redemption' (Hebrews 9:12).

We cannot underestimate the element of grace running through these requirements of law. The very law which showed the awfulness of sin also provided the atonement for sin. Guilt was demonstrated, but grace was there, too, in the fact that God invited his people to draw near, by means of a representative priest, who made atonement for the sins of the people.

Running through the calendar are the sabbatical principles of holiness, rest, consecration and worship which have been part of the experience of man from the beginning, and of Israel since her redemption. In them all, God was teaching his people through symbols and types. These symbols, woven into the religious ceremonies of the Jews, reinforced the moral precepts of the Decalogue; as the people observed the feasts around the tabernacle, the Ten Commandments represented the holiness of God at the heart of the structure. His authority, his holiness, his purity, were what distanced the people, but it was also what lay at the heart of the measures he provided to bring them close to himself. For that reason, while the Sabbath ceremonials have passed away, the Sabbath principle itself remains valid and binding.

Leviticus 25—the Sabbath years

In addition to the weekly Sabbath, and the monthly Sabbath feasts, Israel was commanded to observe Sabbath years, in a marvellous provision which we will allude to briefly. Elaborating on the principle of Exodus 23:10–12, which required that the land be left fallow every seventh year, Leviticus 25 required that

When you come into the land that I give you, the land shall keep a Sabbath to the LORD. For six years you shall sow your field, and for six years you shall prune your vineyard and gather in its fruits, but in the seventh year there shall be a Sabbath of solemn rest for the land, a Sabbath to the LORD ... The Sabbath of the land shall provide food for you, for yourself and for your male and female slaves and for your hired servant and the sojourner who lives with you, and for your cattle and for the wild animals that are in your land: all its yield shall be for food. (Leviticus 25:2–3, 6–7).

In addition to the weekly Sabbath and the additional Sabbaths of the festivals scattered throughout the Jewish calendar, the land, as we have seen, was to rest, to sabbath, every seventh year. The land which has been worked for six years, is to rest, a 'solemn rest' for the land, a 'Sabbath to the LORD'. The seriousness of this precept is registered in the solemn language with which it is made. Just as God entered into a rest after creation, and just as the fourth commandment required rest after the toil of the week, so the land was to rest. And because the people neglected the Lord of the Sabbath, he ensured that the land would have its Sabbath rest during the long years of Babylonian captivity (2 Chronicles 36:21).

In the first instance, the commandment reminded Israel that they were stewards of the land God had given them. The principle running through these regulations, God says, is that 'the land is mine ... you are strangers and sojourners with me' (Leviticus 25:23). Interestingly, God had said much the same thing at Sinai, declaring that 'all the earth is mine' (Exodus 19:5). The Lord of the Sabbath is the Lord of Creation, the sovereign Lord, who has absolute jurisdiction over his people, and who has redeemed them in order that they should serve him. The sabbatical year, just like the Sabbath day, reflects the Lordship of Israel's God over all the earth.

Second, the land rest was good for the soil. The sabbatical year allowed the land to be refreshed and ready for the next period of activity. God's people were being educated in the importance of believing that the God who had given them the land would provide for them in his own way. Again, obedience to his law would be the way to enjoying his blessing and his provision. They needed to believe that, just as he had provided enough manna on the sixth day for two days, so he would give enough harvest. In this way, no one would be burdened with the question 'what shall we eat?' (Leviticus 25:20). Faith always accepts that God will provide.

Third, the land sabbatical would benefit the poor. They would be able to glean and gather the yield. Just as in the fourth commandment, the Sabbath principle has at its heart a concern for the poor and the needy. It is a reflection of the magnanimous and generous heart of God. He is always the God of the poor, and of those who have no help from others. This comes out clearly in the version of the sabbatical year law which we find in Deuteronomy 15, where the motivation for obedience is the promise of blessing, and where the design of God is clearly articulated:

But there will be no poor among you; for the LORD will bless you in the land that the LORD your God is giving you for an inheritance to possess—if only you will strictly obey the voice of the LORD your God, being careful to do all this commandment that I command you today. For the LORD your God will bless you, as he promised you... (Deuteronomy 15:4–6).

A particularly solemn moment occurs in the fiftieth year, called the Year of Jubilee. Again the importance of the number seven and its multiples comes before us. Just as with the Day of Pentecost, which was reckoned by counting seven times seven days plus one, so the Jubilee Year was reckoned by counting seven times seven years plus one. The fiftieth year followed the sabbatical year, so God promised enough harvest for three years in the forty-eighth year (Leviticus 25:20).

Again the regulations emphasize the importance of the creation rest, and the Sabbath commandment. But the Year of Jubilee adds another dimension to the role of the Sabbath in the Old Testament. It is particularly a Sabbath of redemption, in which property is redeemed and restored to its original owner (Leviticus 25:28); those who found themselves in an impoverished condition could be redeemed and restored. The trumpet of jubilee was a great sound of freedom: 'proclaim liberty throughout the land to all its inhabitants' (Leviticus 25:10).[25] Geerhardus Vos brings out the significance of this:

On the Sabbath man and beast rest, in the Sabbathical Year the very soil rests; in the Year of Jubilee the idea of rest is exhibited in its full positive import through restoration of all that was disturbed and lost through sin.[26]

So here it is again: the positive principle of the Sabbath, in its relation both to creation and redemption. It is difficult not to conclude that the great Messianic call of Isaiah 61:1 is not rooted in the regulations governing the Jubilee Year, as Christ says

The Spirit of the Lord God is upon me,

Because the Lord has anointed me to bring good news to the poor, he has sent me to bind up the broken-hearted, to proclaim liberty to the captives, and the opening of the prison to those who are bound, *to proclaim the year of the Lord's favour.*

As Christ cites these words in Luke 4:18–19, applying them to himself, he could also declare that the year of his redemption had come (Isaiah 63:4), the year of God's favour, the year which reminded all Israel of the goal to which God was bringing his creation. Sabbath days, Sabbath months, and Sabbath years all demonstrated God's sovereignty over time, his work in time, and his goal for the universe in future time. Each Sabbath was a reminder of God's intervention in history through grace, in order to deal with the problem of sin.

Numbers 15—the execution of the Sabbath-breaker

There is one other significant passage dealing with the Sabbath in the Mosaic literature. It deals with a specific case of Sabbath desecration:

While the people of Israel were in the wilderness, they found a man gathering sticks on the Sabbath day. And those who found him gathering sticks brought him to Moses and Aaron and to all the congregation. They put him in custody, because it had not been made clear what should be done to him. And the LORD said to Moses, 'The man shall be put to death; all the congregation shall stone him with stones outside the camp.' And all the congregation brought him outside the camp and stoned him to death with stones, as the LORD commanded Moses (Numbers 15:32–36).

At one level this seems a harsh and brutal penalty for gathering sticks. Yet its purpose is obviously to reinforce the sanctity and solemnity with which the Old Testament Sabbath was viewed. In the context of Numbers 15, which deals with laws governing sins committed intentionally or unintentionally, this is a clear example of someone who has committed a sin intentionally. Given that Exodus had already indicated that Sabbath-breaking was punishable by death (Exodus 31:15), the man is clearly acting in a high-handed and rebellious manner.

The fact that Leviticus 24:10–16 reports a similar capital punishment for blasphemy shows that it is not simply the Sabbath command that is held to be authoritative: all the commands are. They are expressions of God's holiness and of his sovereignty, and cannot be discarded or broken with impunity. It is not the action of gathering sticks that is the point, otherwise the penalty would be out of all proportion with the crime; it is that in doing so, the perpetrator was purposely and flagrantly denying the sovereignty of God over him.

Instead, therefore, of knowing God's blessing, which is the way to life, the Sabbath-breaker comes under God's curse, which leads to judgement and to death. That is highlighted in the fact that the penalty is exacted 'outside the camp', away from the place of God's favour and presence, and in the location which speaks of estrangement and malediction.

So although the Sabbath principle spoke of glorious things, bringing before the people the sovereign purposes of the Creator for the world he had made, and highlighting the direction in which God was taking the world even after the Fall, we are reminded that this was the 'ministry of death' and the 'ministry of condemnation' (2 Corinthians 3:7, 9). The Mosaic period was part of a ministry which showed that death was the wages of sin. A sinful world and a sinful people require the grace of law, and there were gracious elements woven into the Old Testament system. But, as Paul reasons, 'will not the ministry of the Spirit have even more glory?' (2 Corinthians 3:8). For us, the redemptive principles which were embodied in the law-focused revelation of the Old Testament are brought into their glorious manifestation in the grace-focused revelation of the New.

And what is it that makes this ministry glorious? Is it not that Christ has suffered for us 'outside the camp' (Hebrews 13:11)? There he has taken all our sins—our law-breaking, including our Sabbath-breaking—'by becoming a curse for us' (Galatians 3:13). He has brought the gracious aspect of redemptive history to its fullest revelation, so that now we see clearly what could only be dimly grasped before.

And at no stage of the transition from the 'ministry of condemnation' to the 'ministry of righteousness' does God do away with the moral precepts which govern his creation and his church, his new creation. The same reverence for God's name, God's day, God's world, and God's ordinances of marriage and of work, carry across from one Testament to the next. What does change is the penalty; now the law-breaker, instead of being stoned to death outside the camp, may come to Jesus, who suffered there for us.

Summary

The Sabbath principle, in various forms, is very clearly an important part of the period of redemptive history which focuses on the leadership of Moses. He is the one to whom God spoke face to face, as a friend (Exodus 33:11), who prophesied of the coming of a prophet like himself (Deuteronomy 18:15), and of whom the closing words of the Pentateuch tell us that 'there has not arisen a prophet since in Israel like Moses, whom the LORD knew face to face' (Deuteronomy 34:10). Moses was the greatest of the Old Testament prophets, fulfilling in his own person and work the role of Redeemer and Saviour, as well as carrying out kingly and priestly functions.

He stands before us then both in comparison and in contrast with Jesus. There are aspects of God's revelation in the Mosaic period which were to be done away with. But there were also aspects which were permanent. We cannot take a dispensational approach to Scripture and say that nothing in the period of Moses is relevant to us today. It is not Christ OR Moses, but Christ IN Moses that must govern our approach to the Old Testament. We must ask: what are the principles of ceremony and of society which were time-bound, cultural and ready to pass away with the coming of Christ, and what are the redemptive, moral and spiritual principles that remain across all the ages?

It seems to me, and I trust our further studies in the Old and New Testaments will confirm it, that at no stage did God ever suspend the moral and creation ordinances which he gave to mankind or covenanted to his people. The Sabbath principle is one of these. It is one law that has never been repealed.

Notes

1 **Jonathan Edwards,** 'The Perpetuity of the Sabbath', p. 95.

2 **T. Longman III,** *Immanuel in our Place: Seeing Christ in Israel's Worship* (New Jersey: P&R Publishing, 2001).

3 **Longman,** *Immanuel in our Place*, pp. xi–xii.

4 **John Murray,** *Principles of Conduct: Aspects of Biblical Ethics* (London: Tyndale Press, 1957), p. 36.

5 **Murray,** *Principles of Conduct*, p. 42.

6 **Sinclair B. Ferguson,** *The Pundit's Folly: Chronicles of an Empty Life* (Edinburgh: Banner of Truth, 1995), p. 20.

7 **Murray,** *Principles of Conduct*, p. 35.

8 **Warfield,** 'The Sabbath in the Word of God', p. 317.

9 **See J.Piper and W. Grudem,** *Recovering Biblical Manhood and Womanhood: A Response to Evangelical Feminism*, Wheaton: Crossway Books, 1991, especially Appendix 1: 'The Meaning of *Kephale* ("Head"): A Response to Recent Studies', by Wayne Grudem (pp. 425–68).

10 **Peter C. Craigie,** *The Book of Deuteronomy*, NICOT, (Grand Rapids: Eerdmans, 1976), p. 158.

11 **J. Murray,** *Principles of Conduct* (London: Tyndale Press, 1957), p. 33.

12 **J.L. Mackay,** *Exodus: A Mentor Commentary* (Fearn, Tain: Mentor, 2001), p. 520.

13 **Mackay,** *Exodus*, p. 520.

14 **John M. Frame,** *The Doctrine of God* (Phillipsburg: P&R, 2002), p. 296.

15 **Glen Knecht,** *The Day God Made* (Edinburgh: Banner of Truth, 2003), p. 50.

16 **G. Vos,** *Biblical Theology* (Grand Rapids: Eerdmans,1948), p.157.

17 **J.M. Boice,** *Foundations of the Christian Faith* (Leicester: IVP, 1986), p. 235.

18 **E.A. Martens,** *God's Design: A Focus on Old Testament Theology* (Leicester: Apollos, 1994), pp. 103–4.

19 **Vos,** *Biblical Theology*, pp. 170–1.

20 Vos. *Biblical Theology*, p. 171.

21 John M. Frame, *The Doctrine of God* (Phillipsburg: P&R, 2002), p. 654.

22 A. Bonar, *The Book of Leviticus* (London, 1846), p. 386.

23 Kevin J. Conner, *The Feasts of Israel*, (Portland: Bible Temple—Conner Publications, 1980), p. 14.

24 Warren W. Wiersbe, *Be God's Guest: Feasts of Leviticus 23*, (Lincoln: Back to the Bible, 1982), p. 53.

25 These words are inscribed on the famous liberty bell in Philadelphia, the birth place of independent America.

26 Vos, *Biblical Theology*, p. 159.

The Prophets and the Sabbath

Keep the Sabbath day holy, as I commanded your fathers. Jeremiah 17:22

The foundation of the apostles and prophets, Ephesians 2:20

'Text messaging' is all the rage in our house, as it is among most of today's teenage mobile phone population. With the pressing of a few buttons, messages can be written up, posted and received on an electronic handset. What did we do before the mobile phone revolution?

Of course, I refuse to bow to the current trend of writing in text messaging shorthand. My children send messages to me in codes that would tax Da Vinci himself. 'C U l8r' is short for 'see you later', but I have too much grammar overload in my blood cells to allow me to commit such barbarity and submit the English language to such a distortion. No—although it takes me ten times as long to write and send a text message, I send it as it ought to be written.

Communication is vitally important, and at so many different levels of experience, we depend on receiving accurate information about all kinds of things, just as others expect us to communicate in that way with them. It is nothing short of remarkable that the communications revolution has come so far that we can relay a message at astonishing speed to almost anywhere in the world.

In times past, as the opening words of Hebrews puts it, God continuously spoke to the forefathers by the prophets. They were in the message business—receiving messages from God and relaying these to the people of God. Sometimes prophets spoke without having received a word to speak. Sometimes the prophets used symbols, drama and action to communicate the message from God to his people. At other times the people refused to listen to what the prophets had to say.

But the role of the prophets as communicators of God's word is fundamental to any study of biblical doctrine and theology. That is why it is necessary to turn to their writings and to ask, 'What is the message of the prophets about the Sabbath, and the principles connected with it?'

The role and ministry of Israel's prophets has received much scholarly attention and study.[1] As we come to ask the specific question of the attitude of the prophets to the Sabbath, we come with certain presuppositions.

First, we assume that the prophets were not merely interpreters of their circumstances but those who were called by God to communicate his word to his people. That did mean a degree of interpretation, both of their own personal circumstances and of the circumstances of their people. It involved an assessment of the people in the light of their history and privileges, but the prophets themselves were never the originators of their message. What they spoke, they received, and their ministries were integral to God's revelation of himself to the world.

The word 'prophet' appears first in Genesis 20:7, where God describes Abraham in this way. This tangential use of the title is not unimportant, since God's covenant with Abraham will carry the message of salvation to the ends of the earth. God not only purposes and promises to save mankind through a covenant with Abraham, but also establishes a means by which his will may be known as his 'prophets' communicate the message of salvation.

But we can say that it is with Moses that classic prophecy truly begins. 'By a prophet the LORD brought Israel up from Egypt, and by a prophet he was guarded' (Hosea 12:13). The prophetic role of Moses is integral to God's redemptive work. So, too, is the promise that God will raise a prophet like Moses who will communicate his word to his people (Deuteronomy 18:18). When the Old Testament observes that no prophet ever arose in Israel like Moses (Deuteronomy 34:10), we are being told that the Old Testament anticipated the coming of Jesus Christ as the one by whom, supremely, God's will for the covenant redemption of the world would be made known.

O. Palmer Robertson summarizes:

… prophetism in Israel had its origin with the establishment of the theocratic nation in the Mosaic period. As the foundational law of the covenant was being revealed, the prophetic office came into being. As a consequence, in stark contrast with a long history of negatively critical reconstruction, law and prophecy do not stand over against one another. Instead, prophetism originates with the mediation of God's law.[2]

Second, what the prophets spoke was consistent with previous revelation. It was not their intention or purpose to discard or replace what God had spoken previously, but to build on it and advance it. Hebrews 1:1 says that God *spoke* to the fathers by the prophets in different ways and at different times. The tense of the verb is significant—it means that God 'kept on speaking', and did so with a message that was consistent across the ages. Indeed, the argument of Hebrews is that the consistency continued into the New Testament, since the same God who spoke continuously in the Old Testament has spoken definitively and finally to us in Jesus Christ.

Professor John Mackay is correct, therefore, to say that

The prophets were not so much concerned with imparting new truth as with the implementation of existing truth. In practice this meant that they exhorted the people to return to, and to maintain, the standards of the covenant delivered through Moses.[3]

It is not surprising, therefore, to find the prophets mentioning the Sabbath. The continuity of revelation was such that they knew that the Sabbath had not been superseded; their call was to the people to honour the claims of God's truth and apply the standards of God's law. They have no new sabbatarianism, but wish to effect a return to the law that marked the boundary line of covenant blessing for the people of God.

Third, what the prophets spoke forth in the Old Testament had a special and unique reference to Jesus Christ. The relation between Christ and the prophets is very intimate, so much so that Peter can say that it was the Spirit of Christ that was in them (1 Peter 1:11), and Christ can say that they spoke about himself (Luke 24:25–27). Their message was one which anticipated the finality of his words, and which prepared the way for his coming .As they spoke God's word, the prophets were looking forward to the day when the Word would become incarnate, and would actually dwell among men (John 1:14). Christ was truly the Christ of the prophets.

So, what was the prophetic message concerning the Sabbath? It will be helpful to examine four key Old Testament places where the prophets address this subject directly. In addition, we will look at one passage which demonstrates very clearly the application of the prophetic word in the life of the covenant people, and at passages which anticipate the 'new covenant', with its implications for Sabbath-keeping.

The Sabbath in Isaiah

The Book of Isaiah is a remarkable example of the retrospective and prospective elements of Old Testament prophecy. Isaiah reminds God's people of many aspects of their past, such as the fact that they have been redeemed (43:1–3) and preserved by God's covenant faithfulness (54:9). But he also anticipates the coming of Christ in a remarkable way, with references in his prophecy to the virgin birth of Jesus (7:14; *cf.* Matthew 1:22–23) and to the suffering of the Servant of Jehovah (53:7–9; *cf.* Acts 8:32–35).

Isaiah mentions the Sabbath in three contexts.

The first is in 56:1–8:

Thus says the LORD:
'Keep justice, and do righteousness,
for soon my salvation will come,
and my deliverance be revealed.
Blessed is the man who does this,
and the son of man who holds it fast,
who keeps the Sabbath, not profaning it,
and keeps his hand from doing any evil.'
Let not the foreigner who has joined himself to the LORD say,
'The LORD will surely separate me from his people';
and let not the eunuch say,
'Behold, I am a dry tree.'
For thus says the LORD:
'To the eunuchs who keep my Sabbaths,
who choose the things that please me
and hold fast my covenant,
I will give in my house and within my walls
a monument and a name
better than sons and daughters;
I will give them an everlasting name

that shall not be cut off.
'And the foreigners who join themselves to the LORD,
to minister to him, to love the name of the LORD,
and to be his servants,
everyone who keeps the Sabbath and does not profane it,
and holds fast my covenant—
these I will bring to my holy mountain,
and make them joyful in my house of prayer;
their burnt offerings and their sacrifices
will be accepted on my altar;
for my house shall be called a house of prayer
for all peoples.'
The Lord GOD,
who gathers the outcasts of Israel, declares,
'I will gather yet others to him
besides those already gathered.'

The prophecy of Isaiah has suffered considerably at the hands of modern Old Testament scholars. Since the nineteenth century heyday of critical views of the Bible, it has been increasingly fashionable to speak of more than one author of this book of the Old Testament; commentators will speak of First (or Proto-) Isaiah as having authored chapters 1–39, Second (or Deutero-) Isaiah has having authored chapters 40–66, with perhaps a Third (or Trito-) Isaiah posited for some sections of the book also.

In his commentary on Isaiah, George Adam Smith (1856–1942) argues that chapter 56 'proves' that even if we take the position that there was a second author (or editor) of the later material, we cannot say that his work has a coherent unity. He says that the section beginning at 56:9 'is one of the sections which almost decisively place the literary unity of "Second Isaiah" past possibility of belief',4 since it contains elements that cannot apply to Israel in exile, while the earlier part of chapter 56 deals with Israel on the eve of return from exile.

As O.T. Allis pointed out a long time ago, however, 'biblical prophecy and the unity of Isaiah stand or fall together'.5 To appreciate the unity of Isaiah is to see the prophet in his true historical and biblical context. It is to see his place on the timeline of God's redemptive history, and to appreciate how the work of the prophets anticipated the coming of the Lord Jesus Christ.

What Isaiah is anticipating is a decisive work of God in history, restoring the fortunes of his people, and enabling them to enjoy his covenant blessing, once again, in the land of covenant promise. The background to the promised blessings of Isaiah 56 is the anticipation of a return from exile and restoration in their own land. In the foreground, however, is the promise to those who will keep God's law that they will have a place in God's house. Philip Hacking is correct to emphasize the link between restoration and Sabbath-keeping, the latter being a thanksgiving for the former: 'when the deliverance from exile would happen the Sabbath would once again be a mark of thanksgiving'.[6] The 'eunuchs' of the passage would keep Sabbath not out of legalistic obedience but out of grateful hearts and as a result of God's deliverance and sovereign intervention.

Who are the eunuchs of the passage? They are those who have been emasculated, and, in the light of Deuteronomy 23:1, cannot be admitted to the assembly of God. Yet now the promise is that what the law could not do, in that it has been made weak through the flesh, God has done. He makes membership of the covenant community possible for those who are excluded. This is further emphasized in the astonishing claim that the Temple is to be for all people, not just Jews (56:8). Isaiah is the prophet with the large vision, the prophet who can dream that the blessings which have belonged to the Jewish people are to be enlarged and extended to a much greater constituency.

Running through this passage are the twin themes of Isaiah's prophecy—indeed, the twin themes of the Old Testament: first, that salvation is all of grace, and second, that salvation is not experienced apart from obedience to God's requirements. The first of these themes is highlighted in the emphasis that salvation is from God—It is *my* salvation (56:1), God says; and throughout the passage there is a stress on God's sovereign activity (56:5,7–8). No salvation blessing is ever entirely dependent on our responses to God's demands, but is very clearly the result of God's sovereign grace.

Yet no salvation blessing is enjoyed by us in isolation from God's law either. Just as the blessings of the covenant were to be experienced within the terms of God's law, so Isaiah depicts the gracious blessings of God's salvation as coming upon those who keep the law of God. Of course, the very ability and desire to keep God's law are themselves the result of God's grace and God's work in men's hearts.

In this connection, it is interesting that it is the Sabbath law that is highlighted in verse 2. The blessing of God's salvation and deliverance is clearly related in this verse to the keeping of the Sabbath. This is stated both positively ('blessed is the man who does this, and the son of man who holds it fast, who keeps the Sabbath…') and negatively ('… not profaning it, and keeps his hand from doing any evil').

The promise of 56:2 is couched in individualistic terms: it is 'the man' who keeps the Sabbath who is blessed. The same blessing is reiterated in 56:6 in more universalistic terms; with the expanded vision of the prophet in this chapter, the blessing is now applied to foreigners, to 'everyone who keeps the Sabbath and does not profane it, and holds fast my covenant'.

This passage is of critical importance. Isaiah looks forward to the day when the good news of God's salvation expands to embrace those whom the Old Testament does not allow into the communion of Israel—notably the eunuchs and the foreigners. The experience of Pentecost (Acts 2) represents a fulfilment of these promises: the light of the Gospel now extends to all men everywhere. And, according to Isaiah's teaching in this chapter, the nature of that New Testament Gospel is the same as the Old Testament message of salvation: it is through God's covenant that men and women are saved.

More importantly, for our purposes, Isaiah envisages a keeping of the Sabbath during that era of expansiveness and fulfilment. There is a promise in the present to those who keep the Sabbath (56:2) but there is also a promise in the future for those who keep the Sabbath (56:6). Sabbath-keeping is not merely an Old Testament phenomenon; it is something which Isaiah intimates here as remaining during the era of world history in which the light of the truth will spread its rays to the ends of the earth.

There is another strand to this prophecy which clearly links it to the New Testament. In 56:7, Isaiah says that those who will keep the Sabbath and hold fast to God's covenant will have a place in God's house, 'for my house shall be called a house of prayer for all peoples'. These are the words which Jesus cites when he cleanses the Temple (Matthew 21:13, Mark 11:17; Luke 19:46) from those who had defiled it. In John's account, the cleansing of the Temple is also related to the resurrection of Jesus (John 2:21), in which the raised body of Christ will function as a rebuilt Temple, a paradigm for the church, the spiritual temple (Ephesians 2:19–22). According to Paul in Ephesians 2, foreigners (*cf.* Isaiah 56:6) will be fellow citizens with saints in the spiritual temple, built on the foundation of the apostles and prophets.

In tying all these strands together, and doing justice to the flow of the Bible's narrative, we need to realise that the Sabbath element is carried across the Testaments; it would be very strange indeed were Isaiah's prophecy of a future temple, housed by foreigners who keep the Sabbath, not to be assumed in Paul's teaching of the church as a temple. This New Testament temple, the church, inhabited by foreigners, is also a Sabbath-keeping temple, because it is also a covenant community which loves to serve God and to honour his law. We fail to understand Isaiah and Paul together if we can drop the Sabbath between the testaments and between the epochal eras of revelation.

Before we leave this section, it is interesting to note how a premillennial scholar like Warren Wiersbe interprets it. He wants to make a clear distinction between the Old Testament Sabbath and the New Testament Lord's Day. He argues that to call Sunday the 'Christian Sabbath' is to confuse two different entities.[7] He correctly sees that 'God never before asked the Gentiles to join the Jews in keeping the Sabbath but here he does so';[8] but then he engages in theological cart-wheels by insisting that there will be a future restoration of the Jews to their land, a restoration of Temple worship, and a literal Sabbath-keeping at the end of human history.[9]

The plain truth of the Scripture is, however, that there is now a breadth and comprehensiveness to the publication of the Gospel message which brings to fulfilment all that the Temple represented under the old covenant. Now there is a new Sabbath-keeping, which is the privilege of both Jew and Gentile, who honour God's covenant, who worship his name, and who keep sacred time.

Isaiah has a second reference to the Sabbath in chapter 58:13–14:

If you turn back your foot from the Sabbath,
from doing your pleasure on my holy day,
and call the Sabbath a delight
and the holy day of the LORD honourable;
if you honour it, not going your own ways,
or seeking your own pleasure, or talking idly;
then you shall take delight in the LORD,
and I will make you ride on the heights of the earth;
I will feed you with the heritage of Jacob your father,
for the mouth of the LORD has spoken.

This conditional statement (*'if you ... then I ...'*) comes as part of an analysis of true and false religion. In the first part of the chapter, God takes issue with the religious practice of the people, who believed that the lengths to which they went in fasting would make them acceptable to God. The spirit of the Sermon on the Mount runs through these verses, as Isaiah rounds on this external religiosity much as Christ did in Matthew 6:16–18.

The theme running through the chapter is that if we give God the worship and service he requires, then he will bless us; but if we are content with mere outward performance, then he will not accept this from us. In religious matters, and not least in the matter of the Sabbath, man looks on the outward appearance, while God looks on the heart (1 Samuel 16:7).

The reference to the Sabbath in this passage comes in the form of a conditional promise: if God's people do something, then he promises to do something for them in return. The first part of the condition is that they should 'turn back their foot from the Sabbath', a metaphor for taking care of how they live and behave on the Sabbath day. It is not a day for people to do their own pleasure, to go their own ways or even to talk idly. It is a day, rather, in which God's people should delight, regarding the day as an honour and also honouring the day.

For Isaiah, therefore, Sabbath observance is not just a matter of foregoing certain practices. It is a matter of attitude and of affection before it is a matter of habit and practice. God's call to his people through Isaiah at this point is that they should positively *enjoy* God's holy day, taking delight in it. For God's covenant people, there ought to be an element of *pleasure* in the keeping of God's commandments.

This is not a note unique to Isaiah. David could describe God's commandments as being 'sweeter also than honey and drippings of the honeycomb' (Psalm 19:10), and expresses his love for the law of God time and again in Psalm 119 (such as at verses 97 and 113). In the New Testament, Paul also testifies of his affection for God's commandments:

'So the law is holy and the commandment is holy and righteous and good ... I delight in the law of God in my inner being ...' (Romans 7:12, 22).

For Isaiah, therefore, to teach that God's people ought to find the Sabbath a source of real joy is nothing other than the experience of God's people in every generation, as they reflect on the nature of God's law and the desire they have to please God in every aspect of life and living. The world may find the Sabbath day a burden; but those who love the Lord find it a delight.

So the reward of which Isaiah 58:14 speaks is the way God meets this attitude of joy and exuberant delight in his day, as he promises to exalt his people, and feed them with the heritage of Jacob. This is the language of covenant, tying together the Old Testament promises of land and inheritance with faithful obedience to the demands of the covenant Lord. It echoes the words of Psalm 37:3–6:

Trust in the LORD and do good; dwell in the land and befriend faithfulness.
Delight yourself in the LORD, and he will give you the desires of your heart.
Commit your way to the LORD, trust in him, and he will act.
He will bring forth your righteousness as the light, and your justice as the noonday.

The burden for the Christian, therefore, ought not to be in keeping the law of God, but in not keeping it. That was the struggle Paul faced in Romans 7—the real burden of having any propensity to sin, and finding in himself that which moved him to disobey God's commandment. He looked for release from that burden, in order to please God, for he knew that the religion of the Bible is one that lifts the heart heavenward, and looks to God for all joy and pleasure.

This is precisely what Jonathan Edwards is referring to when he says that

Those who have a sincere desire to obey God in all things, will keep the Sabbath more carefully and more cheerfully, if they have seen and been convinced that therein they do what is according to the will and command of God, and what is acceptable to him; and will also have a great deal more comfort in the reflection upon their having carefully and painfully kept the Sabbath.[10]

For Edwards, keeping the Sabbath 'painfully' is the result of keeping it joyfully!

There is another important reference to the Sabbath in Isaiah 66:22–23

'For as the new heavens and the new earth
that I make
shall remain before me, says the LORD,
so shall your offspring and your name remain.
From new moon to new moon,
and from Sabbath to Sabbath,
all flesh shall come to worship before me,
declares the LORD.'

These verses form part of the conclusion to the prophecy, as Isaiah anticipates the future. It is important to note here that he uses vocabulary and phraseology which will be taken up by New Testament writers. The phrase 'new heavens' and 'new earth' appear, for example, in 2 Peter 3:13 and Revelation 21:1. Indeed, Isaiah has already used the phrase in 65, in the following verses:

For behold, I create new heavens and a new earth, and the former things shall not be remembered or come into mind. But be glad and rejoice for ever in that which I create; for behold, I create Jerusalem to be a joy and her people to be a gladness (65:17–18).

Isaiah anticipates a new day in the future, in a prophecy which we believe contains several layers of meaning. There is an anticipation of the New Testament era, with the coming of Christ and his death and resurrection.

There is a looking forward to the age of the Holy Spirit when God will build his spiritual Jerusalem, and establish his spiritual kingdom in the hearts and lives of his people, a kingdom characterized by righteousness, peace and joy (Romans 14:17). But, ultimately, Isaiah's horizon stretches beyond even the present, glorious age of the Spirit, to the time when all things will be made new, and God will finally banish all sadness and death (Revelation 21:4).

So, the great prophecy ends with the realization that the King will come for judgement (66:15–16) and to gather together his people. The principle that comes before us here is that of the continuity of God's work across all the ages: what he inaugurated in the Old Testament he will consummate and complete with the final vindication of his people who shall spend eternity with him. He will always have a people to worship and serve him: a remnant, chosen by grace (Romans 11:5).

And this is the language used by Isaiah to describe the ages across which the work of salvation rolls: 'from new moon to new moon and from Sabbath to Sabbath'. The phraseology appears like this elsewhere in the Old Testament (*cf.* 2 Kings 4:23). Isaiah might easily have said, 'from month to month and from week to week', but he does not. He characterizes the month by the term 'full moon' and the week by the term 'Sabbath'. This builds, of course, on the promise given to Noah that 'while the earth remains, seedtime and harvest, cold and heat, summer and winter, day and night shall not cease' (Genesis 8:22). But this is now nuanced through the prophet's vision to include the weekly cycle of Sabbath observance, and the monthly cycle of the new moon, so important for other religious rituals in Israel (*cf.* Psalm 81:3).

In other words, Isaiah anticipates a continuation of the Sabbath, paralleling the continuation of God's purpose and plan of grace across the ages. Just as the work of grace will continue until the words of Isaiah are fulfilled in their highest sense, so the Sabbath will not cease. Isaiah's prophecy concludes with one of the clearest indications of Scripture that the Sabbath was not a temporary institution, but one which God intended to be permanent, a point which Christ himself reinforces.

The Sabbath in Amos

We know very little about the prophet Amos. We can gather from this collection of his writings that he lived in Tekoa, near Bethlehem, and that he was called by God to be a prophet while he was looking after sheep and goats (7:14–15). His ministry is reckoned to have lasted from 765–760BC.[11] Amos has an interesting way of getting his message across: he begins with oracles against the nations round about Israel, messages of judgement with which one might imagine Israel agreeing. But then, all of a sudden, the message of judgement focuses on Israel itself (2:6ff), and continues in an analysis of the sins of the northern kingdom. In other words, Amos has turned the self-centred worldview of Israel on its head, proclaiming that past privileges do not secure immunity from judgement: they merely add to guilt and condemnation. The result, as Walter Kaiser puts it, is that 'Instead of the day of the Lord being a panacea for all the nation's ills, it would bring disaster, as perverted religion and empty ritual must lead to political and economic crashes'.[12]

The theme of the 'Day of the LORD' appears elsewhere in the prophets (Isaiah 2:12, Joel 1:15); it would seem that by the time Amos uses it, it is one of these theological phrases that is current in the conversations of the covenant people. So as Amos looks into the future, challenging the false hopes and optimism of the people, he has 'that day' in view (Amos 8:3). Because of the false religiosity, hypocrisy and legalism that have been so much a part of the life of the nation, 'that day' will be a day of darkness (8:9) and of spiritual famine (8:11–12).

One of the reasons for this judgement concerns the Sabbath, as Amos makes clear in the following passage (8:4–7):

Hear this, you who trample on the needy
and bring the poor of the land to an end,
saying, 'When will the new moon be over,
that we may sell grain?
And the Sabbath,
that we may offer wheat for sale,
that we may make the ephah small and the shekel great
and deal deceitfully with false balances,
that we may buy the poor for silver
and the needy for a pair of sandals

and sell the chaff of the wheat?'
The LORD has sworn by the pride of Jacob:
'Surely I will never forget any of their deeds.'

This is not so much an attack on Sabbath-breaking as a tirade on those corrupt businessmen who took advantage of the poor and needy in society. Yet the reference to the Sabbath is an interesting one. The implication is that a kind of lip-service was paid to the Sabbath day, but in their hearts these people were saying 'When will the Sabbath be over, so that we can get back to exploiting the poor and cheating on those who deal with us?' Indeed, perhaps their deepest thought was not when the Sabbath day would be ended, but when the Sabbath would be gone for ever.

There is a tacit admission in this passage that one of the functions of the Sabbath was precisely to prevent exploitation. The people suspended their ordinary activity, and in doing so, the poorer classes had respite. The commandment was designed as much to protect the servants and the strangers as to provide rest for the covenant people.

In fact, there is an interesting wordplay in the Hebrew construction of this passage. The motive of those who trample the needy is to bring the poor of the land 'to an end'. The Hebrew form of that phrase is similar to the word for 'Sabbath', and shows how the people were actually perverting God's original intention both for his law and for his people. The law was intended to help his people, given for their spiritual advantage, so that all would benefit from its regulations and precepts. Now, however, the people are using it for their own advantage; as Gary Smith comments, 'their goals were directly contrary to Yahweh's purpose of protecting the poor'.[13] The result is that God will bring an 'end' on them (8:2).

Amos' prophetic word is as relevant today as ever it was. The same materialistic impulse, fuelled by the secularization of our modern society, drives out the Sabbath principle in its protection of the poor. The principle of rest, applied to the economic situation of our contemporary world, acts as an effective barrier to the amorality of the free market in which business is conducted in the Western world. As Rev. Fergus Macdonald put it in a moderatorial address before the General Assembly of the Free Church of Scotland:

Today our most effective advocacy of the Sabbath commandment would, I believe, be to carry the Sabbath principle into the public square and demonstrate to political and business leaders alike its penetrating prophetic critique of unfettered capitalism and its deep pastoral concern for the human and ecological casualties of a myopic pursuit of wealth.[14]

That is precisely what Amos is doing, and his message is as relevant today as ever it was.

The Sabbath in Jeremiah

Jeremiah was one of the great prophets of the Old Testament, called to a forty-year ministry which coincided with the last four decades of Judah's history before the captivity of 587BC. His message was largely the message of that approaching judgement, with the gleam of light that anticipates restoration to the covenant land (30:18; 31:17), and a future re-casting of God's covenant purposes in the form of a 'new covenant' (31:31ff).

Jeremiah's call to public ministry is outlined in the opening chapter. In particular, God says to him:

Behold, I have put my words in your mouth. See, I have set you this day over nations and over kingdoms, to pluck up and to break down, to destroy and to overthrow, to build and to plant' (1:9–10).

O. Palmer Robertson suggests that these six infinitives, appearing regularly at critical points throughout the book, form the key structural basis for Jeremiah's message.[15] They are 'a theme round which Jeremiah perceived his ministry to centre'.[16] The six words contain four negative words (plucking up, breaking down, destroying and overthrowing) and two positive words (building up and planting). They bring together the twin messages of judgment and hope, of demolition and of building up.

This language appears in the passage in which Jeremiah addresses the Sabbath issue, in chapter 17:19–27:

Thus said the LORD to me: 'Go and stand in the People's Gate, by which the kings of Judah enter and by which they go out, and in all the gates of Jerusalem, and say: "Hear the word of the LORD, you kings of Judah, and all Judah, and all the inhabitants of Jerusalem, who enter by these gates. Thus says the LORD: 'Take care for the sake of your lives, and do not bear a burden on the Sabbath day or bring it in by the gates of Jerusalem. And do not carry a burden out of your houses on the Sabbath or do any work, but keep the Sabbath day holy, as I commanded your fathers.' Yet they did not listen or incline their ear, but stiffened their neck, that they might not hear and receive instruction.

'"But if you listen to me, declares the LORD, and bring in no burden by the gates of this city on the Sabbath day, but keep the Sabbath day holy and do no work on it, then there shall enter by the gates of this city kings and princes who sit on the throne of David, riding in chariots and on horses, they and their officials, the men of Judah and the inhabitants of Jerusalem. And this city shall be inhabited for ever. And people shall come from the cities of Judah and the places around Jerusalem, from the land of Benjamin, from the Shephelah, from the hill country, and from the Negeb, bringing burnt offerings and sacrifices, grain offerings and frankincense, and bringing thank offerings to the house of the LORD. But if you do not listen to me, to keep the Sabbath day holy, and not to bear a burden and enter by the gates of Jerusalem on the Sabbath day, then I will kindle a fire in its gates, and it shall devour the palaces of Jerusalem and shall not be quenched."'

The passage ends with the threat of destruction and of demolition, just as God had intimated to Jeremiah at the outset. In this case, the argument of the prophet is clear: desecrating the Sabbath leads to judgement. God is jealous for his honour, and jealous for his day.

John L. Mackay draws our attention to the fact that in Exodus 31:13, 17, the Sabbath day, in addition to its being incorporated and guarded in the Ten Commandments, was also given the position of a 'sign' of the covenant. 'As such,' Professor Mackay concludes, 'it was a key index of the nation's spiritual commitment to the Lord, challenging them as to whether God or their own economic and personal interests were to be the ultimate determinant of their lifestyle'.[17] It was not, therefore, merely a matter of observing one day and expecting God's blessing, as if that day was a talisman or a good-luck charm: Jeremiah took the attitude of the people to the Sabbath as a sign of their attitude to the whole of God's law, and, ultimately, as a sign of their attitude to God himself.

Jeremiah's word is addressed to the people and to their leaders. It is a message addressed to the commercial world of his day, and to the business activities which were going on in Jerusalem. Clearly there was nothing to distinguish the Sabbath from any other day: burdens were being carried in and out—'on the seventh day of the week it was business as usual in Jerusalem'.[18] The prophet's controversy is not with the people engaging in business, but with the fact that they were neglecting God's prescription as to how such business ought to be conducted.

Jeremiah reminds the people that God had given a law that was specific in its standards. No burden was to be carried *in* on the Sabbath, and no burden was to be carried *out*. Work was forbidden, and the day was to be kept holy. Later, Jewish rabbis would nuance these parameters even further than God himself intended; and this would be evidenced in the way in which Jesus would be accused of breaking the commandment by plucking grains of corn.

But the abuse of a law does not negate that law. The ethic of the commandment still stood: this was what God had commanded their fathers (17:22), and they had stubbornly resisted. That reference seems to confirm Jeremiah's earlier observation in this same chapter that 'the heart is deceitful above all things and desperately sick: who can understand it?' (17:9). Just as those to whom the Sabbath law had been given in the first place found it easy to stray from it and to break it, so, too, had the Judah of Jeremiah's day rebelled against God by failing to honour his day.

What is perhaps surprising in this passage is the exuberant and exaggerated blessings which God outlines for those who do respect his day and his law. As a consequence of Sabbath-keeping and Sabbath-obedience, Jeremiah promises a succession of Davidic kings, a Jerusalem forever inhabited, and a stream of foreigners coming to Jerusalem to worship the true God (17:25–26). On the other hand, a continued disrespect for the Sabbath would result in the destruction of Jerusalem.

In spite of the fact that some liberal commentators have suggested that this passage was a later addition to the book, Jeremiah's word on the Sabbath day and its importance rings true. This is part of God's work to 'tear down' before he 'builds up'. The fire of judgement is kindled in Jerusalem, and the exile into Babylon is a direct consequence of the people's neglect of God and his law. This is made clear in Jeremiah 25, where the prophet intimates that for twenty-three years 'the word of the Lord has come to me, and I have spoken persistently to you but you have not listened' (25:3). As a consequence, God says that he will banish the voice of joy from the land: 'this whole land shall become a ruin and a waste, and these nations shall serve the king of Babylon seventy years' (25:11). Elsewhere, this notification of God's judgement is described as a Sabbath:

[Nebuchadnezzar] took into exile in Babylon those who had escaped from the sword, and they became servants to him and to his sons until the establishment of the kingdom of Persia, to fulfil the word of the LORD by the mouth of Jeremiah, until the land had enjoyed its Sabbaths. All the days that it lay desolate it kept Sabbath, to fulfil seventy years (2 Chronicles 36:20–21).

So here is an interesting and instructive commentary on the exile and the reason for it: God's people failed to honour him. Their neglect of the Sabbath was one symptom of that dishonour. Their commercial activity on the Sabbath day was a public protest against the authority of God over them and their lives. Their attitude was that the Sabbath was like any other day: there was no need to keep it holy, or to keep it as a day of rest.

So, in spite of the many repeated warnings they received, God himself forced a Sabbath rest on the land. His patience ran its course, and judgement came upon them. The land enjoyed its Sabbaths, its seventy long years of rest, showing that God was not to be mocked. The Babylonian captivity was a Sabbath for the land, which the people could not enjoy, and was a direct consequence of their failing to honour God by giving him the Sabbath he asked for in his law.

The principle which comes clearly before us in Jeremiah is simply this: that God honours those who honour him (1 Samuel 2:30). Individuals and nations have a responsibility to give to God the respect, reverence and 'fear' that he is due. His day cannot be despised lightly. Just as Sabbath-keeping, in Jeremiah's day, was a badge of the people's submission to God in every area of their lives, so, too, their Sabbath-breaking was a visible and public mark of their rebellion. God tolerates that sin so far, but draws a line eventually. How much we need to heed Jeremiah's message and remind ourselves that God is not mocked!

To do servile work on the Sabbath shows an irreligious heart, and greatly offends God. To do secular work on this day is to follow the devil's plough; it is to debase the soul. God made this day on purpose to raise the heart to heaven, to converse with him, to do angels' work; and to be employed in earthly work is to degrade the soul of its honour. God will not have his day entrenched upon or defiled in the least thing. The man that gathered sticks on the Sabbath he commanded to be stoned (Numbers 15). It would seem a small thing to pick up a few sticks to make a fire; but God would not have this day violated in the smallest matters. Nay, the work which had reference to a religious use might not be done on the Sabbath, as the hewing of stones for the building of the sanctuary. Bezaleel, who was to cut the stones, and carve the timber out for the sanctuary, must forbear to do it on the Sabbath (Exodus 31:15). A temple is a place of worship, but it was a sin to build a temple on the Lord's day.

Thomas Watson, *A Body of Divinity* (London, 1898), p. 294

The Sabbath in Ezekiel

With its 48 chapters, the Book of Ezekiel is one of the major books of the Old Testament, yet is probably one of the most neglected. Part of the historical importance of this prophecy is its setting: Ezekiel is one of the few prophets who continued a prophetic ministry while the nation was in captivity in Babylon. Ezekiel, who functioned as a priest (1:3) as well as a prophet, focuses much of his message around the priestly ministry and the temple services.

One of the themes running through the book, with its review of Jerusalem's condition before the exile (in chapters 1–24), its judgement against the nations (in chapters 25–32) and its anticipation of future restoration (in chapters 33–48), is that of the glory of God. In intricate, visionary material in chapter 1, Ezekiel says that he saw 'the likeness of the glory of the LORD. And when I saw it, I fell on my face, and I heard the voice of one speaking' (1:28). This is similar to John's experience on the isle of Patmos (Revelation 1:12–17). The glory of the Lord is what commissions Ezekiel, and is further developed in subsequent chapters (*cf.* 3:12, 23).

However, as Ezekiel becomes aware of the sins of the covenant people, and the abominations of the Temple, the prophet sees the glory of God moving from its central location in the Temple precincts, to dwell at the threshold of the house (9:3; 10:4), moving then towards the cherubim (10:24), and out of the city altogether (11:23). Unbelievably, the glory of God, which the covenant people knew, was going to dwell among the heathen nations (39:21). The image is one of a departed glory, an 'Ichabod' (1 Samuel 4:21), an experience in which God is exiled from his dwelling-place. The inevitable consequence is that God's people will be exiled from theirs.

And Ezekiel has no doubt as to the reason for this departure:

I gave them my Sabbaths, as a sign between me and them, that they might know that I am the LORD who sanctifies them. But the house of Israel rebelled against me in the wilderness. They did not walk in my statutes but rejected my rules, by which, if a person does them, he shall live; and my Sabbaths they greatly profaned (20:12–13).

Drawing on Exodus 31, with its doctrine of the Sabbath as covenant-sign, Ezekiel declares that the Sabbath desecration of which the people were guilty was evidence of a deeper rejection of God and rebellion against his law. As the review of Israel's past continues in Ezekiel 20, so the charge of having polluted the Sabbaths becomes an increasing part of the case against Israel (see 20:21, 24). The judgement continues in 22:8—'You have despised my holy things and profaned my Sabbaths'. The priests are guilty of failing to distinguish between the sacred and the secular:

They have made no distinction between the holy and the common, neither have they taught the difference between the unclean and the clean, and they have disregarded my Sabbaths, so that I am profaned among them (22:26).

There can only be one consequence: 'Therefore I have poured out my indignation upon them' (22:31).

If that were the sum and substance of the message, it would be a dark one indeed. But there is more: the glory returns to a new Jerusalem and a new Temple: 'as the glory of the LORD entered the temple by the gate facing east, the Spirit lifted me up and brought me into the inner court; and behold, the glory of the LORD filled the temple' (43:4–5). God's purpose is not exhausted with the captivity. He will restore the fortunes of his people, and will turn their captivity (cf. Psalm 126:1–2).

It is in this context that Ezekiel mentions the Sabbath, describing the worship of a renewed, restored and spiritual Temple in 46:1–12:

Thus says the Lord GOD: The gate of the inner court that faces east shall be shut on the six working days, but on the Sabbath day it shall be opened, and on the day of the new moon it shall be opened. The prince shall enter by the vestibule of the gate from outside, and shall take his stand by the post of the gate. The priests shall offer his burnt offering and his peace offerings, and he shall worship at the threshold of the gate. Then he shall go out, but the gate shall not be shut until evening. The people of the land shall bow down at the entrance of that gate before the LORD on the Sabbaths and on the new moons. The burnt offering that the prince offers to the LORD on the Sabbath day shall be six lambs without blemish and a ram without blemish. And the grain offering with the ram shall be an ephah, and the grain offering with the lambs shall be as much as he is able, together with a hin of oil to each ephah. On the day of the new moon he shall offer a bull from the herd without blemish, and six lambs and a ram, which shall be without blemish. As a grain offering he shall provide an ephah with the bull and an ephah with the ram, and with the lambs as much as he is able, together with a hin of oil to each ephah. When the prince enters, he shall enter by the vestibule of the gate, and he shall go out by the same way.

When the people of the land come before the LORD at the appointed feasts, he who enters by the north gate to worship shall go out by the south gate, and he who enters by the south gate shall go out by the north gate: no one shall return by way of the gate by which he entered, but each shall go out straight ahead. When they enter, the prince shall enter with them, and when they go out, he shall go out. At the feasts and the appointed festivals, the grain offering with a young bull shall be an ephah, and with a ram an ephah, and with the lambs as much as one is able to give, together with a hin of oil to an ephah. When the prince provides a freewill offering, either a burnt offering or peace offerings as a freewill offering to the LORD, the gate facing east shall be opened for him. And he shall offer his burnt offering or his peace offerings as he does on the Sabbath day. Then he shall go out, and after he has gone out the gate shall be shut.

One of the difficulties of this section is to identify the 'Prince', who leads the worship of God in Ezekiel's Temple. He alone eats bread in God's presence (44:3) and is in a position of particular closeness to him. Does he represent Christ? Or is he an ideal king figure? Given the nature of Ezekiel's writings, it does seem fair to say that 'we should not expect the "prince" to emerge as any one figure of definable identity … what we have in these chapters is an entire impressionistic tableau'.[19]

And what we also have here is the use of the phrase 'Sabbath and new moon'. In 46:1, the east gate, that is, the gate by which the glory of God returned to the Temple (44:2) is to remain closed, except on the Sabbath day and on the day of the new moon. Ezekiel's vision clearly draws on traditional, Mosaic teaching regarding the marking of special, sacred times of worship and communion with God, but nuances these differently. The people are to gather to the eastern gate on the Sabbaths and new moons, when offerings will be offered to the Lord (46:4, 12), officiating on behalf of the people in the presence of a God who dwells among them again.

Things will be different in the future, but the Sabbath principle will remain. The blessings of communion with God, of which the Sabbath speaks so eloquently, will be enjoyed in new measure by the people of God. Iain Duguid brings out the importance of this, when he comments on the 'lack of timelessness' so often found in eschatological visions in the Bible.[20] He goes on to say that 'in Ezekiel's reordering of the festival calendar, time itself is brought under the discipline of the new age',[21] and he goes on to apply this to Christian worship today. And although he does not explicitly speak of the Sabbath factor in Christian worship, that is surely one of the main lines along which Ezekiel's vision takes us: to the realization that just as Jesus is our sacrifice and Prince, and just as we are a spiritual temple in him, so he has given us a new sacred 'time', a new Sabbath, a Sabbath of the eighth day (*cf.* 43:27), our Lord's Day Sabbath.

The Sabbath in Nehemiah

To complete this survey of the Sabbath in the prophetic writings of the Old Testament, we need to turn to someone who was not a prophet, but who nonetheless plays an important part in the affairs of God's people following their return from exile. Nehemiah had risen to an important position under Artaxerxes of Persia. The Persians were used by God to deliver his covenant people out of the power of the Babylonians, and now Nehemiah, hearing of the sorry fortunes of those exiles who had returned to Jerusalem, receives the king's permission and blessing to join them. He set about rebuilding the wall of Jerusalem, but discovered a deeper problem. Walter Kaiser summarizes:

> There were new problems for Nehemiah to face: loss of income for the workers, who had left farms and homes, was forcing some of them into debt as they mortgaged their fields and vineyards to pay their taxes and provide for food … Nehemiah was angered by the way the wealthy class was using this national crisis to make an inordinate amount of money for themselves.[22]

This was part of the deep moral and spiritual crisis which still remained, even after the years of exile. Not surprisingly, the Sabbath issue was symptomatic of this moral crisis, and it is raised in three passages in Nehemiah.

First, in Nehemiah 9:14, there is a reference to the Sabbath commandment given many years before: 'and you made known to them your holy Sabbath and commanded them commandments and statutes and a law by Moses your servant.' The context of this is important; it is a setting of worship, in which the spiritual and temporal leadership of the people combine to bring about a rededication and recommitment to the Lord. Part of the worship ceremony is a rehearsal of the past, a summarizing of the history and the spiritual inheritance of the children of Israel.

This is an important reference, since it reminds us of the continuity of God's moral law across the generations. After the exile, the community of God's people stood in solidarity with their forefathers, and acknowledged the many covenant blessings and privileges which they had been given. Among them was the Sabbath principle, and, along with other laws and commandments, the people had disregarded it. The prophets had warned that disobeying God's law would lead to exile; now, after the exile, the people acknowledge the reality of that threat, and the truth of that prophetic word.

Second, the Sabbath is mentioned in Nehemiah 10. The result of the worship service is a confession of sin and a renewal of covenant commitment and obligation. The people responded to the reading and explanation of the law in the following manner:

The rest of the people, the priests, the Levites, the gatekeepers, the singers, the temple servants, and all who have separated themselves from the peoples of the lands to the Law of God, their wives, their sons, their daughters, all who have knowledge and understanding, join with their brothers, their nobles, and enter into a curse and an oath to walk in God's Law that was given by Moses the servant of God, and to observe and do all the commandments of the LORD our Lord and his rules and his statutes. 'We will not give our daughters to the peoples of the land or take their daughters for our sons. And if the peoples of the land bring in goods or any grain on the Sabbath day to sell, we will not buy from them on the Sabbath or on a holy day. And we will forego the crops of the seventh year and the exaction of every debt' (10:28–31).

The pledge of the people is more than a recognition of the authority of God's law: it is a very public promise to be separate, and to be different from other people. That is why we ought to pause at the reference to 'peoples of the land' bringing in goods to sell on the Sabbath day. As Charles Fensham points out in his commentary on Nehemiah:

For a small religious community in a larger world of heathens who did not hold the sabbath law, it became more and more difficult to keep it. The foreign merchants arrived in Jerusalem on the sabbath and wanted to do business. The way of least resistance was for the Jews to accommodate themselves to these foreign customs. But in this verse the Jews put themselves under obligation to withhold from participating in any transactions on the sabbath.[23]

In other words, this was a willing and public subjection to the Sabbath law which was going to be costly. It was a pledge that a people, reminded of their privileges and covenant blessings, were willing to make. The Sabbath was then, as it is now, a public badge of what God meant to this people.

However, there is a *third* passage in Nehemiah which refers to the Sabbath, and which shows that the promises made by the people were quickly forgotten. Consider what Nehemiah says in 13:15–22:

In those days I saw in Judah people treading winepresses on the Sabbath, and bringing in heaps of grain and loading them on donkeys, and also wine, grapes, figs, and all kinds of loads, which they brought into Jerusalem on the Sabbath day. And I warned them on the day when they sold food. Tyrians also, who lived in the city, brought in fish and all kinds of goods and sold them on the Sabbath to the people of Judah, in Jerusalem itself! Then I confronted the nobles of Judah and said to them, 'What is this evil thing that you are doing, profaning the Sabbath day? Did not your fathers act in this way, and did not our God bring all this disaster on us and on this city? Now you are bringing more wrath on Israel by profaning the Sabbath.'

As soon as it began to grow dark at the gates of Jerusalem before the Sabbath, I commanded that the doors should be shut and gave orders that they should not be opened until after the Sabbath. And I stationed some of my servants at the gates, that no load might be brought in on the Sabbath day. Then the merchants and sellers of all kinds of wares lodged outside Jerusalem once or twice. But I warned them and said to them, 'Why do you lodge outside the wall? If you do so again, I will lay hands on you.' From that time on they did not come on the Sabbath. Then I commanded the Levites that they should purify themselves and come and guard the gates, to keep the Sabbath day holy. Remember this also in my favour, O my God, and spare me according to the greatness of your steadfast love.

In surveying the country of Judah, Nehemiah came across places where the Sabbath was forgotten, and where commercial activity was going on, in direct contradiction of the law of God. Nehemiah's anger is fuelled, first, by the realization that God's covenant people have become just like the peoples round about them. The Sabbath covenant sign signifies nothing. What ought to have been a badge of their distinctiveness as a people set apart for Jehovah's honour and glory has long since ceased to be worn. The literal wall around the city set Jerusalem apart; but the spiritual wall was still in need of repair.

Nehemiah is also angry because the people have learned so little from their history. Have they not appreciated that the neglect of the Sabbath, symbolic of rebellion and disobedience in the past, was one of the very reasons God visited his people with judgement, in the form of exile and banishment? Sometimes the lessons of history are the most difficult to apply; Nehemiah discovered a generation for whom that was certainly the case.

Nehemiah took practical steps to correct this situation, first of all positioning his own servants outside the gate to prevent this commercial activity going on; and secondly, giving the duty of protecting the city on the Sabbath to the Levites. It is interesting to note that this duty of Sabbath-keeping is specifically given to the priests, so that, just as in Ezekiel's prophecy and vision, the restoration of a spiritual worship among God's people focuses on the Temple and the priestly office.

The book of Nehemiah makes an important contribution to our understanding of the relationship that there ought to be between church and state. Nehemiah was not a prophet; he acts as a public political figure. Yet he sees himself as under God, obligated to serve him, and to make use of those in religious office to that end. Some theologians have argued that there ought to be complete separation between church and state, and that any state connection is a dangerous thing for the church. Yet it is difficult to argue that point on the basis of the Book of Nehemiah, where political and religious offices combine to support, defend and maintain the worship of God's people.

It seems to me that there is evidence here that God's people ought to be public in their defence and support of the Sabbath, and that those whom God has set over us in public office ought also to support these principles. As the history of the people of God in the Old Testament draws to a conclusion, the Sabbath principle is maintained. It does not recede into the background. We are not allowed to forget the holy day God gave his people, and the obligation they are under to serve and obey him in all things.

The New Covenant

The prophets were commissioned, as we have seen, to deliver God's word to God's people. But they looked forward, too, and anticipated the glories of the New Testament era, the coming of Jesus Christ, and the superiority of his work on the cross. Jeremiah speaks in terms of a new covenant:

Behold, the days are coming, declares the LORD, when I will make a new covenant with the house of Israel and the house of Judah, not like the covenant that I made with their fathers on the day when I took them by the hand to bring them out of the land of Egypt, my covenant that they broke, though I was their husband, declares the LORD. But this is the covenant that I will make with the house of Israel after those days, declares the LORD: I will put my law within them, and I will write it on their hearts. And I will be their God, and they shall be my people. And no longer shall each one teach his neighbour and each his brother, saying, 'Know the LORD,' for they shall all know me, from the least of them to the greatest, declares the LORD. For I will forgive their iniquity, and I will remember their sin no more.

Let us remind ourselves, before we leave our study of the Sabbath in the prophets, that Jeremiah's vision of a 'new covenant' includes the writing of God's law on the hearts of his people. Just as law was integral to the covenant arrangement earlier in the Old Testament, so it will be an integral element in the New Testament arrangement. It is a fallacy to think that the new covenant is lawless, as if it did not bind us to the law given at Sinai. What is different is not the laws to which we are bound, but the emphasis on internalization and spirituality—these laws are now written on our hearts. Thus, for those who are in a new covenant with God in Christ Jesus there is no abrogating of the Sabbath command; but, along with the other laws, that commandment has been given new significance, and God's people have a new propensity and motive to honour God's day.

As O. Palmer Robertson puts it, 'the substance of the law itself, apart from any externalised ritualistic details, becomes directly a part of the heart of the new covenant participant'.[24] Thus the believer is now freed from the law as a basis of salvation (as in the old covenant of works), and is freed to keep the law as a result of the covenant of grace. We therefore must read all the Old Testament passages on Sabbath-keeping and other law matters into the Jeremiac vision of an internalized law provision. And that will be further developed by Christ and the apostles in the New Testament.

Conclusion

The prophets, as we saw at the outset of this chapter, were commissioned and called by God to proclaim his word. That meant remaining faithful to the revelation that he had given. He spoke in many ways to the fathers by the prophets, but he never wavered from setting his moral, Sinaitic law before them as the standard of their obedience. The prophets remind Israel of their past, challenge their behaviour in the present, and point into the future. The law of which the Sabbath commandment is a part is the touchstone by which their loyalty to the God of the covenant is measured. And when they experience exile, they have only themselves to blame. No small part of their captivity is their neglect of the Sabbath. And no small part of their hope for the future is the restoration to the land of covenant promise, and the development of the Sabbath principle in ways hitherto unrealized.

Notes

1 For an excellent up to date treatment of this theme, *see* **O.P. Robertson,** *The Christ of the Prophets* (Philadelphia: Presbyterian and Reformed, 2004).

2 **Robertson,** *Christ of the Prophets*, p. 29.

3 **John L. Mackay,** *Jeremiah: An Introduction and Commentary*, Volume 1: Chapters 1–20 (Fearn, Tain: Mentor, 2004), p. 72.

4 **G.A. Smith,** *The Book of Isaiah*, Vol II, The Expositor's Bible (London: Hodder and Stoughton, 1892), p. 409.

5 **O.T. Allis,** *The Unity of Isaiah* (Nutley, NJ: Presbyterian and Reformed, 1977), p. 122.

6 **P. Hacking,** *Isaiah: Free to Suffer and to Serve*, Crossway Bible Guides (Nottingham: Crossway Books, 1994), p.178.

7 See **W. W. Wiersbe,** *Be Comforted: Isaiah* (Buckinghamshire: Scripture Press Foundation, 1992), p.144.

8 **Wiersbe,** *Be Comforted*, p. 144.

9 **Wiersbe,** *Be Comforted*, p. 145.

10 **J. Edwards,** 'The perpetuity and change of the Sabbath', in *Works*, Vol II, p. 93.

11 **Gary V. Smith,** *Amos: A Mentor Commentary* (Fearn, Tain: Mentor, 1998), p. 16.

12 **Walter J. Kaiser,** *A History of Israel from the Bronze Age Through the Jewish Wars* (Nashville: Broadman and Holman), 1998, p. 354.

13 **G.V. Smith,** *Amos*, p. 341.

14 **F.A.J. Macdonald,** 'Public Truth and Spiritual Freedom', *The Monthly Record*, June/July 2004, p. 7.

15 O.P. Robertson, *Christ of the Prophets*, p. 270.

16 J.L. Mackay, *Jeremiah: A Mentor Commentary*, Vol 1, Mentor, 2004, p. 104.

17 Mackay, *Jeremiah*, Vol 1, p. 524.

18 Philip G. Ryken, *Jeremiah and Lamentations: From Sorrow to Hope* (Wheaton, IL: Crossway books, 2001), p. 284.

19 D. Thomas, *God Strengthens: Ezekiel Simply Explained*, Darlington: Evangelical Press, 1993, p. 287.

20 I.M. Duguid, *Ezekiel*, The NIV Application Commentary (Grand Rapids: Zondervan, 1999), p. 524.

21 Duguid, *Ezekiel*, p. 524.

22 Kaiser, *History of Israel*, p. 443.

23 F. Charles Fensham, *The Books of Ezra and Nehemiah*, New International Commentary on the Old Tesatment (Grand Rapids: Eerdmans, 1982), pp. 239–40.

24 O.P. Robertson, *The Christ of the Covenants* (Phillipsburg NJ: Presbyterian and Reformed, 1980), p. 292.

Jesus and the Sabbath

The Son of Man is lord even of the Sabbath. Mark 2:28

Now after the Sabbath, towards the dawn of the first day of the week ...
an angel of the Lord descended from heaven and rolled back the
stone ... Matthew 28:1–2

My daughter and some of her friends are currently into wearing
wristbands. The current fashion is to wear coloured bands, with a
variety of issues and causes represented by them: 'cancer
awareness', 'against racism' and so on. Then there are the wristbands with a
message in the initials: P.U.S.H. for 'pray until something happens', F.R.O.G.
for 'fully rely on God', or the favourite: W.W.J.D.—'what would Jesus do?'

It is an interesting question, of course, which can be applied to all kinds
of situations: what would Jesus do if he were confronted with some of the
situations in which we find ourselves today? If our supreme concern is to
follow his example, and to be like him in all that we do, surely it is only right
that we should ask how he would respond and react to these issues.

Yet I have a sneaking suspicion that it is the wrong question to ask. On
the one hand, Jesus was not confronted with the modern issues which face
us. We don't, therefore, have direct access to information that would enable
us to answer the question 'what would Jesus do?' in every situation. Would
he use the Internet? Watch television? Send text messages? Wear
wristbands? Confronted with clear moral and ethical choices, we know
that he would always do what God required of him; but sometimes our
choices are not quite that clear. Would he ordain a minister who had been
unbiblically divorced? Would he employ musical instruments in worship?
Would he compete in sports events? Or attend the theatre?

On the other hand, there is a question we can ask: 'what *did* Jesus do?' I
wonder if asking 'what *would* he do?' masks our ignorance about what we
are in fact told about Jesus. I don't wear the wristband. I do want to be like
Jesus in all I say and do, and in all that I am. So the first thing I need to find
out about Jesus is what he said, or did, about the Sabbath principle.

It seems to me that there is a twofold fallacy in the minds of many Christians regarding Jesus' teaching on the Sabbath. First, many people assume that Jesus said little about the Sabbath day; and second, that the little he did say was an attack on Sabbath-keeping. The first of these fallacies is belied by the fact that all four Gospels contain several references to the Sabbath. It is not, in fact, true that Jesus had nothing to say about this special, covenantal day. Both in his teaching and by his example, as we shall see, he reinforced the responsibilities of the fourth commandment. Nor is it the case that of all Ten Commandments, this was the one that Christ did not underline. In fact, the teaching of the Gospels makes it clear that the Sabbath is of permanent duration, and is binding on us still.

The second fallacy has more than a grain of truth in it. Much of what Jesus said about the Sabbath was, in fact, in the context of a polemic, or argument, against the Pharisees and other Jews of his day, whose religion was legalistic in the extreme. There were some things at which they would draw a line, while there were other things they were ready to tolerate. Their religion was hypocritical. It is true: Jesus did attack their Sabbath-keeping.

But that does not mean that he attacked all Sabbath-keeping. In fact, the idea of hypocrisy has no meaning unless the practice itself is valid. It is possible to be a hypocrite in religion only because there is such a thing as a valid religion. And it is possible to be hypocritical in our Sabbath-keeping, only because there is such a thing as biblical Sabbath-keeping. Jesus' attack on the Pharisees for their Sabbath-keeping does not make all Sabbath-keeping wrong.

THE SABBATH OF THE LORD

It is clear from the Gospel records that Jesus was brought up to respect the commandments. Luke tells us that as a youth, Jesus 'grew and became strong, filled with wisdom. And the favour of God was upon him' (Luke 2:40). He was the God-man, to be sure, but for him that meant living in a world in a state of humiliation, dependent on God his Father, and dependent on other human beings, not least on Mary and Joseph.

We know very little about Jesus' young life. That is perhaps wise; we might have become fascinated by the development of Jesus from foetus to baby, from baby to toddler, from toddler to teenager. We might have been distracted by questions about his psychology, his pastimes, his friends. It may be frustrating, but we need to learn that there are questions the Bible does not even ask, and questions about the growth and development of the human Jesus are among these.

Nonetheless, we are not left entirely in the dark. We know that Mary and Joseph were faithful believers, whose relationship and home were characterized by a fear of God and a love for his law that make the holy family an exemplary family. One of the features of their family life was the habit of worship. They observed the annual religious festivals of Israel, for Luke tells us that Jesus' parents 'went to Jerusalem every year at the Feast of the Passover' (Luke 2:41). By the time Jesus had grown into manhood, the habits of piety and of religious worship had been carefully sown in his life by his parents.

Of course, in the case of Jesus, other factors feed into the equation. In him the fullness of the godhead dwelt bodily (Colossians 2:9), and therefore the Holy Spirit ministered to him in a unique way. The Word of God was also integral to his commitment to the Father's will, so that by the time he commences his public ministry he can say that he is fulfilling, and the fulfilment of, the Old Testament (see, for example, Luke 4:21). At the age of twelve he knows that his life's work is to be in his Father's house (Luke 2:49), and his subsequent ministry will demonstrate his understanding that to do the Father's will is to be his food and drink (John 4:34).

One of the habits that were developed in the life of Jesus was observance of the Sabbath, and attendance at the synagogue. Luke tells us that

He came to Nazareth, where he had been brought up. And, as was his custom, he went to the synagogue on the Sabbath day, and he stood up to read (Luke 4:16).

The events that are going to take place in Nazareth will demonstrate the truth of John's claim that Jesus 'came to his own, and his own people did not receive him' (John 1:11). The rejection of his ministry and his work began early; the cross was the culmination of three years of antagonism to the one who claimed to be Messiah.

Luke's detail is important, however. His visit to the synagogue was not the first. This was his custom, his habit. Some commentators argue that the 'custom' to which Luke refers was the custom of *teaching* in the synagogue, but that is to confine the text too narrowly. Jesus had received a good upbringing, and a good deal of religious training in it. New Testament scholar Ben Witherington says that

There were two conditions that had to be met if a young boy was to receive religious training: (1) a synagogue in the town or village where he lived, and (2) pious parents who wanted him to be trained in this manner. Both of these conditions seem to have been met in the case of Jesus, and probably in the case of many other Galileans.[1]

Or, as Darrell Bock puts it, 'Jesus is a pious Jew, who attends synagogue regularly'.[2]

Indeed, we need to emphasize more than this. Not only did the custom of synagogue worship demonstrate Jesus' subjection to the fourth commandment; so too did his employment. In Matthew 13:55, Jesus is called 'the carpenter's son', showing that Joseph was a carpenter. But in Mark 6:3 he is called simply 'the carpenter', showing that for the years of his obscurity he had developed a trade.

This is not unimportant; after all, the fourth commandment had said more than simply to keep the Sabbath day holy. It had also spoken about the need to work for six days. By the time Jesus begins his public ministry, he has been engaged in a secular profession, legitimating work and honouring the demands of God's law. Although some scholars like Geza Vermes have suggested that Talmudic teachers used the word 'carpenter' in a metaphoric sense to describe a learned man, there seems no reason to depart from the picture of Jesus as a tradesman of Galilee.[3] In this way, the life of Jesus shows the totality of his devotion to the law of God.

Vermes is correct, however, to say that 'whatever he did to earn a living before he entered public life, the New Testament record leaves no room for doubt that during his ministry Jesus practised no secular profession but devoted himself exclusively to religious activities'.[4] And the interesting thing is that it was on a Sabbath that he publicly did so.

Before leaving Luke 4:16, one or two other observations are in order.

First is that of Nigel Lee. He says:

Arriving in Nazareth, the Lord went into the synagogue on the sabbath day 'as his custom was'—thus proving his regular attendance at communal sabbath worship in his office as the Second Adam. As the Second *Adam*, his example probably establishes that the first Adam also so worshipped or was to have so worshipped; as the *Second* Adam his example is mandatory for all his federal descendants, his sabbath-keeping children.[5]

We have already looked at the way in which God's pattern of creation was to be a pattern of worship for man made in his image. Whether or not Adam ever managed to keep a Sabbath day devoted to the Lord is a moot point: the important point here is that the one who is to restore what we have lost in Adam appears as the Sabbath-keeper, the law-keeper, whose covenant obedience and faithfulness will be the basis of our restoration and salvation. And as the promised seed of the covenant, Christ does set before us the example of Sabbath-keeping as the way to honour the God who has saved us.

A second observation is that of Samuele Bacchiocchi, who argued that by beginning his ministry on the Sabbath with a quotation from Isaiah 61:1–3, Jesus 'announces his messianic mission in the language of the sabbatical year'.[6] We have discussed the importance of non-weekly sabbaths, such as the Jubilee year, and their relation to the weekly Sabbath in Israel; and although Max Turner goes on to dismiss Bacchiocchi's position, it is an interesting suggestion nonetheless. The combination of custom and citation at the commencement of public ministry shows that for Jesus the meaning of the Sabbath, as well as the weight of Old Testament prophecy, was concentrated in a unique way on his Person and Work.

Whatever his own habit, however, it is clear that the sabbatarianism of Jesus was to lead to controversy. Darrel Bock is correct, in his commentary on Luke 4:16, to see a relation between the stress on Jesus' personal Sabbath-keeping and the subsequent controversial nature of his teaching.[7] We will look at the six passages in Luke's Gospel which show Jesus clashing with the religious leaders on this issue.

Chapter 4

Luke 4:16–30: Christ's rejection at Nazareth

As we have noted, this was the commencement of Christ's public ministry, and on this particular Sabbath day, it led to a riot. Christ claimed that the prophecy of Isaiah 61:1–3 ('the Spirit of the LORD is upon me...') was fulfilled in their hearing. The audience was amazed; but then their wonder grew to incredulity as they listened to his claims. He declared himself to be the prophet sent by God, just as Elijah and Elisha were prophets of God in the Old Testament. The characteristic of their ministries to which Jesus refers is the fact that they were not sent to their native people, but to individuals and peoples outside of Israel (Elijah to Zarephath and Elisha to Syria).

The implication of his exposition was that God's judgment lay on Jesus' audience, as his judgement had been on Israel in the Old Testament. The crowd becomes violent, and Jesus' life is threatened: 'they drove him out of the town and brought him to the brow of the hill on which their town was built, so that they could throw him down the cliff. But passing through their midst, he went away' (Luke 6:29–30).

The ministry of Jesus is going to be one of conflict, just as was predicted by Simeon in Luke 2:34, when he said that 'this child is appointed for the fall and rising of many in Israel and for a sign that is opposed'. Not the least area of conflict will revolve around the Sabbath itself. But how interesting that these pious, Sabbath-keeping, synagogue-going worshippers could so soon demonstrate the murderous intent of their hearts! Surely one of the main points of the episode is to highlight the contrast between the Saviour's Sabbath-keeping and that of his audience. There is a Sabbath-keeping that demonstrates loyalty to Jesus; there is also a Sabbath-keeping that has in it no love for the Saviour at all, but accompanies the same kind of enmity as we read of in Luke 4, and leads to the same kind of rejection.

Luke 4:31–37 Christ heals a man with an unclean demon (see Mark 1:21–28)

Four of the passages in Luke which deals with Christ and the Sabbath centre on his miracles of healing. For Luke, there is a close connection between the healing miracles (in which, as a doctor himself, he has a great interest) and the special, messianic role of Jesus as the Saviour and

Mediator of his people. In Luke's second volume, the Book of Acts, we find the following words of Peter recorded:

God anointed Jesus of Nazareth with the Holy Spirit and with power. He went about doing good and healing all who were oppressed by the devil, for God was with him ... to him all the prophets bear witness that everyone who believes in him receives forgiveness of sins through his name (Acts 10:38, 43).

For Luke, therefore, the healing miracles were attestations both of the fact that Jesus was the fulfilment of prophecy and that he was the Christ, the Messiah, the anointed One.

The healing of the man with the unclean spirit takes place on a Sabbath in Capernaum. It is the first of a succession of miracles which take place that day. After the synagogue service is over, Jesus heals Peter's mother-in-law and then heals many sick people at sunset (Luke 4:40).

But there is another dimension to the first of these miracles: by healing the man, Jesus is openly declaring himself to be standing in opposition to the kingdom of darkness. He has already faced the devil (Luke 4:1–13), standing against the temptation where the first Adam yielded. Now, having drawn attention to the ministries of Elijah and Elisha, two miracle-working Old Testament prophets, Jesus faces the devil in the experience of the man who cries, 'What have you to do with us, Jesus of Nazareth? Have you come to destroy us? I know who you are—the Holy One of God'.

As Royce Gruenler points out, this is all part of the declaration that Christ has come to confront the forces of spiritual darkness:

As the king of the heavenly kingdom, Jesus opposes the reign of Satan and his minions. Barely a dozen verses in Mark's abbreviated account separate Jesus' confrontation of Jesus in the wilderness and an evil spirit in Capernaum (Mark 1:21–28). Other healings and exorcisms follow in rapid succession ... The progressive nature of the atoning warfare of invasion is illustrated in Jesus' accompanying teaching in parables, which both reveal and mask the deep significance of what he is doing ... Jesus personifies the reign of God in the spiritual realm.[8]

In other words, the healing is an attack on Satan's kingdom, an intimation of John's later assertion that 'the reason the Son of God appeared was to destroy the works of the devil' (1 John 3:8). But the point is also made that there is a clear connection between the Sabbath teaching, which came with an authority that led the people to be amazed (Luke 4:31), and the Sabbath healing. The salvation Christ was bringing was not only in word, but also 'in power and in the Holy Spirit and with full conviction' (*cf.* 1 Thessalonians 1:5). Like the revelation of God's salvation in the Old Testament, it was both a word and an action—it *declared* life and it *brought* life. It stood opposed to anything that threatened the good of man, and addressed itself to man's needs.

The activity of Jesus on the Sabbath, therefore, brings us to the heart of the business in which he was engaged, as the one who declared the word of God and demonstrated the power of God.

Luke 6:6–11 Christ heals a man with a withered hand

In Luke 6, our attention is drawn to two important incidents which took place on the Sabbath. We will look at the first of these in some detail; here, we will note the second. By the time Jesus came to this point in his miracle, the Pharisees were making it their business to find some reason for raising a case against him—'they watched him to see whether he would heal on the Sabbath, so that they might find a reason to accuse him' (Luke 6:7).

The rabbinic tradition held the Sabbath-breaker to be as guilty before God as the person who blasphemes God's name—a sin punishable by death. In discussing Numbers 15:32–36, in which a Sabbath-breaker was stoned to death, the rabbis cite Leviticus 24, with its prescription for the judicial death of the blasphemer.[9] So the high view of the Sabbath held by the scribes and Pharisees in Jesus' time equates with their high view of the Name of Jehovah. Neither his name nor his day could be treated lightly. For the scribes and Pharisees, 'blasphemy represents an offense against God and a violation of a fundamental principle of the faith'.[10] Sabbath-breaking was no less a violation, and no less an offence.

Hence the care with which the leaders of Israel observed Jesus. Luke tells us, however, that 'Jesus knew their thoughts' (Luke 6:8). Mark's account uses more emotive language; having posed the question 'is it lawful on the Sabbath to do good or to do harm, to save life or to kill?', Jesus 'looked round at them with anger, grieved at their hardness of heart' (Mark 3:4–5). B.B. Warfield does not want us to modify this ascription of anger to Jesus in any way:

What is meant is simply that the spectacle of their hardness of heart produced in him the deepest dissatisfaction, which passed into angry resentment.[11]

But Warfield also observes that

The fundamental psychology of anger is curiously illustrated by this account; for anger always has pain at its root, and is a reaction of the soul against what gives it discomfort. The hardness of the Jews' heart, vividly realised, hurt Jesus; and his anger rose in repulsion of the cause of his pain.[12]

In fact, the feelings of Jesus also illustrate the explicit point of the question he asked. Which is lawful on the Sabbath: to do good or to do harm? The unbelief that was ready to allow the man to suffer longer had a deeper motivation of hatred for the Saviour. The scribes and Pharisees

are no longer passive witnesses. Their 'watching' Jesus takes the character of 'spying' with the intent of bringing formal charges against him. These 'regulators' thus function as barriers to the healing of this man, and in fulfilling this role they also represent the synagogue and Sabbath as entities segregating this needy man from divine help.[13]

The importance of this miracle, therefore, cannot be underestimated. In spite of all that the Sabbath had represented to Israel, as a sign of the covenant, functioning as a visible token of God's interest in his people, those who set themselves up as defenders of the Sabbath were the very ones who were preventing people from knowing the blessing of the God whose day it was.

Jesus heals the man, once again demonstrating both his conviction that the Sabbath was God's 'Yes' to man's need, and also that his own unique power was legitimately employed when it was used to heal a man on that day.

Luke 13:10–17 Christ heals a woman with a disabling spirit

The same features of confrontation are to be found in the other two miracles of healing which took place on the Sabbath day. The first was that of a woman who had been disabled and crippled for eighteen years. However, there are important contextual considerations.

First, Luke has already told us that Jesus' ministry is now being carried out with Jerusalem, and the sufferings he must endure there, very clearly in view (9:51). The fact that Jesus returns to a synagogue (mentioned in both verse 10 and verse 14) shows a continuity with his earlier ministry, but also highlights that the intimation he had given earlier about his being the fulfilment of Old Testament prophecy now has a narrower focus as the cross beckons.

Second, Jesus has already said that the synagogue will be a place of testing and of trial. In Luke 12:11, he says, 'when they bring you before the synagogues and the rulers and the authorities, do not be anxious about how you should defend yourself'. Yet he takes no steps to avoid the danger himself; in fact he faces it by deliberately turning to the synagogue where the confrontation will be very public.

Third, the Sabbath is mentioned five times in this passage. There is established a congruity between the reason for the Sabbath and the reason for the mission of Jesus. He has not come to abolish the Sabbath, any more than he has come to abolish any of the laws of God; he has come to fulfil. His activity on this occasion serves to remind us that while the Sabbath calls us to glorify God in our lives, sin prevents us from doing so. The mission of Jesus is to free people from whatever it is that may hinder them from 'glorifying and enjoying' God, and enabling them to do so. For this reason, the result of the healing is that the woman 'was made straight and glorified God' (Luke 13:13).

These are important issues. We cannot appreciate the meaning of the Sabbath until we appreciate the meaning of Christ's ministry and mission. And we cannot understand his work except in the light of the very principle for which the Sabbath was given—as a gracious sign of God's love, mercy and covenant faithfulness. By the very act of healing 'a daughter of Abraham whom Satan bound for eighteen years' (Luke 13:16), Jesus is proving himself to be the essence of the covenant of grace for a fallen world.

More than this, however, Jesus takes the opportunity to remind the audience of the weight of the Old Testament witness, and the burden of its message. The ruler of the synagogue is introduced in this narrative, who comes in complaining that 'there are six days in which work ought to be done. Come on those days and be healed and not on the Sabbath day' (Luke 13:14).

It has to be admitted that the argument did have a compelling ring to it. Jesus had 'worked' on the Sabbath, and the Sabbath was not a day for working. Yet Jesus' response is to describe his opponents as 'hypocrites'. The twofold response was, first, that they themselves did the very thing that they were saying Jesus should not do. 'Does not each of you on the Sabbath untie his ox or his donkey from the manger and lead it away to water it?' he asks in verse 15. Joel Green is right to draw our attention to the fact that Jesus is here asserting his authority as teacher in the synagogue, in contrast with the false teaching of the ruler of the synagogue.[14]

The reference to the ox or the donkey is a reminder of the scope of the fourth commandment. It did not simply govern human beings in their relation to God, but in relation also to people and animals. Jesus' accusation of hypocrisy is a two-edged sword: on the one hand, if the ruler is right, then arguably their own nourishing of the life of their animals on a Sabbath day is equally a breach of the fourth commandment. On the other, by what standard can it be deemed right to look after an animal, but not another human being?

Undergirding Jesus' response is the fact that when our relationship with God is out of step, it will affect everything else. Jesus is the one who is without sin, who observes the fourth commandment perfectly. His relationship with God is the relationship all men ought to have with God. Because that is so, he is able to heal the woman (and, indeed, answer his accusers). But the Pharisees, whose relationship to God is all wrong (as is evidenced by their legalistic view of the Sabbath), also have wrong attitudes to others. Their lack of spiritual life is seen in their antagonism to Jesus and their indifference to the needs of others.

Additionally, Jesus is accusing them of not seeing the wood for the trees, of ignoring the substantial spirit of the law, which always has as its end that God will be glorified and that men's lives will be saved. How much they needed to recover the fundamental principle that God's word was never intended to bring bondage—*man's* word often does that—but to bring life, liberty and healing.

There may well be another consideration here. The Pharisees were prioritizing the Sabbath commandment over the healing of the woman, but in point of fact the ethics of life take priority over the ethics of the Sabbath. God created life on the sixth day, the day before the Sabbath. Following the pattern of Genesis we can say that, in terms of timescale at least, the care and consideration which God put into shaping and fashioning man in his image came before the rest and consecration of the Sabbath.

There may, then, be something in the way Jesus describes the woman as a 'daughter of Abraham' in Luke 13:16, contrasting with the perception the scribes and Pharisees had of themselves as true 'sons of Moses'. However, in the same way that the promise of life to Abraham was not contradicted by the word of law spoken to Moses (Galatians 3:16–17, 21), so the Sabbath commandment could not contradict the healing of this woman. She was an heir of life; the Pharisees were using the law to prohibit and prevent life reaching her, and were showing their radical departure from the faith they professed.

Luke 14:1–6 Christ heals a man with dropsy

A similar incident takes place in Luke 14:1–6, although this time the setting is not the synagogue but the private home of the ruler of the Pharisees. Given the build-up of the tension thus far, it may appear strange to us that Jesus will go to the house of a prominent Pharisee. But he is not given to avoiding confrontation, any more than he is given to passing up an opportunity for Gospel witness. In fact, the meal in the Pharisee's house enables him to demonstrate in his teaching what it means to have true fellowship at God's table and at God's banquet.

Again we are informed that the Pharisees are 'watching him carefully' (verse 2). This may well be the reason why the invitation was extended to him in the first place. Given the recent history, one can hardly imagine that Jesus would have been first on the invitation list. It is more likely that his being there would give the Pharisees an opportunity to spy on him. On the other hand, we know that there were some members of the Pharisee circle (like Nicodemus, in John 3 and John 7:45ff) who did acknowledge his status as teacher.

The presence of the man with the dropsy is equally surprising. His medical condition, due to excess fluid, would be enough for the Pharisees to regard him as ritually and ceremonially unclean. His presence at the table is an indication that the good news Jesus is preaching is to the poor (*cf.* Luke 4:18–19).

Our attention is drawn here, not to the miracle, but to the discussion regarding the Sabbath. When Jesus asks 'Is it lawful to heal on the Sabbath or not?' the Pharisees remain silent. This advances on previous similar episodes, by showing that the Pharisees had not embraced Jesus' earlier teaching. They were still unwilling to trust themselves to the interpretation of the fourth commandment which Jesus had already advanced.

Equally significant is the fact that the Pharisees found the logic of Jesus' conclusion equally compelling, yet unanswerable: 'they could not reply to these things' (verse 6). Jesus has the last word, and Luke is reminding us of the inherent authority he possesses as teacher of the law and as one who understands not only its meaning, but the way in which it ought to be observed.

However, the most controversial incident requires further comment, since it introduces us to one of the most staggering claims made by Jesus.

Lord of the Sabbath (Luke 6:1–5; see also Matthew 12:8 and Mark 2:28)

Unlike other Sabbath incidents, this particular controversy took place after Jesus had plucked and eaten some corn while walking through the grainfields on the Sabbath. Jesus was accused by the Pharisees of being a Sabbath-breaker. In response to the accusation, Jesus not only claimed that he was a Sabbath-keeper, but, in fact, that he was 'Lord of the Sabbath', precisely because he was the Son of Man.

In fact, the way in which Jesus defends himself against the accusation of Sabbath-breaking is interesting. He refers to 1 Samuel 21:1–6, a passage situated in the context of David's enforced exile. Coming to Ahimelech, the priest, David asked for bread. All the priest could offer him was the consecrated bread to be eaten by the priests: 'so the priest gave him the holy bread, for there was no bread there but the bread of the Presence, which is removed from before the LORD, to be replaced by hot bread on the day it is taken away' (1 Samuel 21:6).

As D. Ralph Davis comments on this passage, 'the text neither condemns nor justifies David for his conduct'.[15] What the text does is to show God's remarkable provision for his servant. The bread that was placed before the LORD was able to sustain the fugitive king at a particularly difficult point of his life.

Although there is no explicit reference to the Sabbath in the passage, there is an *implicit* reference in that the bread of the Presence was replaced every Sabbath: 'Every Sabbath day Aaron shall arrange it before the LORD regularly; it is from the people of Israel as a covenant for ever' (Leviticus 24:8). The bread that David ate, therefore, was linked both to the Sabbath and to Israel's covenant relationship with the Lord of the Sabbath.

Christ's use of the incident is interesting, not only for the explicit conclusions he draws from it about his own justifiable sabbatarianism. After all, the attitude of the Pharisees shows that he, too, is a fugitive king, to whom the religious leaders stand opposed.[16] On this occasion, he is also hungry, and his eating of corn on the holy day parallels David's eating of bread in a holy place.

The principle which Jesus enunciates in the light of the Old Testament is that religious ceremony and cultic purity are secondary issues. They are not unimportant, but there are things of greater moment. The prophet Micah puts it in its naked reality as he enumerates the things God really wants:

With what shall I come before the LORD and bow myself before God on high? Shall I come before him with burnt offerings, with calves a year old?

Will the LORD be pleased with thousands of rams, with ten thousands of rivers of oil? Shall I give my firstborn for my transgression, the fruit of my body for the sin of my soul?

He has told you, O man, what is good, and what does the LORD require of you, but to do justice, and to love kindness, and to walk humbly with your God? (Micah 6:6–8).

In Matthew's record of this scene, Christ cites a similar passage in Hosea 6:6—'I desire steadfast love and not sacrifice, the knowledge of God rather than burnt offerings' ('I desire mercy and not sacrifice' in Matthew 12:7). Christ's authority for the statement is clear—'something greater than the temple is here' (Matthew 12:6). Indeed, we might say, something greater than the Sabbath is here also, and one of the lessons Christ wants to teach is that 'canon law and liturgical rubric cannot be used as pretexts for lack of compassion'.[17]

So, in his treatment of the Sabbath principle in the light of 1 Samuel 21, where something that has been consecrated may also be used for a humanitarian purpose, Jesus uses two phrases that deserve our attention. The first is the phrase 'Son of Man', which has received a great deal of attention from scholars. What did Jesus mean by this statement? Interestingly, although others called Jesus the Son of God, no one called him the Son of Man. It was a phrase used of him only by himself. And the title appears in different contexts. Look at the following statements:

The Son of Man has nowhere to lay his head (Matthew 8:20)

The Son of Man has authority on earth to forgive sins (Luke 5:24)

For even the Son of Man came not to be served, but to serve, and to give his life as a ransom for many (Mark 10:45)

The Son of Man must be lifted up (John 3:14)

Who do people say that the Son of Man is? (Matthew 16:13)

One important question that has occupied New Testament scholars is this: is the title 'son of man' simply an elaborate way of saying 'I' or 'me', or was it, in fact, a title, with a very specific referent? Geza Vermes, a careful and exacting scholar of Judaism and of the Dead Sea Scrolls, argued passionately that the title was a 'circumlocution', that is, an elaborate way for a speaker to refer to himself. By contrast, he says, 'no trace survives of its titular use, from which it must be inferred that there is no case to be made for an eschatological or messianic office-holder generally known as "the son of man"'.[18]

But this is a very different approach to the classical Reformed and evangelical view, which has insisted that against the background of Daniel 7, in which Daniel saw 'one like a son of man' receive honour and blessing from God, the phrase cannot simply be a circumlocution. As Geerhardus Vos puts it:

Other names he might acknowledge ... but this name stands alone as the name that was his favorite ... it suggested a messianic career, in which, all of a sudden, without human interference or military conflict, through an immediate act of God, the highest dignity and power are conferred.[19]

In other words, when Jesus refers to himself as the Son of Man, he is self-consciously identifying himself with the cosmic messianic figure on whom the Lord confers the highest glory, and whom he invests with an eternal kingdom. 1 Corinthians 15 is the response to Daniel 7: in the latter passage the Father gives that kingdom to the Son; in the former, the Son returns the kingdom to the Father. Having fulfilled the role of Mediator and Servant, the Son of Man is honoured with the highest honours that heaven can give, and God has all the glory in the work of salvation.

Each reference to the Son of Man is loaded with these ideas of honour, conferment, investiture and glory. That is what makes some of the concepts so mind-blowing: it is the *Son of Man* that is to be lifted up on the cross! The *Son of Man* is to give his life a ransom for many! The *Son of Man*, to whom belong all honour, power and glory, has no place to lay his head!

And it is the same *Son of Man* who is also Lord of the Sabbath. The two titles are linked in the contexts of the Synoptic Gospels in a remarkable way. Part of the glory that belongs to the Son of Man is his lordship over the Sabbath day! What do you think it would have meant for a pious Jew to hear Jesus say that he was Lord of the Sabbath? For the whole of the Old Testament period the Sabbath principle and idea was bound up closely with the idea of the absolute sovereignty of Jehovah. The fourth commandment cited God's example as the reason for the obligation to honour the day. And it receives its seal and owes its force to the fact that these are the absolute standards of the one who says 'I am the LORD your God.'

The law, as we have seen, was the revelation of the holiness, grandeur and majesty of God. Now in the New Testament, that is nuanced for us even further. It is the Son of Man who is Lord of the Sabbath! The Jehovah whose glory is revealed in the law, and who caused Sinai to shake and tremble, is none other than the Jesus who walked among men and worked his great miracles here on this earth.

There is also another important implication of this. In *A Treatise on the Authority, Ends and Observance of the Christian Sabbath*, first published in 1832, Duncan Macfarlan of Renfrew noted that by referring to himself as the Son of Man with lordship over the Sabbath, Christ cut the feet away from those who wish to argue that the Sabbath was a sign between God and ethnic Israel:

The term 'Son of man' is nowhere restricted to any relation in which the Saviour stood to the tribes of Israel, but has always a respect to mankind in general. But if the Son of man is constituted Lord of the Sabbath, in virtue of the Sabbath's having been made for man, it is first clear, as already alleged, that man here means mankind; and then, that even under the special dispensation of the Son of man, the authority of the Sabbath is to be recognised, only it is placed under the direction of him who presides over all the appointments of his Kingdom.[20]

In other words, as long as mankind exists, and Christ rules as Son of man, the Sabbath principle remains under Christ's direction and for the good of all men.

In his commentary on the Gospel of Mark, Professor James R. Edwards makes the important point that 'western indifference toward Sabbath observance puts modern readers at a disadvantage in understanding the importance of the Sabbath in Judaism'.[21] It also places us at a disadvantage when we try to capture the 'register' of these words; Edwards puts it like this: 'God had instituted the Sabbath ... and Jesus now presumes preeminence over it!'[22] The claim is staggering. If Jesus is Lord of the Sabbath, he is God!

But over what is Jesus claiming lordship? Over an Old Testament icon which he was intending to demolish? It makes no sense at all to say that the Sabbath was merely an Old Testament provision, one of the shadows and types which were to be done away in Christ. For Jesus to claim sovereignty over the Sabbath implies that the Sabbath remains under his jurisdiction.

It seems to me that we often fail to do justice to this great statement on the lips of Jesus. How can the Sabbath be altogether dispensed with by Jesus if he is Lord over it? Jesus does not say that he *was* Lord of the Sabbath, but that he *is* Lord of the Sabbath! If language means anything, then in Mark 2:28, Jesus is implying the permanent nature of the Sabbath as something over which he, as universal and eternal Son of Man has absolute authority. The day is his, as much now as ever. As long as Jesus continues to be Son of Man, he continues to be Lord of the Sabbath.

This is no indication, of course, of which day is to be marked out as the Sabbath in the New Testament age. That has to be established on other grounds. But it is a clear indication of the fact that Jesus has not abrogated the Sabbath—he has not cast it into some Old Testament oblivion. The thinking that suggests that the Sabbath is gone cannot be accommodated with the claim that Jesus makes here. If he is Lord of the Sabbath, then the Sabbath remains.

But in what sense is he Lord of this day?

First, Jesus is the Lord of the Sabbath in the sense that *his view of the Sabbath is definitive and normative*. It strikes me as strange that many Christians have a very ambivalent view of Sabbath-keeping. But if being a Christian means anything, it means acknowledging that Jesus is Lord (1 Corinthians 12:3). But when we press that point and try to put substance into it, we see that his lordship extends over the Sabbath. At the very least, there is an inconsistency in our profession if we profess to be subject to the Lordship of Jesus, yet deny the very area over which he claims to have Lordship!

Second, he is Lord of the Sabbath *as the proper object of Sabbath worship*. As Larry Hurtado has pointed out in a recent book, worship of Jesus was not a late, but an early development within the New Testament church.[23] The early disciples unashamedly worshipped Jesus, without any embarrassment. And they also devoted a day, at the beginning of the week, which they observed with all the care of the Old Testament Sabbath.

The New Testament evidence is breathtaking: on a particular day of the week, the early church gathered to worship Jesus, without any sense that they were compromising any of the commandments. They were not worshipping another God. They were not worshipping images. They were not misusing God's name. And they were not neglecting the Sabbath. New Testament worship was cast in a form different from the Old Testament; and part of the reason for that re-casting was the revelation that the Jehovah of the Sabbath was none other than the Lord Jesus Christ.

So—Christ's example, teaching and principles are an all-important part of our approach to Sabbath-keeping. It is not, in fact, the case that Jesus simply spoke about the Sabbath in order to abolish it. Nor is it the case that his attack on legalism means that the Sabbath law is no longer binding. In fact, it is the Sabbath issue that brings us to the very heart of what it is to be a disciple and follower of Christ: to be a Christian is to say 'He is Lord'. And, among other things, He is Lord of this particular day.

Made for man

In this same context, Jesus makes another extraordinary statement, which is also worth pondering. He tells us that the Sabbath day was made 'for man'. His own example showed that he understood the Sabbath to be God's gift for the preservation and for the advancement of life. It was a day which was designed to help man, not hinder him, to be for his benefit, not be imposed on him as a burden.

The Old Testament commandment contained within itself the meaning of this phrase. The Sabbath was made for man to provide him with rest. Physically, there was a day which could give man's body a respite from the exacting work of the rest of the week. Psychologically, the Sabbath allowed man's mind and heart to enjoy a period of quietness and stillness. Spiritually, the Sabbath made provision for man to enjoy God's company and to worship in God's house.

The fourth commandment was also for man in the sense that it guarded the rights both of employers and employees. It legitimatized proper employment, by outlining God's provision for work. It also protected the workers, by giving to them a day of rest.

Everything God does is for our good. Not least of his gifts to us is the gift of his own day as a blessing for our bodies, our minds and our souls. Donald Macleod calls our attention to the protective nature of the Sabbath law: it was, he says, 'the first piece of employee-protection legislation. Such a law, said Jesus, may not be invoked to justify inhumanity'.[24] As Lord of the Sabbath, Jesus, both by precept and example, demonstrates that the Sabbath law has at heart the honour of God and the good of man. Neither of these ideals can be met apart from our worship of the Christ who claims that the day is his.

Jesus and the Sabbath in John's Gospel

There are two passages in John's Gospel which also deserve study in connection with Jesus' relation to the Sabbath day. Both are miracles of healing. The first took place at the pool of Bethesda, where a man who had been an invalid for thirty-eight years was healed. The context is important. John marks the time of the incident as one of the Jewish festivals (John 5:1). We have already noted the relationship between the feasts of Israel and the Sabbath principle, and Christ's presence and activity at these festivals was more than a passing indication of the fact that he was, in fact, the fulfilment of the Old Testament ceremonial.

We are also left in no doubt as to the supernatural nature of the incident. Some manuscripts say that the crowd of invalids were waiting for the waters to move, 'for an angel of the Lord went down at certain seasons into the pool, and stirred the water; whoever stepped in first after the stirring of the water was healed of whatever disease he had' (John 5:5, ESV footnote[25]). Whatever we are to understand by this detail, clearly the immediacy of Christ's healing touch is designed to demonstrate the superiority of Jesus over all other beings.

John customarily brings miracle and doctrine together (*cf.* the feeding of the five thousand followed by the discourse on the bread of life in chapter 6), and here the healing of this individual leads to a discourse on the authority of the Son of God. The themes of Sabbath and Sonship are woven together in such a way that the opposition of the Jewish leaders finds a focal point: 'the Jews were seeking all the more to kill him, because not only was he breaking the Sabbath, but he was even calling God his own Father, making himself equal with God' (John 5:18).

The Sabbath issue arose because the healed man carried his mat. This offended the scruples of those who had hedged the Sabbath commandment around with many regulations of human origin; the scribes had lengthy discussions over what constituted work, and which 'work' was forbidden on the Sabbath. Clearly, carrying one's bed fell into the proscribed category, and the healed man is challenged on that point. Eventually, he identifies Jesus as the one who had urged him so to do, and the opposition intensifies.

The interesting thing about this passage is that, while Jesus' attitude to the Sabbath clearly becomes one of the points of grievance against him, he does not actually give any specific teaching or precept on the subject in this incidence. His attitude is implied; John delays telling us that it was the Sabbath day until after the miracle was performed (John 5:9), and the dialogue between the leaders and the healed man becomes the basis for the ongoing design against Christ.

But clearly the chapter is important. Christ's attitude to the Sabbath, cutting as it did across the cherished traditions of the religious leaders, was closely connected to his own identity as the one who was equal with God. Clearly, therefore, if Jesus claimed equality with God, he was claiming authority over the Sabbath, and he and the Jewish leaders could not both be right. Leon Morris is correct, therefore, to conclude that the Jews 'discerned that the Sabbath-breaking was no isolated, rootless phenomenon. It proceeded from Jesus' view of his person and was consistent with it'.[26]

And the result was a complete reversal of views. The Jews proceeded on the basis that they had a monopoly on interpretation of the Mosaic law. When they applied their standards to Jesus, he came far short. He defends himself against their accusation on the grounds that, as well as law-keeper, he is also the law-giver. The God who gave the law was no person other than the person whom they accused of law-breaking!

Yet at the close of the discourse Jesus turns the searchlight on them: 'There is one who accuses you: Moses, on whom you have set your hope. If you believed Moses, you would believe me, for he wrote of me. But if you do not believe his writings, how will you believe my words?' (John 5:45–47).

This was a staggering claim to make; and its importance for us is that it sets all the discussion about the Sabbath in its biblical context. Not only

was Christ's behaviour consistent with the spirit of the Mosaic covenant—
it was also consistent with the letter of the Mosaic writings. Here was the
great Teacher accusing these acknowledged teachers of the law and experts
in the Old Testament Scriptures that, for all their study, they had failed to
see what was before their eyes.[27] The Jewish authorities accused Jesus of
failing to honour the letter of the Sabbath commandment. Jesus' counter-
accusation was that they had failed to understand the commandment to
begin with, and to grasp the multiple Old Testament witness to his own
Person and Work.

The implication for us is that we will not understand the fourth
commandment properly either, until we appreciate that Christ is at its
heart. The Sabbath law is nothing if it is not Christocentric.

A second important passage in John's Gospel concerns the healing of the
blind man (chapter 9). Having had this impediment since birth, the
recovery of his sight was going to demonstrate God's glory in a remarkable
way (John 9:3). The confrontational aspect begins when the man is taken
before the Pharisees and is asked to explain what has happened. Their
conclusion about Jesus is that 'This man is not from God, for he does not
keep the Sabbath' (John 9:16), although John hints that this was not a
universal opinion, since there was a division among the people.

A second interview between the healed man and the Pharisees leads to
their arrogant claim to be the true disciples of Moses (John 9:28), with the
added assurance that God spoke to Moses. Jesus' credentials, on the other
hand, they regard as questionable. The passage ends with Jesus reassuring
the man of his forgiveness, and the Pharisees of their continued blindness to
spiritual things (John 9:40–41).

And it is precisely this that gives a clue to the whole passage. The man
who was naturally blind is enabled to see spiritually, while those who have
physical sight are shown to be void of spiritual discernment. Part of the
evidence for this is precisely the legalism that blinds the Pharisees to the
wonder of the miracle which has taken place, and leaves them raising the
accusation of Sabbath-breaking. 'There were those so firmly in the grip of
darkness that they saw only a technical breach of their law and could not
discern a spectacular victory of light over darkness. They disputed with the
man and in the process revealed their inward blindness'.[28]

Neither John 5 nor John 9 teaches that Jesus regarded the Sabbath as unimportant. But both incidents demonstrated how far removed people could be from the spirit of the commandment, even as they professed to defend it. In particular, the incongruity of their professed respect for God's law and their simultaneous rejection of Christ demonstrated that they had failed to grasp the message of the Old Testament. The true measure of our Sabbath-keeping may be judged by our devotion to Jesus Christ.

There is another interesting reference to the Sabbath in the teaching of Jesus, to which we must do justice. Matthew (in chapter 24), Mark (in chapter 13) and Luke (in chapter 21) give attention to Jesus' Olivet discourse on the last things. This eschatological discourse promises increased difficulties for his faithful followers—they will be tempted to give up, they will be hated, they will be betrayed. But Jesus promises that the one who endures to the end will be saved (Matthew 24:13).

Then he speaks of a period of tribulation, fulfilling the prophecy of Daniel (in Daniel 9 and 11) regarding the 'abomination of desolation' which will lead to persecution and people fleeing for their safety. Mark 13:18 says, 'Pray that it way not happen in winter'. But Matthew 24:20 lengthens this to 'Pray that your flight may not be in winter or on a Sabbath'. Luke does not include this detail.

The discourse arises out of Jesus' observation that the Temple will be torn down. The immediate focus of his attention is the destruction of Jerusalem by the Romans in AD 70, but it is clear that he is telescoping his discourse to include events which will characterize the end of the world.

Clearly the reference to fleeing Jerusalem in wintertime is a reference to the fact that winter conditions could make travel difficult. But what difference would the Sabbath make? Well, for one thing, we know that Nehemiah instituted the practice of shutting the gates of Jerusalem for the duration of the Sabbath (Nehemiah 13:19). It may be that the continuation of this practice might mean that the ability to leave the city on a Sabbath day would be severely hampered.

Jesus is certainly assuming Sabbath-keeping up to the fall of Jerusalem, if not, indeed, to the end of the world. If he is referring to the Jewish Sabbath, then the concern might be that for true believers to flee Jerusalem on that day might lead to an aggravation of their situation, since, like their Master, they might then be regarded as Sabbath-breakers.

On the other hand, Nigel Lee argued that Jesus is not here necessarily referring to the Mosaic Sabbath. He points out the important fact that Paul, prior to the destruction of Jerusalem, was already arguing that observance of the old Sabbath was not part of the Christian ethic (Colossians 2:16), so that Jesus' remarks would then anticipate the continuance of the Sabbath but a change of the day.[29] Christ's remarks in this instance would indicate that the day of rest and worship for the Christian church would be threatened by the circumstances in which his followers would find themselves, and he urges them to pray that this will not happen.

Obviously the reference to the Sabbath is not the main part of the Olivet discourse, and we should not get bogged down in details. The larger meaning is that following Christ will be costly, both in the immediate aftermath of his ascension, and in subsequent generations to the end of time. Two thousand years later have demonstrated time and again the truth of his prediction. And in a world of hostility to Jesus, the Lord's Day Sabbath rest has been given to us for our encouragement, for respite, and for strengthening. Whatever the inconveniences of our lot, we need the Sabbath day and dare not be without it.

There is a good deal of material regarding the Sabbath in the teaching of Jesus. It is a glib generalization to suggest that all he did was argue against Jewish legalism. Jesus did much more than this: he argued that he was Lord of the Sabbath. That is crucial. If there is no longer a Sabbath day, how can he be Lord of the Sabbath? His teaching indicated that there was a wrong way to keep the Sabbath holy, but not that it was wrong to keep it holy. And it also indicated that what God had enshrined in his moral law for Israel was binding on all men everywhere—all who acknowledge Jesus as Lord must acknowledge that there is a day which is uniquely his. But the events surrounding Jesus' death and resurrection were also crucial both for the continuation of the Sabbath principle and the change of the day.

Now, if on calmly examining all these narratives, we should find, 1. That our Lord always honoured the Sabbath; 2. That he performed miracles of healing upon it, only when important occasions arose, and in order to confirm his doctrine and ensure faith in his messiahship; 3. That these acts were never in violation, but entirely in accordance with the Mosaic law; 4. That they were especially designed to relieve the institution from the oppressive traditions of the scribes and pharisees; 5. That no objections were taken against them at first, and that the cavils afterwards raised were only pretences to cover their hatred to his divine mission; 6. That our Lord's defences of himself and his disciples proceeded on what had ever been the real import of the fourth commandment, though misunderstood, and assumed that the Sabbath itself was of perpetual obligation; 7. That all this is confirmed by our Lord's caution concerning the flight of his disciples at the destruction of Jerusalem; and 8. By the conduct and doctrines of his inspired apostles at the first promulgation of the gospel—then it will be admitted that our Saviour, so far from relaxing the fourth commandment, or abrogating the essential law of the Sabbath, vindicated it, established it, and left it in more than its original authority and glory.

Daniel Wilson, *The Lord's Day* (London: LDOS, 1956), p. 70

The Sabbath and Jesus' death and resurrection

Jesus was crucified around Passover time. The Sabbath of the Passover festival was doubly sacred because of both its weekly and its annual significance. The fact that Jesus was crucified at this time demonstrates God's ordering of the events of history to show that Jesus, as the Passover lamb of the church (1 Corinthians 5:8) had indeed come in the fullness of the times (Galatians 3:4).

He was also crucified on the Preparation day, the day before the Sabbath, that is, Friday of Passover week (John 19:31). There was a deep spiritual significance in all that took place at the cross; as the Jewish people were making preparation for their day of rest, so Christ was making preparation for a Sabbath-rest for all his own people.

Nigel Lee suggests further parallels. The solar eclipse, for example, was not without significance: 'the created sun "sabbathed" in solar "death" for three hours at its noon-day prime, in acknowledgement of that Creator Sun who was about to "Sabbath" in human death at the prime of his earthly life'.[30] The principle of Sabbath rest, so integral a part of the original creation, and proclaiming the essential nature of the provision of God's covenant of grace, was thus in evidence at Calvary, where creation and re-creation coalesced and where the Creator sabbathed in death for his people.

Lee also sees a parallel between the seven days of creation in Genesis and the seven sayings of Jesus from the cross. The sixth saying, for example, was 'It is finished', corresponding to the sixth day of creation, when God completed the work of creation. Much was now completed in the death of Christ, not least the ceremonial ordinances. So while the pre-Israelite, moral principle of the Sabbath remained, Christ brought to an end the temporary expression of that in a seventh-day Sabbath:

> The shadows had now disappeared. It is finished. And the (Saturday) sabbaths were finished too: finished and perfected in the dying body of the Lord of the Sabbath himself; finished when the veil of the temple and the whole Mosaic economy was rent from top to bottom, from God to man, rent when the Second Adam and Mediator of the Covenant who had suddenly come to his Temple was rent apart and breathed his last.[31]

Similarly, the seventh word—'Father, into your hands I commend my spirit'—also corresponded to God's final creation rest, as Christ entered into his sabbath rest, and God sabbathed, his justice resting where his righteousness was vindicated, in the finished work of his Son. And, interestingly, in his burial, Christ observed the Sabbath rest of the old covenant by sleeping in death on Israel's High Sabbath day, showing himself to be Lord of the Sabbath, Mediator of the Covenant, and Passover Lamb all in one. While he slept in death, keeping Sabbath, his opponents, who had consistently declared themselves to be the students of Moses and the guardians of the Sabbath, worked to secure his incarceration in the tomb. But the resurrection demonstrated that the one who has the key of David (Revelation 3:8) had turned the key in the lock of the Sabbath with his rest, in order to open a new Sabbath door for his people.

For he did not rise from the tomb on Israel's Sabbath, 'but deliberately passed it by in death, and fulfilled the prophecy to rise on the third day by rising on Sunday, the day after the Saturday sabbath, thus turning Sunday, not Saturday, into the day of joy.'[32] His subsequent appearances to his people, both on the resurrection day and later, as well as the established pattern of apostolic worship on the Lord's Day, demonstrate with clarity that Jesus had maintained the principle of Sabbath rest, while changing the structure of things for his people. The place that the seventh day of the week had in the old covenant was now superseded by the place to be given to the first day of the week in the new.

Let's always bear in mind that the transition from Old to New Testament is characterized in that way in all its parts. There is a unity of God's purpose of salvation—the gospel is preached in both Old and New Testaments, the church exists in both, the line of God's grace runs from Genesis to Revelation, unbroken and complete.

Yet the structures around which the Old Covenant was centred give way. The essence of the covenant of grace continues, although the structures show themselves to be temporary. Tabernacle and Temple give way to the spiritual reality of the spiritual temple which is the church. Circumcision gives way to baptism. Passover gives way to the Lord's Supper. Israel gives way to the church. The work goes on in unbroken unity, but the old forms demonstrate themselves to be temporary. What Christ has done brings to light what is permanent and unalterable.

And the change effected by the resurrection is equally staggering, as the seventh day Sabbath gives way to the first day Sabbath, transferring the day signifying spiritual rest from the end of the week, as something longed for and anticipated, to the beginning of the week, as something established and secured. That was enough for the early church. With their high view of Scripture, they had no difficulty in accepting the abolition of the old order, with its old Sabbath, and the introduction of a new order, with its new Sabbath. For that reason, the apostles met on a different day. Christ had taken the Mosaic Sabbath into the grave with him, and he had left it there. But more than that, he had taken a new one out of the grave with him, to be a day of joy and gladness for his people until the end of time.

There are at least two passages that confirm this. The first is the account of Pentecost, in Acts 2. The story of how the Holy Spirit descended in power is staggering, and it is recorded very carefully by Luke. We are reminded, for example, that Old Testament prophecy was fulfilled with the coming of the Holy Spirit, as Acts 2:17–21 cites Joel 2:28–32. But in the background there is also the teaching of Jesus that *he* would send the Spirit (see John 7:39 and 16:7). Luke therefore reminds us in the course of the chapter that Jesus has poured out the Holy Spirit having been exalted to God's right hand (Acts 2:33). In a remarkable way, therefore, Pentecost bears testimony to the glory of the risen Christ.

And Luke tells us that this happened 'when the day of Pentecost arrived' (Acts 2:1), or 'was fully come' (AV). Pentecost (the Greek word for 'fiftieth') always fell on the fiftieth day after the first sheaf of the harvest was presented to the Lord (Leviticus 23:15–16). This corresponded to the seven weeks between the original Passover in Exodus and the arrival at Sinai with the giving of the Law (which is why Exodus 19:1 supplies the detail that the people arrived at Sinai in the third month after leaving Egypt). In reading Acts 2, therefore, with the coming down in glory of the Holy Spirit who would write the laws of God on the hearts of his people (Jeremiah 31:33), we have an echo-fulfilment of Exodus 19ff, when the glory of God came down and gave laws to Israel.

Pentecost always fell on the first day of the week, on the day after the old Sabbath. Kevin Connor, whose work on the Feasts of Israel is rich in supplying the spiritual truths embedded in Israel's ceremony, is correct to suggest that Pentecost anticipated the end of the seventh day Sabbath, but wrong to suggest that it anticipated the end of the day. He says that 'the Sabbath was the sign and seal of the old or Mosaic Covenant. The New Covenant sign and seal is the Baptism in the Holy Spirit. One was a day of rest. The other is the Spirit of rest'.[33] The reality was that Pentecost always demonstrated that the first day of the week was to be significant, and that the old Sabbath was ready to give way to something better. The fact that Christ poured out his Holy Spirit on the first day of the week verified the typology, and showed that what the Old Testament had longed for was now here. The Day of Pentecost had, in fact, arrived; it *was* fully come, not just because it was the fiftieth day after Passover, but also because the fullness of God's saving grace was to be realized fully and finally. There was to be no more Pentecost, just as there was to be no more Passover.

Secondly, when John tells us in the Book of Revelation that he was 'in the Spirit on the Lord's Day' (Revelation 1:10), he is, at the very least, reminding us of the importance which the New Testament church attached to this particular day. For John, the significance of this particular Lord's

Day was the revelation he had of the glory of Jesus Christ, reminiscent of what he had seen on the transfiguration mountain, with all its overtones of the theophany of Sinai.

We will discuss the apostolic observance of the Lord's Day in the next chapter; here our interest is in the relation of a special day of Spirit-filled worship to the risen Lord. It is not at all insignificant that John says immediately that when he was in the Spirit on this particular day 'I heard behind me a loud voice like a trumpet'. Simon Kistemaker comments that while the voice was startling, 'the resonance of the trumpet, however, told him of its heavenly origin. John was reminded of God giving the Ten Commandments at Sinai where the Israelites heard a trumpet sound (Exodus 19:16, 19; 20:18). The beginning of the New Year was marked by trumpet blasts … in short, the sound of the trumpet introduced the advent of a new interval'.[34] The correspondence between the sounding of the trumpet and the giving of the Sabbath law with the Spirit-filled Lord's Day and the voice of the risen Christ sounding as a trumpet is surely significant. For John, this was the day the Lord had made; the new covenant Sabbath was the day on which he gave his Spirit to his people, and the day on which he gave his apocalypse to his servant.

To argue that there is no relation between these movements of revelation is to break the equilibrium of the Scriptures. As we study Christ, both in his teachings and in his actions, we discover the glory of the New Covenant. Old structures give way to permanent, spiritual realities. And not the least of these is the Sabbath, now given to the church in the form of the Lord's Day. We shall see in the next chapter how the apostles accommodated this change in their own religious practice and teaching.

Hence the Scriptures teach that Christ, the Sun of righteousness (Malachi 4:2) was resurrected on Sunday, on which day he appeared to his congregated church; that eight days later, that is, on the following Sunday … he again appeared to his congregated church; after, after his ascension into heaven, he gave his spirit to his congregated church on Pentecost Sunday; that he caused his holy supper to be celebrated in his congregated church on Sunday; that he caused contributions for the saints to be made by his congregated Church's members every Sunday; and that he himself appeared on Sunday, the Lord's Day, to his messenger the Apostle John in order to transmit his seven letters to his congregated churches in Asia Minor. In short, the weekly Sunday became the weekly Sabbath day—the day of the congregation of the Church in order to worship her God in a restful manner … The weeks, previously demarcated since the fall by a holy termination day of the week, swung round the resurrection of Christ as the hinge of history, as it were, and, never broken, the series of weeks are henceforth demarcated by a holy commencement day of the week.

Nigel Lee, *The Covenantal Sabbath,* p. 201

Notes

1 **Ben Witherington III,** *The Jesus Quest: the third search for the Jew of Nazareth* (Downers Grove: IVP, 1997), p. 38.

2 **D.L. Bock,** *Luke,* Volume 1: Luke 1:1–9:50, Exegetical Commentary on the New Testament (Grand Rapids: Baker Books, 1999), p. 402.

3 See **G. Vermes,** *Jesus the Jew* (London: SCM Press, 1994), p. 22.

4 **Vermes,** *Jesus the Jew,* p. 22.

5 **F.N. Lee,** *The Covenantal Sabbath: the weekly sabbath scripturally and historically considered,* (London: LDOS, 1966) p. 193.

6 Discussed by **M.M.B. Turner,** 'The Sabbath, Sunday and the Law in Luke/Acts', in **Carson,** *Sabbath to Lord's Day,* pp. 102ff.

7 See **Bock,** *Luke,* Vol 1, p. 402–3.

8 **R.G. Gruenler,** 'Atonement in the Synoptic Gospels and Acts', **C.E. Hill and F.A. James III** (eds.), *The Glory of the Atonement: Biblical, Theological and Practical Perspectives* (Downers Grove: IVP, 2004), p. 101.

9 See **D.L. Bock,** *Blasphemy and Exaltation in Judaism: The Charge Against Jesus in Mark 14:53–65* (Grand Rapids: Baker Books, 1998), pp. 90–91.

10 **Bock,** *Blasphemy and Exaltation,* p. 111.

11 **B.B. Warfield,** 'The Emotional Life of our Lord', in **B.B. Warfield** *The Person and Work of Christ* (edited by **S.G. Craig**) (Philadelphia: Presbyterian and Reformed), p. 108.

12 **Warfield,** *Emotional Life,* p. 108.

13 **J.B. Green,** *The Gospel of Luke,* The New International Commentary on the New Testament (Grand Rapids: Eerdmans, 1997), p. 255.

14 **Green,** *Luke,* p. 523.

15 **D. Ralph Davis,** *1 Samuel: Looking on the Heart*, (Fearn, Tain: Christian Focus, 2000), p. 175.

16 Some modern scholars suggest that the narratives of opposition in the Gospels were written more to encourage Gentile Christians in the first century. **E.P. Sanders,** for example, describes himself as 'one of a growing number of scholars who doubt that there were any substantial points of opposition between Jesus and the Pharisees', and states that the Gospel records to that effect seem artificial (*Jesus and Judaism* (London: SCM Press, 1985), pp. 264–5). This seems a very arbitrary conclusion, however, given the deliberate policy of the Pharisees to try to ensnare Jesus.

17 **D. Macleod,** 'Jesus and Scripture', in **P. Helm and C.R. Trueman** (eds.), *The Trustworthiness of God: Perspectives on the Nature of Scripture* (Grand Rapids: Eerdmans, 2002), p. 84.

18 **Vermes,** *Jesus the Jew*, p. 168.

19 **Geerhardus Vos,** *The Self-Disclosure of Jesus*, (New York, 1926), p. 256.

20 **D. Macfarlan,** *A Treatise on the Authority, Ends and Observance of the Christian Sabbath*, (Glasgow, 1832), p. 56.

21 **J.R. Edwards,** *The Gospel According to Mark*, Pillar New Testament Commentary, (Leicester: Apollos, 2002), p. 93.

22 **Edwards,** *Mark*, p. 95.

23 **L.W. Hurtado,** *Lord Jesus Christ: Devotion to Jesus in Earliest Christianity*, (Grand Rapids: Eerdmans, 2003), p. 2.

24. **D. Macleod,** 'Jesus and Scripture', p. 84.

25 The detail is missing from many manuscripts, raising doubts over whether it was an authentic part of the original text.

26 **Leon Morris,** *The Gospel of John*, New International Commentary on the New Testament, (Grand Rapids, Eerdmans, 1995), p. 275.

27 cf. **C.G. Blomberg:** 'Perhaps most pointedly of all, Jesus challenges their ability to read and understand the Scriptures' (*The Historical Reliability of John's Gospel*, (Leicester: Apollos, 2001), p. 116.

28 **Leon Morris,** *John*, p. 423.

29 **See Lee,** *Covenantal Sabbath*, p. 198.

30 **Lee,** *Covenantal Sabbath*, p. 199.

31 **Lee,** *Covenantal Sabbath*, p. 199.

32 **Lee,** *Covenantal Sabbath*, p. 200.

33 **K.J. Conner,** *The Feasts of Israel* (Portland: Bible Temple Publishing, 1980), p. 36.

34 **S.J. Kistemaker,** *Exposition of the Book of Revelation* (Grand Rapids: Baker Books, 2001), p. 92.

The Apostles and the Sabbath

On the first day of every week. 1 Corinthians 16:2

There remains, therefore, a Sabbath rest for the people of God. Hebrews 4:9

Some years ago a new war memorial was constructed on a piece of waste ground in our community. It was designed and constructed beautifully, with a central cairn indicating the purpose of the stones, surrounded by standing stones representing local villages, each with the names of those lost in past conflicts.

The Bible talks about stones speaking out, and I often reflect on what these standing stones might say, what story they might tell, and what past they might unfold. They stand as silent witnesses to families who spent months on end in fear for the safety of loved ones, to mothers whose hearts broke over lost sons, to a widowed generation. These are beautiful stones, telling about great actions in the past.

The memorial was located on a high point in the district, looking out to sea. Two powerful spotlights were situated in front of the central cairn, with the result that even in the darkest night, one can see into the past. The lights illuminate a cairn which speaks louder than any man.

As we approach the New Testament writings, it seems to me that they function a little bit like these spotlights, casting their illuminating rays back on the cross, which is itself rooted in the great acts of God in redemptive history. Everything that God did in the Old Testament anticipated the cross; and everything that we read in the New Testament explains the cross. It is only in the light of what Jesus did, and continues to do, that we can approach the place of the Sabbath/Lord's Day. Let's turn on the lights!

The question we are asking in this chapter is whether the writings and the example of the apostles furnish us with evidence that the fourth commandment is still binding on the Christian Church. Indeed, are any of the commandments still binding on us in this age of the Holy Spirit? How much of the material in the Acts of the Apostles ought to be replicated in our churches? And is it permissible to speak of the Lord's Day as the 'Christian Sabbath'?

To begin answering these questions, we need to lay down certain principles. First, we recognize that there was much in the experience of the early New Testament church that was temporary, precisely because it was a transitional period. The Old Covenant realities were giving way to New Covenant realities, and the era in which the incarnate Jesus was present on earth was giving way to the era of the permanent Holy Spirit. Just as in the Old Testament, it is not surprising that a new chapter in redemptive history should be accompanied and authenticated by unusual phenomena. Among these I include tongue-speaking and various miracles. I do not believe they are valid for the church now, as she is in possession of an infallible and complete Bible. But God worked through them, as important accompaniments of the gospel in the infancy of the New Testament.

Secondly, we also recognize that the experiences of the Acts of the Apostles need to be read through the development of doctrine represented in the New Testament epistles. As Paul puts it in 1 Corinthians 14:32, 'the spirits of prophets are subject to prophets'—in other words, the canonical Scripture, and not any experiences or unusual phenomena, must be our final court of appeal.

Thirdly, we recognise that the particular issue we are studying—the place of the Sabbath principle in the Christian life—is part of a wider subject: the subject of the law of God and the new covenant believer. To answer the question about the 'Christian Sabbath' requires that we look at passages which speak of our relation to God's law, on this side of the resurrection. This is such an important element of the discussion, that it is with this that we shall begin.

What is the law?

It is clear that the New Testament uses the word 'law' in several different ways. Paul says in Romans 10:4 that 'Christ is the end of the law for righteousness to everyone who believes', a phrase which seems to equate 'law' with the whole of Old Testament revelation. Paul can also speak of the 'law of Moses' in 1 Corinthians 9:9, when he is citing a passage from Deuteronomy 25:4. He can also use the word 'law' to mean a 'principle', such as in Romans 7:21, in his phrase 'I find it to be a law that when I want to do right, evil lies close at hand'. He can talk of the 'law of the Spirit of life' in Romans 8:2, or the 'law of Christ' in Galatians 6:2. On a very simple reading, therefore, the word 'law' can be used in different senses in the New Testament.

On the other hand, there are passages in which the word 'law' very clearly refers to the Ten Commandments. Consider the following line of reasoning in Romans 2:21–23:

> While you preach against stealing, do you steal? You who say that one must not commit adultery, do you commit adultery? You who abhor idols, do you rob temples? You who boast in the law dishonour God by breaking the law.

Just as in the teaching of Jesus himself, the apostle Paul clearly uses the word 'law' in certain contexts to refer to the Ten Commandments. These he regards as inviolable; his argument in the passage above in Romans 2, for example, would make no sense if Paul believed the Ten Commandments to have been abrogated.

This is also the case in Romans 7, in a notoriously difficult passage which I take to be a description by Paul of himself at the time of writing, expressing the struggle he finds in himself, as at one and the same time a justified man and a sinner. Paul's testimony is this:

> ... if it had not been for the law, I would not have known sin. I would not have known what it is to covet if the law had not said 'you shall not covet' ... I was once alive apart from the law, but when the commandment came, sin came alive and I died ... the law is holy, and the commandment is holy, and righteous and good (Romans 7:7, 9, 12).

Again, for Paul in this passage, 'law' means the Ten Commandments. He recognizes the uniqueness of the Decalogue as a revelation of the moral standards of God in a way that is not true of other Old Testament legislation.

The same point may be illustrated from Romans 13:8–10:

> Owe no one anything, except to love each other, for the one who loves another has fulfilled the law. The commandments, 'You shall not commit adultery, You shall not steal, You shall not covet', and any other commandment, are summed up in this word:

'You shall love your neighbour as yourself'. Love does no wrong to a neighbour; therefore love is the fulfilling of the law.

This closely packed passage further illustrates our point. In highlighting the relationship between law and love, Paul illustrates the Decalogue with a sample of three of the commandments, to which he adds, 'and any other…'. He is not teaching that loving our neighbour is *replacing* the commandments, but that it is *fulfilling* them. Loving our neighbour is not a substitute for stealing from our neighbour, but is the way we demonstrate and exercise that love that fulfils the law. Again, the Ten Commandments have continuing prominence; if they are to be relegated to a past dispensation, and our tie to them completely severed, then Paul's argument here makes no sense whatsoever.

So, although the word 'law' can be used in different senses in the New Testament, we cannot ignore the fact that it is also used in the sense of the Ten Commandments. The question we must now ask is—what is the relation of the New Testament believer to these Ten Commandments?

We shall ask that question, first, of the apostle James. Although questions of authorship and dating for the New Testament letters can be difficult, a good case can be made for the position that this letter was written by our Lord's brother, some time in the AD40s. That would make it one of the earliest of the New Testament epistles.

One of James' main, and powerful, arguments, in his letter, is that although we are saved through faith alone, we are not saved by a faith which is ever alone. Faith is always accompanied and evidenced by its actions, or its works (James 2:26), not in the sense that the believer's works are regarded by God as being meritorious, but in the sense that they demonstrate that the person really is a believer, and is resting on Christ alone for salvation.

So as he urges his readers not just to accept the word of the gospel, but also to live lives that conform to God's requirements, James argues:

If you really fulfil the royal law according to the Scripture, 'You shall love your neighbour as yourself', you are doing well. But if you show partiality, you are committing sin and are convicted by the law as transgressors. For whoever keeps the whole law but fails in one point, has become accountable for all of it. For he who said 'Do not commit adultery' also said, 'Do not murder'. If you do not commit adultery but do murder, you have become a transgressor of the law. So speak and so act as those who are to be judged under the law of liberty. For judgement is without mercy to one who has shown no mercy. Mercy triumphs over judgement (James 2:8–13).

There are several important points here. First, there is James' description of God's law as 'the royal law', the law that is 'according to the Scripture', and the law that is 'the law of liberty'. Is he referring to the Ten Commandments in each of these instances? Clearly he is, since he ties together the Ten Commandments with the summary principle of loving one's neighbour; his whole argument hinges on the fact that we do not enjoy any liberty or peace with God as long as one sin, one broken law, stands ready to condemn us. Just as we have received mercy, so we must show mercy, honouring God's law out of gratitude, and applying its standards in every area of our lives. As Nigel Lee puts it,

The thrust of James' argument is inescapable: the royal law is the Ten Commandments, the law of the royal Messenger of the Covenant and the Lord of the Sabbath, which he himself gave at Sinai and which he taught and lived out during His earthly life, and which must hence be kept by the justified children of the covenant as the permanent rule of their lives too.[1]

Indeed, it is a point to which James returns in 4:11 where he identifies the works of faith with keeping God's law. Either one is a 'doer of the law' or a judge of the law. Faith, which rests alone on Christ for salvation, nevertheless evidences itself not by judging the commandments to see which are relevant and which are not, but by letting the commandments judge us, and willingly submitting to them as the rule of our life and practice.

But does not the New Testament teach that if we are in Christ, our relationship to the law is altered? Does Paul not say that 'you are not under the law but under grace' (Romans 6:14)? Does he not also urge us to 'avoid foolish controversies', which might include 'quarrels about the law' (Titus 3:9)? Does the letter to the Hebrews not emphasize that we have not come to Mount Sinai but to Mount Zion (Hebrews 12:18–24), thereby drawing a clear and sharp division between the law and the Gospel?

As with every passage of Scripture, we need to interpret these passages very carefully. In the same letter to the Romans, Paul argues that while the law cannot condemn us if we are in Christ, nevertheless we now live a life of faith in Christ 'in order that the righteous requirement of the law might be fulfilled in us, who walk not according to the flesh but according to the Spirit' (Romans 8:4). In other words, while it is true that we have been saved by the gracious work of Christ on our behalf—in which his perfect law-keeping is the very basis of our acceptance before God, our justification and our pardon—it is still the case that the law has a role to fulfil in our lives. Whatever might be foolish questions about the law, clearly this is not one of them—Paul is teaching us that we show the newness of our lives in Christ by our obedience to him and his sovereign law. In other words, we have been set free from the law's condemnation and curse, and freed in order to keep it to the glory of God.

That is precisely the teaching of Hebrews also. There were many things in the Old Testament, such as the sacrificial system and other elements of typology, which in themselves were unable to secure full pardon for the sinner. They anticipated the coming of Jesus Christ, whose work at Calvary rendered every other sacrifice and every other basis of our acceptance as obsolete and defunct. But it did not set aside the Ten Commandments; that point is made explicitly in Hebrews 10:16, with the writer's citation of the prophecy concerning the new covenant, which we looked at in the previous chapter. The writer's argument is that the Old Testament bore witness to the greater work of God in the New, and explicitly stated that the law given to his covenant people would be written on the hearts of his own.

In the light of this, the writer urges that we go forward, serving God acceptably. This is the argument he uses: 'for if we go on sinning deliberately after receiving the knowledge of the truth, there no longer remains a sacrifice for sins, but a fearful expectation of judgement ...' (Hebrews 10:26–27). But how can a believer know if he or she is sinning? Only by the law, for 'apart from the law, sin lies dead' (Romans 7:7). Yet the new covenant believer, living for God's glory, wishes to avoid sin and to overcome sin. We need God's holy law to teach us what sin is, so that we will avoid it more and more.

In terms of the general point regarding the law, then, the New Testament seems to be teaching that there are many laws and regulations from the Old Testament which functioned like the scaffolding around a building, and for which there is no more need once the building is complete. Jesus has fulfilled the typology, and it remains true that in Jesus Christ 'forgiveness of sins is proclaimed to you, and by him everyone who believes is freed from everything from which you could not be freed by the law of Moses' (Acts 13:38–9).

By our own efforts at law-keeping, we could never be freed, pardoned or justified. We could never know peace with God, or enjoy a saving relationship with him. Christ has kept the law in our place, so that his law-keeping, his righteousness, is credited to us. Similarly, our sins have been credited to him, so that the penalty which the law pronounced against sin, he has endured on the cross, once and for all. In him, there is no more condemnation (Romans 8:1).

Yet those who are in him—those 'new covenant' believers—are not without a rule of life. God has written his law on their hearts. Just as in the Old Testament, pardon and forgiveness were not matters of mere outward religion—they were matters of the heart. That is why Paul begins dealing with the subject of justification by faith, not with Christ, but with Abraham, whose relationship with God depended on faith just as much as ours does today (see Romans 4:1–12). And those who believe, and who are pardoned, freed and justified, are those who love to obey God, to yield the members of their bodies as servants to righteousness, to law-keeping. They keep God's commandments, not in order *to be* saved, but because *they already are* saved.

This comes out clearly in Paul's letter to the Galatians, an extremely important epistle for our purposes, since it addresses the very issue of the place of the law in the Christian life. There were some believers in the regions of Galatia who were in danger of standing the gospel of God's grace on its head by their insistence that their own law-keeping could supplement the work of Christ on the cross and be an adequate basis for their justification. Paul describes this as foolishness, and as a new bondage (3:1, 5:1). So insistent is he on the fact that 'all who rely on works of the law are under a curse' (Galatians 3:10) that any attempt to win favour by God through law-keeping is a perversion of the gospel.

On the surface of it, therefore, Paul seems to be arguing that the law has finished its work once it brings us to Christ (Galatians 3:24). But what is our responsibility now as Christians? According to Galatians 6:2, it is to 'fulfil the law of Christ'! Outward symbols of covenant membership, like circumcision, count for nothing, now that Christ has offered himself up for us. In him, we are 'a new creation' (Galatians 6:15). Instead of being slaves to sin, shut up under the law, we are now redeemed from the law's curse, and we serve God, not as slaves, but as sons (Galatians 4:7).

The life of faith is what matters now, not slavish obedience to legal practice and old ritual: 'in Christ Jesus, neither circumcision nor uncircumcision counts for anything, but only faith, working through love' (Galatians 5:6). But what is love? It is, according to Romans 13:10, the fulfilling of the law!

Being a Christian means knowing where to place law-keeping in the scheme of God's salvation. It means knowing that our law-keeping can never make us acceptable to God. It means knowing that Christ's law-keeping on our behalf is the only ground of our justification. And it also means knowing that, out of grateful and gladsome hearts, God calls his justified sons and daughters to serve him by fulfilling his law, by keeping his commandments, and by seeking for themselves the way of the cross: the way of obedience to his revealed will.

The law is good and holy because it expresses the holy will of our holy God. The effect of the law on sinners who understand it is to lead them to despair of their own efforts to save themselves. The law also drives them to rest in Christ, who alone can fulfill the law for them. Those who find forgiveness of sin in Christ are completely free of the law as a means of justification. They have died to the law, and it no longer has any power to condemn them. But those who are justified will love the law as an expression of God's will for them. These Christians will study and treasure the law as a guide for them as they seek to subdue sin in their lives and to live in a holy way.

W. Robert Godfrey, *An Unexpected Journey: Discovering Reformed Christianity* (Phillipsburg, P&R, 2004), pp. 121–2

So how does this affect the New Testament's perspective on the fourth commandment in particular?

From Sabbath to Lord's Day

It is interesting to note that the word 'Sabbath' appears in the book of Acts in connection with the evangelistic work of the early church. In Acts 13:14, for example, Paul and his companions came to Pisidian Antioch, 'and on the Sabbath day they went into the synagogue and sat down'. Following the sermon on that occasion, the people begged them to tell them the same gospel message 'the next Sabbath' (Acts 13:42). The same idea is found at Acts 16:13, in connection with Lydia's conversion, in Acts 17:2, where Paul taught the Gospel in a synagogue in Thessalonica for three successive Sabbaths, and in Acts 18:4, where he preached in a Corinthian synagogue 'every Sabbath'.

Yet, at the same time, the early believers were congregating to worship God on a different day. Just as Pentecost fell on the first day of the week, so, too, did the weekly commemoration of Christ's resurrection, and clearly the early church held their regular services on that day. So, in Acts 20:7, Luke begins his account of Paul's visits in Macedonia and Greece in the following way:

On the first day of the week, when we were gathered together to break bread, Paul talked with them, intending to depart on the next day, and he prolonged his speech until midnight.

This is further corroborated in 1 Corinthians 16:2, with Paul's advice that

On the first day of every week, each of you is to put something aside and store it up, as he may prosper, so that there will be no collecting when I come.

And in connection with this, we should also note John's reference in Revelation 1:10, when he says that 'I was in the Spirit on the Lord's day'.

So there are two strands of evidence here. On the one hand, there are passages which show clearly that Sabbath day (i.e. seventh day) worship was going on in the synagogues week by week. In order to preach the message of the gospel, the apostles attended these services. That was reasonable and logical; after all, they wanted to preach that Christ had fulfilled the prophetic word of the Old Testament, and it was in the synagogues that the Old Testament was being read. The disciples knew the synagogue practices; they had been brought up in them, and their interest was to reason in the synagogues about the status of Jesus Christ in the light of prophecy.

But the seventh day Sabbath was not their preferred day of meeting. The believers made it their habit and practice to meet on the first day of the week, the day following the Sabbath. That was the day that became known as 'the Lord's Day'. Modelling their practice on the Old Testament Jewish Sabbath, these early Christians maintained the practice of a regular, weekly, holy day, but changed the day on which they met. Now they met on the first day of the week.

There are several important things to note here.

First, even with their high regard for the fourth commandment—or perhaps because of it—the disciples had no difficulty in re-arranging their week so as to place their day of rest and worship at the beginning of the week, rather than at the end. They gather together for worship on a weekly basis, knowing that this is at the heart of the fourth commandment. But, as with so much else in the Old Testament, they do so knowing that the teaching has been nuanced and filtered through the teaching of Jesus, who declared himself to be Lord of the Sabbath.

So the disciples have allowed the Lord of the Sabbath to dictate for them the ordering and arranging of their time. It is still, for the early church, a case of labouring for six days and resting on the seventh: only now, their day of rest and worship has been altered. The commandment remains in force, but the day has been changed.

Secondly, the disciples did not just choose a convenient day. There is a sense, of course, in which Christ had sanctified all of time for them: every day was a 'holy' day in the sense that now, in the age of the Spirit, all time was to be 'redeemed' (Ephesians 5:16) and all of life was to be a sacrificial service to Christ (Romans 12:1). Yet the unmistakable fact of New Testament history remains: the disciples set aside one specific day of the week as a day of worship.

How did they know which day to choose? Might they not have chosen any day of the week? Shall we not answer that question by saying that the Lord of the Sabbath himself showed them which day he claimed as his own, by his resurrection on the first day of the week (John 20:1)? This single fact was enough to sanctify and consecrate one day in particular as a holy day for the early church. Just as God had demonstrated, by the commands governing the manna in Exodus 16:23ff, which day was to be the old covenant Sabbath, so he demonstrated, in raising Jesus on a particular day, which day was to be the new covenant Sabbath.

Thirdly, Paul could counsel the believers in Corinth to contribute to the needs of the church, knowing that they were habitually gathering together on the Lord's Day. Let's remember that 1 Corinthians was written sometime in the mid AD50s, some twenty years after the resurrection and ascension of Jesus Christ. And still the practice had been sustained, for these two decades, of regular, first day of the week gatherings for worship. Over ten years later, Revelation is written, and John can still refer to a special, weekly, holy day, which he names as 'the Lord's Day'. By the time the New Testament is complete, the Christian church is meeting on a specific day every week.

Christian Sabbath?

This raises another important issue. Is it right to talk of a 'Christian Sabbath'? Is that what the Lord's Day was? Should we apply the language of Sabbath to the first day of the week, or should we confine it to the seventh?

It is true that there is no New Testament evidence of this usage. Nowhere do the apostles speak of the Christian Sabbath. Of course, nowhere do they speak of the Trinity either; and there are other theological terms which are not found explicitly in the Scriptures: you won't find 'supralapsarianism', or 'variegated nomism' or 'open theism' referred to explicitly in these terms in Scripture, yet they are the stuff of our theological reflection.

So we find the Westminster Confession of Faith, for example, describing the Lord's Day in the following terms:

As it is of the law of nature, that, in general, a due proportion of time be set apart for the worship of God; so, in his word, by a positive, moral and perpetual commandment, binding all men in all ages, he hath particularly appointed one day in seven for a sabbath, to be kept holy unto him; which, from the beginning of the world to the resurrection of Christ, was the last day of the week; and from the resurrection of Christ, was changed into the first day of the week, which in Scripture is called the Lord's Day, and is to be continued to the end of the world, as the Christian Sabbath (XXI.7).

The same point is made in the Westminster Assembly's *Larger Catechism*, Question 116, which says that

The fourth commandment requireth of all men the sanctifying or keeping holy unto God such set times as he hath appointed in his word, expressly one whole day in seven; which was the seventh from the beginning of the world to the resurrection of Christ, and the first day of the week ever since, and so to continue to the end of the world; which is the Christian Sabbath, and in the New Testament called The Lord's Day.

In his commentary on the Larger Catechism, Johannes Vos argues that

The Christian Sabbath, or the Lord's Day, is on the first day of the week in remembrance of Christ's resurrection from the dead. Thus it may be said that the Old Testament Sabbath commemorated God's original creation, while the Christian Sabbath in addition calls attention to God's new creation, his great work of redemption in Jesus Christ.[2]

The great American theologian, Robert L. Dabney, in an essay defending the idea of the Christian Sabbath, says that 'the professed Christian has two reasons for observing the Sabbath: every human being has one'.[3] Just as mankind needs a day of rest, so the Christian, in addition, has this reason for keeping a holy day to the Lord: that a new creation has been inaugurated in Christ. So Dabney describes Pentecost as an event 'meant by God as a forcible precedent, establishing the Lord's day as our Christian Sabbath'.[4] So, for generations the phrase 'the Christian Sabbath' has summarized the mainstream view that the Lord's Day replaces the Sabbath as a new day of rest for new covenant believers.

Several theologians argue strenuously, however, that the phrase 'Christian Sabbath' is invalid, teaching that we should not transfer

Sabbath-theology to the New Testament Lord's Day practice. Andrew Lincoln, for example, in an important essay on 'From Sabbath to Lord's Day', highlights the similarities between the Sabbath and the Lord's day in terms of recognizing the distinctiveness of one day in seven, their celebration of redemption, the fulfilment of one in the other and the fact of worship.[5] Yet he distances himself from 'those who view Sunday as the Christian Sabbath'.[6] Similarly, James Montgomery Boice, in his fine theological summary, *Foundations of the Christian Faith*, argues that 'the sabbath was a uniquely Jewish institution and was neither given to nor fully observed by any other race or nation either ancient or modern'.[7] In other words, although there are, in Boice's view, sound reasons for observing what he calls 'the Christian Sunday' as a day of celebration, it is not to be equated in any sense with a Sabbath, or even with the Sabbath.

Interestingly, while these theologians deny the validity of the term 'Christian Sabbath', they call it such in all but name. Their description of the Lord's Day as 'a day of joy, activity and expectation, the character of which is set by the events of the first Lord's Day, on which Christ arose',[8] is precisely what we say about the Christian Sabbath. In common with the other commandments, this fourth commandment is nuanced in a way that is positive, gladsome and filled with delight.

An important consideration in this regard is precisely the term John uses in the Book of Revelation, the phrase 'the Lord's Day', a phrase which is 'clearly and consistently used of Sunday from the second half of the second century on'.[9] Richard Bauckham is correct to argue that, in its context, the vision of the glorified, sovereign Christ—so much the theme of the Book of Revelation—informs the meaning of the phrase:

The total situation of [Revelation] 1:9 and the specific occasion of the weekly day of worship (1:10) are for both John and his churches interrelated by the implications of their confession of the lordship of Jesus Christ.[10]

But in the light of this, it is strange to find him arguing that the Lord's Day was 'not a substitute for the Sabbath nor a day of rest nor related in any way to the fourth commandment',[11] since this is precisely how God defines the Sabbath in the Old Testament. It is 'a Sabbath to the LORD' (Exodus 20:8,

Leviticus 23:3)—it is the Lord's day! Indeed, in Isaiah 58:13, God calls the Sabbath 'my holy day', and in Isaiah 56:4 he speaks of 'my Sabbaths'. In the Old Testament, the Sabbath is, in a carefully defined sense, the Lord's Day. It is not surprising, therefore, to find the phrase 'the Lord's Day' in the New Testament. There is both continuity and discontinuity here: the Old Testament Jewish Sabbath is the Lord's Day, and the New Testament Lord's Day is the Christian Sabbath. There is no reason, therefore, to abandon the phrase. Both 'the Lord's Day' and 'the Christian Sabbath' are, in my view, legitimate phrases to describe the first day of the week.

But what about ...?

But what about passages in the New Testament which seem to argue against any sabbatarianism in this Christian era? In particular, what about Colossians 2:16–20, which says

Therefore let no one pass judgement on you in questions of food and drink, or with regard to a festival or a new moon or a Sabbath. These are a shadow of the things to come, but the substance belongs to Christ ... If with Christ you died to the elemental spirits of the world, why, as if you were still alive in the world, do you submit to regulations ...?

On the surface of it, Paul seems to be arguing that the Sabbath regulations, like much else of the Old Testament, only anticipated the coming of Jesus Christ and his work, and is now, therefore, obsolete. He seems to be saying that no one has the right to impose any restrictions on our behaviour on the Lord's Day, since Sabbath laws are no longer binding. Indeed, in a very perceptive comment, F.F. Bruce says that 'the *onus probandi* [the burden of proof] lies on those who argue that the weekly sabbath is not included in this reference'.[12] How can we accept Paul's injunction to let no one judge us with respect to a Sabbath day, and yet still maintain that the weekly Sabbath, in the form of the Lord's Day, is binding on Christians?

Dabney's answer to that question is to suggest that the days themselves are not the issue; that the reference to 'new moons' and 'Sabbath days' refer not to the sacred times themselves, but to the festivals associated with them. The 'shadows of things to come', he says, were not the days themselves, 'but only the typical services appointed on them'.[13] This hardly avoids the problem, however, since it is precisely in relation to the Sabbath that Paul addresses the point.

And other passages seem to raise the same problem for sabbatarians. In Romans 14:5–6, Paul argues as follows:

> One person esteems one day as better than another, while another esteems all days alike. Each one should be fully convinced in his own mind. The one who observes the day, observes it in honour of the Lord. The one who eats, eats in honour of the Lord, since he gives thanks to God, while the one who abstains, abstains in honour of the Lord and gives thanks to God.

Here, the point seems to be that Christians are free to make up their own minds about holy and special days. There seems to be a *prima facie* case for saying that our consciences on this point have been liberated by God, and therefore we ought to respect the decisions to which other believers come on the matter of holy days. To do otherwise seems to run contrary to Galatians 4:9–11:

> But now that you have come to know God, or rather to be known by God, how can you turn back again to the weak and worthless elementary principles of the world, whose slaves you want to be once more? You observe days and months and season and years! I am afraid I may have laboured over you in vain.

Let's take a moment to see what Paul is actually saying in these passages. In Colossians 2:16, it is clear that Paul is addressing an error to which the believers there were prone—the error of 'supplementing' their faith in Christ with practices that Christ's coming had, in fact, abolished. So, when the issue of the Sabbath is addressed, it is clear that Paul is referring to the old, Jewish, seventh day of the week Sabbath. That was, indeed, part of the shadow which anticipated the coming of a new revelation.

But Paul does not say in this passage that there is no Sabbath-keeping in the New dispensation! Let us not forget that he contrasts *shadow* with *substance* in Colossians 2:17. There is something substantial throughout the Old Testament period of revelation, something which belongs to and is orientated around the work of Jesus Christ. The shadow is gone, but the substance remains. And as far as the fourth commandment is concerned, the shadow (the old, week-end Sabbath) has gone, but the Christ-substance appears before us now in a week-beginning Sabbath, the Christian Lord's Day.

Even so, of course, it still remains the case that it is possible to pervert the new Sabbath with legalism, asceticism and other self-centred practices which give no glory to God, and which 'are of no value in stopping the indulgence of the flesh' (Colossians 2:23). To that extent, anything in our observation of the Lord's Day as the New Testament Sabbath which compromises our Christian liberty, or which is done merely for an outward show, is not going to be pleasing to God.

It is not difficult to see how the early church, with the major transition from Judaism to Christianity which was going on across the Testaments, found it easy to fall into the error of thinking that rites and rituals from the older covenant should be carried over into the new. Paul's argument, here and elsewhere, is not that everything in the older covenant is gone; it is that it is re-cast, preserved in a new shape and form. We need to appreciate the glory of the Lord's Day Sabbath, while being aware of how easily we can drift into a legalistic observation of it.

It does not seem to me, however, that there is anything in Colossians 2 that requires the belief that the Sabbath principle is abolished. Indeed, Paul's argument is not that there should not be a Sabbath-keeping, but that there should be no judging regarding Sabbath-keeping. Once you go into the area of prescribing and proscribing rules, Paul says, you have missed the whole point of the transition from symbol to substance that is the characteristic of the movement from old covenant to new. That is to become self-centred, legalistic and pharisaic.

But a wrong application of a law does not make the law itself wrong. As John Murray pertinently asks, 'why should insistence upon Sabbath observance be pharisaical or legalistic? The question is: is it a divine ordinance?'[14] If we keep that principle before us, and interpret Colossians in the light of other Scriptures, we will see that the Lord's Day is indeed a Christian Sabbath by divine ordinance, the day over which the Son of Man is Lord. It is necessary to bring Colossians 2 into play only when that principle is abused.

Chapter 5

So what about Romans 14 and Galatians 4? Do these not rule out a Sabbath-keeping principle on the grounds that observing particular days is a matter of personal freedom, and that we have no right to insist on the performance or non-performance of any action on any particular day?

To be sure, in these passages Paul is addressing the whole question of our legitimate freedoms in Christ. This was a theme considered so important by the compilers of the Westminster Confession of Faith—with their view that the Lord's Day is the Christian Sabbath—that they dedicated a chapter to the issue of 'Christian Liberty and Liberty of Conscience' (Chapter 20). In it, they insist that

> God alone is lord of the conscience, and hath left it free from the doctrines and commandments of men which are in any thing contrary to his word, or beside it, in matters of faith or worship. So that to believe such doctrines or to obey such commandments out of conscience is to betray true liberty of conscience ...[15]

So Paul argues both in Romans and in Galatians that there is a freedom that is ours in Christ: not an absolutely libertarian freedom in which we may do anything we like. It is possible for Christians to do things that are wrong (14:23), and sin cannot be excused on the grounds of liberty of conscience. In things, however, that God has pronounced neither good nor bad (such as abstaining from certain foods), there is no absolute rule, so we cannot pass judgement on others, or make our personal preferences the rule of someone else's conscience or conduct. It is enough for each of us to remember that 'each of us will give an account of himself to God' (Romans 14:12).

But is it in fact the case that the issue of a New Covenant Sabbath—the Lord's Day—is an indifferent matter? Surely not, if our exegesis of other Scriptures has been right. The fourth commandment is still binding upon us, and our freedom is the liberty to keep it! We may wish, for personal reasons, to observe other days as days of particular religious interest, and we may exercise a degree of freedom therein. But the Son of Man, the Lord of the conscience, is also Lord of the Sabbath! Do his sovereign prerogatives over my conscience somehow cancel out his prerogatives over his own day? Not at all! In fact, the freedom that is mine in him is the liberty that enables me to love him and keep his commandments.

The same must be true regarding the teaching of Galatians 4. These 'days and months and years' were referring to man-appointed days, man-made rules, and man-centred teachings which compromised and perverted the gospel. Can we really imagine that the apostle Paul, with his knowledge of the regular, weekly meeting of Christian believers on the first day of the week, would teach that to observe such a day signalled that he had laboured in vain? No, but when he saw them going beyond the bounds of their Christian responsibility, and insisting on other holy times, he despaired. Pleasing God is not a matter of heaping up merit by observing more and more holy moments. It is a matter of using wisely and well the holy time he has given us, with all the joy and exuberance of the new covenant Sabbath.

Geerhardus Vos summarizes the situation well when he says:

The Sabbath was under the Old Testament an integral part of a cycle of feasts which is no longer in force now. The type embodied in it was deepened by the Sabbatical year and the Year of Jubilee. On the Sabbath man and beast rest, in the Sabbatical year the very soil rests; in the Year of Jubilee the idea of rest is exhibited in its full positive import through restoration of all that was disturbed and lost through sin. From all this we have been released by the work of Christ, but not from the Sabbath as instituted at Creation. In this light we must interpret certain New Testament statements such as Romans 14:5–6, Galatians 4:10, Colossians 2:16–17.[16]

Hebrews 4 and the abiding significance of the Sabbath principle

One of the most important passages regarding the significance of the Sabbath is Hebrews 4. The author of this letter is moving forward his argument that Jesus is greater than Moses. By examining these two lives, he sees a continuity in God's scheme of redemption: Moses was a servant in God's house, but Christ is a son (Hebrews 3:6)—they are both, however, in the same house. There are changes and discontinuities, but these are within the same scheme of redemption. We must never lose sight of the one story which the whole Scripture tells us.

In Hebrews 3:6, the writer uses the experience of the Israelites in the wilderness of Sinai as a powerful argument in this epistle of warning. Many of those who left Egypt perished in the wilderness, and did not reach the promised land. They did not enter into the 'rest' which God promised (Hebrews 3:11, quoting Psalm 95:11; see also 4:3,5). The point of the citation is not to teach us that it is possible for us to be redeemed and subsequently lost, which is what happened to all but two of those who left Egypt. As with so many other citations and quotations from the Old Testament, the passage is highlighted in order to focus in on one point in particular: this whole matter of entering God's rest.

Interestingly, the writer then links the 'rest' of the land of Canaan with God's rest at creation (Hebrews 4:4). The thought is that as God entered into 'rest' on the seventh creation day, so he provided a 'rest' which his people could enjoy in their inheritance of the promised land. Yet, as verse 8 demonstrates, Canaan could never have been the total fulfilment of the promise that God would give his people 'rest'. Ultimately, that rest is ours in the glory of heaven, the full and consummate enjoyment of the communion we have with God through the mediatorial work of Jesus Christ.

So, the writer says at verse 9, 'there remains a Sabbath rest for the people of God'. The important thing here is the change of word which the writer uses for 'rest'. Throughout the passage, he has used the Greek word *katapausis*, but now he uses the word *sabbatismos*, which belongs to the Old Testament word group referring to the Sabbath rest. When we read, for example, in Exodus 16:30 that 'the people rested on the seventh day', the meaning is that they 'sabbathed', observing as a holy day the day of the week which God designated as his own.

No reader of the letter to the Hebrews, full as it is of Old Testament imagery, allusion and vocabulary, could fail to pick up the nuance of this word injected into the argument at Hebrews 4:9. It is not that there is a *katapausis*, a state of final cessation from labour, for God's people—but that there is an ongoing enjoyment of that spiritual rest which is ours in Christ, fully to be realized in heaven, but expressed symbolically in the Sabbath-keeping of the New Covenant—the observing of the Lord's Day.

As Joey Pipa argues, if the writer had simply wished to say that we enter spiritual rest in Christ, which will be fully ours in glory, he could have used the word *katapausis*.[17] Instead, he deliberately uses a word with an entirely different connotation:

The uniqueness of the word suggests a deliberate, theological purpose. He selects or coins *sabbatismos* because, in addition to referring to spiritual rest, it suggests as well an observance of that rest by a 'Sabbath-keeping'. Because the promised rest lies ahead for the New Covenant people, they are to strive to enter the future rest. Yet, as they do so, they anticipate it by continuing to keep the Sabbath.[18]

There are those who read Hebrews 4:9 differently. While acknowledging that the writer has deliberately inserted a word here which means 'Sabbath-keeping', Andrew Lincoln argues that there is no hint here of a Sabbath-*keeping* on the part of God's people, but of a Sabbath-rest for the people of God which has found its fulfilment in Christ and is ours now in a spiritual sense. He says that

The New Covenant people of God discharge their duty of Sabbath observance, according to this writer, by exercising faith ... This Christian Sabbath-keeping will involve the realization of everything that God had intended by His own Sabbath rest.[19]

But will it? If the Sabbath-keeping which remains for the people of God is merely a matter of believing in Christ, where does that leave his lordship over the Sabbath? If we love him, we keep his commandments; if we believe in him, we join with his disciples in gathering for worship on the Lord's Day. By doing so, we enjoy the New Covenant Sabbath keeping, with all its joyful declarations of fulfilment and accomplishment on the part of Christ for us, and we anticipate the coming glorious rest which will be ours in heaven. Joey Pipa is right: 'the theology of accomplished redemption does not annul a continued Sabbath-keeping but requires it'.[20]

'In the Spirit on the Lord's Day'

We have already quoted this phrase from Revelation 1:10, a phrase which appears in the introductory passage to the great Book of Revelation. It seems an almost incidental reference, yet it is packed with significance. It tells us, as we have seen, that by the time the New Testament canon of Scripture is closed, there is a regular, weekly day being observed, hallowed and sanctified by the first century followers of Jesus Christ. For them, the 'day of the Lord' comes round in a weekly cycle, just as God's Sabbath did in the Old Testament. Now, instead of observing a holy day at the end of the week, a new and different Sabbath rest is observed at the beginning of the week.

However, it has become a virtual truism in the contemporary evangelical church that the re-configuration of time under the Gospel means that every day—and not just one day of the week—is holy to the Lord. In this vein, Tremper Longman argues that

Even though we do not have an explicit command to change the day, I think that the church is more than justified to meet on Sunday rather than Friday evening or Saturday. After all, Christ has made every day holy, though there is also the command to meet together in formal worship of God. We are not to forsake the assembly of the saints … What better day to meet than Sunday? All days are holy, but there is a need for a special day. The early Christians met on Sunday. We cannot think of Sunday as a uniquely holy day, but it is a special day …[21]

The best that Tremper Longman can suggest here is that Christians need a 'special' day for worship, and that there are good reasons why the early Christians met on Sunday. We may, or may not, do the same.

But does this not create an additional problem—the problem of authority? If there is no weekly Sabbath, no day which is especially to be consecrated to the Lord, then what we are left with is a moral and ethical vacuum regarding the assembling of Christians. The day and time of church meeting become matters over which men and women are supreme! *We* decide which day to give to God in public, formal worship. *We* decide how to regulate our week. *We* decide what proportion of our time to give to worship.

Is that what makes Sunday special? Surely not! Sunday cannot be special in any sense if all days are equally holy! If everything is holy, nothing is holy. The reality is that by resurrection power, Jesus took a new Sabbath out of the grave, and gives us a new desire to honour the laws he has written on the hearts of his New Covenant children. Included in these laws is the Sabbath law. We worship the Lord of the Day, and we do it, as John did it, on the Day of the Lord.

No one needed to tell John, in his lonely exile on Patmos, that God could bless on any day of the week, or that he could worship on any day of the week. No doubt God blessed John many times, and no doubt John worshipped God often. But every time a new week began, John dedicated its first day to his Redeemer. He knew believers everywhere were doing the same, 'sabbatising' the first day of the week, using it to focus their minds and hearts in a special way on the One who had triumphed over death for them. As they did so, they no doubt reflected on the fact that under the Old Covenant, the day of rest and worship was something which lay before them, awaiting fulfilment, and on the complementary fact that on the New Covenant side of the cross, the day of rest and worship comes before everything else. In the Old Testament, you lived out your week with the prospect of keeping Sabbath; in the New Testament, you lived out your week under the shadow of a Sabbath already kept. In Patmos, John would have difficulty with the idea that Sunday was just 'convenient'. For him, it was holy.

Secondly, John knew that keeping holy time was of no benefit apart from the Holy Spirit's power and blessing. Many Lord's Days passed, on which he prayed for the Holy Spirit to come as he had come on that Pentecostal Lord's Day in Jerusalem. But Patmos was not Jerusalem: this was lonely, difficult and tough.

On one particular Lord's Day, however, a blessing came John's way that made this day memorable. Apart from the first, resurrection Sunday, he had never experienced anything like it. He saw the Lord of the Day on the Lord's Day, and the vision of heaven which was to open up eventually before him took his breath away, as he heard the risen Lord declare, with all the echoes of Genesis creation, 'Blessed are the dead who die in the Lord from now … that they may rest from their labours, for their deeds follow them!' (Revelation 14:13–14).

This was what 'being in the Spirit' on the Lord's Day meant for John— new visions of Jesus, new insights into his plan and purpose of grace, new awareness of what God has prepared for those who love him. And that is precisely the nature of the New Covenant Sabbath. Away with the thought that we observe the first day of the week legalistically! Perish the thought that all we are doing is returning to the elements of bondage from which we have been redeemed! No—the Lord's Day is for us to seek the Lord's Spirit, so that we, too, through our gathering together around and under the word on the Lord's Day, after the example of the early church, and subject to the authority of the Son of Man, may, through the blessing and illumination of the Spirit, see more of the Christ of the Gospels in all his glory.

But, as Duncan Macfarlan, a nineteenth century Scottish minister, reminds us, the whole phrase—'I was in the Spirit on the Lord's Day'—adds weight to the matter of Sabbath observance:

For why at all mention the day of the week, unless the writer attached some special importance to that particular day? Suppose, for example, that John had been in the Spirit on the second, or third, or fourth, day of the week, would it not be altogether unlike the usual practice of the New Testament writers to mention the day? They are accustomed to take notice of the day, should it happen to be on any of those held sacred; such as the Passover, Pentecost, and the weekly Sabbath: but it was certainly not their practice to notice ordinary days, undistinguished by any particular observance.[22]

So both the 'being in the Spirit' and the being in the Spirit 'on the Lord's Day' combine to highlight for us the unique and high place given to the Lord's Day by the Lord's last apostle. How much we need to pray for a recovery of a sense of the importance of the Lord's Day in the church today, with the prayer that we, too, will know the power of the Holy Spirit as we gather for the preaching of the gospel on the Lord's Day week by week!

Notes

1   **Francis Nigel Lee,** *The Covenantal Sabbath* (London: LDOS, n.d.), p. 211.

2   **J.G. Vos,** *The Westminster Larger Catechism: a commentary* (Phillipsburg NJ,: Presbyterian and Reformed, 2002), p. 323.

3   **R.L. Dabney,** 'The Christian Sabbath: its nature, design and proper observance', in *Discussions of Robert Lewis Dabney*, Vol 1 (Edinburgh: Banner of Truth, 1982), p. 548.

4   **Dabney,** 'The Christian Sabbath', p. 532.

5   **A.T. Lincoln,** 'From Sabbath to Lord's Day: A Biblical and Theological Perspective' in D.A. Carson (ed.), *From Sabbath to Lord's Day: A Biblical, Historical and Theological Investigation* (Grand Rapids: Zondervan, 1982), pp. 398–99.

6   **Lincoln,** 'From Sabbath to Lord's Day', p. 401.

7 **J.M. Boice,** *Foundations of the Christian Faith* (Leicester: IVP, 1986), p. 234.

8 **Boice,** *Foundations*, p. 235.

9 **G.K. Beale,** *The Book of Revelation*: The New International Greek Testament Commentary (Grand Rapids: Eerdmans, 1999), p. 203.

10 **R.J. Bauckham,** 'The Lord's Day', in Carson (ed), *From Sabbath to Lord's Day*, p. 241.

11 **Bauckham,** 'The Lord's Day', p. 240.

12 **F.F. Bruce,** *T he Epistles to the Colossians, to Philemon and to the Ephesians*, New International Commentary on the New Testament (Grand Rapids: Eerdmans, 19840, p. 115, n. 105.

13 **R.L. Dabney,** 'The Christian Sabbath', p. 530.

14 **J. Murray,** *Collected Shorter Writings*, Volume 1 (Edinburgh: Banner of Truth, 1976), p. 214

15 Westminster Confession of Faith, chapter 20.2. Interestingly, Colossians 2:20–23 is among the proof texts cited for this paragraph.

16 **G. Vos,** *Biblical Theology* (Grand Rapids: Eerdmans, 1948), p. 159.

17 **J.A. Pipa,** *The Lord's Day* (Fearn, Tain: Christian Focus Publications, 1997), p. 117.

18 **Pipa,** *Lord's Day*, p. 117.

19 **A.T. Lincoln,** 'Sabbath, Rest and Eschatology in the New Testament', in *From Sabbath to Lord's Day*, p. 213.

20 **Pipa,** *Lord's Day*, pp. 117–18.

21 **Tremper Longman III,** *Immanuel in our Place: Seeing Christ in Israel's Worship* (Phillipsburg: P&R Publishing, 2001), pp. 180–1.

22 **D. MacFarlan,** *A Treatise on the Authority, Ends and Observance of the Christian Sabbath* (Glasgow: Collins, 1832), pp. 72–3.

The Puritans and the Sabbath

Christ wrought most of his miracles upon the Sabbath; so he does still: dead souls are raised and hearts of stone are made flesh. How highly should we esteem and reverence this day.

Thomas Watson, *A Body of Divinity*, p. 292

On this day Christ doth indeed delight to distribute gifts, and blessings, and joy, and happiness, and will delight to do the same to the end of the world. O, therefore, how well it is worth our while to improve this day, to call upon God and seek Jesus Christ!

Jonathan Edwards, *Works*, Vol II, p. 102

It was with fear and trepidation that I went to my school reunion some years back. In our part of the world, school reunions have become an annual event, and are held to coincide with the BIG birthdays. I went along on the year that most of my class were turning forty.

A bit of me was rehearsing C.S. Lewis, whom I had read somewhere as saying that old College reunions were just attempts to get back to the Garden of Eden, so he never went. Of course childhood was long gone, as were its innocence, its safety, its excitements and its experiences.

My main concern was probably whether anyone would recognize me. Forty years can take its toll on an otherwise healthy and slim body! But I wouldn't have missed it for the world. Some of these men and women had been my constant companions before my age reached double figures, yet most I had not seen since we left school.

I think I realized just how much I owed them all—even the ones I hadn't known well in school. Yet their presence, their influence, their homes and families all contributed to the person I have since become. And I am grateful to God for that.

But others can be our companions and can influence us in other ways. Isn't it amazing that we can have friends, brothers and sisters in Christ who lived at different times and eras, yet who embraced the same faith as we do? I think that is one implication of the timelessness of God: his people can enjoy a reunion often! In this chapter we are going to turn to the class of '60.

The year 1660, that is.

It would be possible to fill several pages—and probably several books—with an historical account of sabbatarianism in church history. That has been surveyed fully elsewhere.[1] It is clear—and it is not surprising—that the patristic period (the second century) was one in which a clear distinction was made between the Sabbath and the Lord's Day. This was a period anxious to defend the liberty of believers in the Gospel against the perversions and heresies of which the apostles had warned.

Yet, as Joey Pipa reminds us, it was also a period in which doctrine took a long time to be accurately formulated. He argues that, just as the church struggled to appreciate the doctrine of the incarnation, so she struggled to see the significance of the Sabbath-keeping principle of the new covenant.[2] Yet, even in the struggles of the church fathers, there is an indication that the choice of day should influence the lifestyle of believers; thus Ignatius, writing around the turn of the second century, talks about 'no longer living for the Sabbath but for the Lord's Day'.[3] Even if the language blurs the continuity between Old Covenant and New Covenant Sabbath, the sabbatarian principle is still there: believers should live around one day in seven set apart for a holy purpose.

In other writers, such as Eusebius, there is an identification of Sabbath and Lord's Day, in the observation that the Word (Jesus) had 'exchanged and transferred the feast of the Sabbath to the Lord's Day'.[4] F.N. Lee also claims that Origen used the term 'the Christian Sabbath'.[5]

It is perhaps invidious to single out any particular period of church history as a high-water mark of theological acumen and biblical understanding, but I believe that seventeenth and early-eighteenth century Puritanism represents such a period. Following the break with Medieval superstition and legalism, and even the 'tangled web'[6] of Reformed theology, the Puritan theologians—John Owen, Thomas Watson, Richard Sibbes, Jonathan Edwards and others—brought massive learning, combined with deep piety, to bear on important questions of theology and church life. In the Puritan outlook we find the maturing of theological discussion and insight from which we do well to learn.[7]

I am not saying that the Puritans got everything right. The Holy Spirit is still at work in the church, giving new insights and enabling us to test all the Puritan spirits in the light of the Word of God. But the Puritan worldview is one that the modern church desperately needs to recover:

> They applied their understanding of the mind of God to every branch of life, seeing the church, the family, the state, the arts and sciences, the world of commerce and industry, no less than the devotions of the individual, as so many spheres in which God must be served and honoured. They saw life whole, for they saw its Creator as Lord of each department of it, and their purpose was that 'holiness to the Lord' might be written over it in its entirety.[8]

This holistic approach to the Christian life is the answer we need to the subjectivism and individualism that blights so much of contemporary Christianity. Each man is now encouraged to be persuaded in his own mind to the extent that the doctrine of the church is marginalized. I firmly believe that one reason we need to recover the Puritan doctrine of the Sabbath is because we need to recover the Puritan doctrine of the church, and to discover our part in the body of Christ. So what did the Puritans teach about the Lord's Day? And who were they, anyway?

The Puritan Sabbath

The term 'Puritan' is often used to mean something that is dull and joyless, legalistic and oppressive. For some, therefore, to talk about a 'Puritan Sabbath' is to talk about the very worst kind of Sabbath-keeping, and the kind of thing the modern evangelical church needs to get rid of.

But this attitude grows out of a caricature of the Puritans. Just as there was ignorance about the Puritans in their own time (indeed, the word 'Puritan' was coined as an offensive nickname), so there is much ignorance about the Puritan ethos and ideal today. We have much to learn from the Puritan movement, not least in the whole area of Sabbath-keeping.

So who were the Puritans? Puritanism really began with the arrival in England of William Tyndale's translation of the English New Testament in 1526. Ten years later, under Henry VIII, the Church of England formally separated from the Church of Rome, and when Edward VI became king in 1547, the Reformation of the Church of England continued.

However, in 1553 Queen Mary, a Roman Catholic, succeeded to the throne, and some three hundred Protestants were put to death. Many more fled to the continent. Her reign of five years set back the Reformation work in the Church of England. Mary was succeeded by Elizabeth I, who tried to effect a compromise which allowed for the preaching of Reformed doctrine, but authorized the Anglican Prayer Book in worship.

The Puritan movement grew out of a dissatisfaction with this 'semi-Reformation'. The Puritans refused to conform, and came into conflict with many of the civil and religious authorities. Their goal was a complete reform of the Church of England, and a thoroughgoing application of the Reformation principle of 'Scripture alone'.

Andrew Thomson, in his biographical sketch of John Owen, puts it this way:

John Owen belonged to a class of men who have risen from age to age in the church, to represent great principles, and to revive in the church the life of God. The supreme authority of the Scriptures in all matters of religion, the headship of Christ, the rights of conscience, religion as a thing of spirit, and not of form ... the church as a society distinct from the world, these principles, often contended for in flames and blood, were the essence of that Puritanism which found one of its noblest examples in Owen.[9]

Puritanism, therefore, was a religious reform movement of protest. There are at least three reasons why they are important in our discussion of the Sabbath.

First, we can identify with them: their battle is our battle. We, who love the Bible as they did, wish to see it applied in every area of life. We would love to see a reformed church in a reformed commonwealth. Christ's church is still contending for his supremacy in all matters of faith and life. James Packer says that

The Puritans lost, more or less, every public battle that they fought. Those who stayed in England did not change the Church of England as they hoped to do, nor did they revive more than a minority of its adherents ... They hung on by the skin of their teeth.

But the moral and spiritual victories that the Puritans won by keeping sweet, peaceful, patient, obedient and hopeful under sustained and seemingly intolerable pressures and frustrations give them a place of high honour in the believers' hall of fame.[10]

The church which contends for the truth of God's word will find itself in a similar situation, and needs to hold on to the same encouragement by the help of the same grace.

Secondly, the magnificent statement on the Sabbath in the Westminster Confession of Faith is rooted in Puritan theology and doctrine. Confessional evangelicalism needs to recover its roots, in an age where, as David Wells argues, theology is fast disappearing from the life of the church. He says:

It is proper to speak of the disappearance of theology. It is not that the elements of the evangelical credo have vanished: they have not. The fact that they are professed, however, does not necessarily mean that the structure of the historic Protestant faith is still intact. The reason, quite simply, is that while these items of belief are professed, they are increasingly being removed from the center of evangelical life where they defined what that life was ... [11]

There seems to be a growing reluctance among professing evangelical churches to be confessional. Yet David Wells is correct: it is the church's confessional position that defines the very nature of her evangelicalism. We need the Puritans, therefore, to make us *radical*, in the sense of helping us to recover our roots, our *radix*. Otherwise we drift, and we lose our sense of what the church is called to be.

Thirdly, we need the Puritans because of the important *practical* strain of their theology. Matthew Henry outlined his approach to interpreting the Bible in this way:

We are concerned not only to understand what we read, but to improve it to some good purpose, and, in order thereunto, to be affected with it, and to receive the impressions of it ... we must, therefore, in searching the scriptures, enquire, not only 'What is this?' but 'What is this to us?' What use may we make of it? How may we accommodate it to some of the purposes of that divine and heavenly life which, by the grace of God, we are resolved to live? ... [I am] aiming in all to promote practical godliness.[12]

Similarly, John Owen, in a preface to his work on the Sabbath, says that

There are two great concerns of that religion whose name thou bearest—the profession of its truth, and the practice or exercise of its power. And these are mutually assistant unto each other. Without the profession of faith in its truth, no man can express its power in obedience, and without obedience, profession is of little worth.[13]

So the Puritan theology is constantly being subjected to a public test, to the test of character, of integrity, of public obedience. Far from being dry theoreticians, the Puritans were practitioners of the faith. Not least in the area of the Sabbath, they enrich us both by their doctrine and their practice.

So what was the Sabbath day like in seventeenth-century England? To answer that question we need only quote from Thomas Watson's discussion of the fourth commandment:

The Sabbath day in England lies bleeding, and oh! That our parliament would pour some balm into the wounds which it has received! How is this day profaned by sitting idle at home, by selling meat, by vain discourse, by sinful visits, by walking in the fields and by sports! ... When one of Darius's eunuchs saw Alexander setting his feet on a rich table of Darius's he wept. Alexander asked him why he wept? He said it was to see the table which his master so highly esteemed made a footstool. So may we weep to see the Sabbath day which God highly esteems ... made a footstool and trampled upon by the feet of sinners.[14]

Owen's biographer sets Owen's treatise on the Sabbath in context this way, describing the Sabbath as a means by which God protected his church:

...in seeking to preserve this precious fence which the goodness of God has drawn around the vineyard of his church, and which he found assailed on the one hand by fanatics, who denounced it as a mere ceremonial and carnal observance, and by the more numerous and noisy disciples of the 'Book of Sports' who hated it for its spirituality.[15]

Chapter 6

The *Declaration of Sports* was published by King James I in 1618, and allowed for popular sports to be played after church on Sundays. Like many other attempts at large-mindedness, it only 'opened a flood-gate to all manner of licentiousness'.[16]

This is obviously a large area, but one which will repay careful discussion. We may look at three areas: the Puritan *doctrine* of the Sabbath, Puritan *descriptions* of the Sabbath, and Puritan *directives* for the Sabbath.

The Sabbath—Puritan Doctrine

The Puritans, as we have noted, built on a solidly biblical foundation and basis. Leland Ryken describes their sabbatarianism as having 'a multiple biblical basis'.[17] In this practice, too, we may learn from them; we have noted time and again that our Christianity needs to be *biblical* and not merely drawn from the New Testament. This biblical basis drew on the creation rest of God, the manna provision in the desert, the practice of Christ and the apostolic doctrine of the New Testament.

But it was in their exegesis of the fourth commandment that the Puritans excelled. For Calvin and other Reformers, the Sabbath was a Jewish sign which foreshadowed a future provision. In this sense, they argued that the Sabbath was abrogated, and that the Lord's Day is not a Sabbath. Yet they still wanted to maintain that the fourth commandment is in some sense binding. James Packer is correct to describe this as 'a standing puzzle',[18] an inconsistency which the Puritans rectified.

For the Puritans, no part of a permanent moral code can be temporary. Jonathan Edwards address this very issue in one of his sermons on 'The perpetuity and change of the Sabbath':

Some say that the fourth command is perpetual, but not in its literal sense ... They say that it stands in force only in a mystical sense, viz. as that weekly rest of the Jews typified spiritual rest in the christian church; and that we under the gospel are not to make any distinction of one day from another, but are to keep all time holy, doing every thing in a spiritual manner.

But this is an absurd way of interpreting the command, as it refers to Christians. For if the command be so far abolished, it is entirely abolished ... if it stands in force now only as signifying a spiritual, christian rest, and holy behaviour at all times, it doth not remain as one of the ten commands, but as a summary of all the commands.[19]

For Edwards, the fourth commandment helps set the parameters for genuine worship of God, showing that God alone is to be worshipped (first commandment), showing that he is to be worshipped only in the way prescribed and mandated in his Word (second commandment), showing that he is to be worshipped reverently (third commandment), and showing that he has appointed stated times of worship (fourth commandment). To argue for the abrogation of the fourth commandment, therefore, is to invalidate the whole structure and purpose of the Decalogue.

Coupled with this is the observation that there was, in fact, something which was temporary: that was the Old Covenant practice of sanctifying the seventh day of the week. But the Puritans insisted that the fourth commandment did not say 'Remember the seventh day to keep it holy' but 'Remember the *sabbath* day to keep it holy'. They wished only to go as far as the commandment itself would allow, and they saw the commandment as teaching a specific principle, that of one day out of seven to be observed holy for the Lord. In this way, they could argue both for perpetuity and change. So Thomas Watson could write:

The old seventh-day Sabbath, which was the Jewish Sabbath, is abrogated, and in the room of it the first day of the week, which is the Christian Sabbath, succeeds. The morality or substance of the fourth commandment does not lie in keeping the seventh day precisely, but keeping one day in seven is what God has appointed.[20]

Owen argues very closely and with great precision on this point. He says:

Herein the day originally fixed in the covenant of works is again limited unto this people, to continue unto the time of the full introduction and establishment of the new covenant. And this limitation of the seventh day was but the renovation of the command when given unto them in the way of an especial ordinance (Exodus 16) and belongs not to the substance of the command itself.[21]

And again:

I have also proved that the observation of the seventh day precisely was a pledge of God's rest in the covenant of works, and of our rest in him and with him thereby … therefore although the command for the observation of a sabbath to the Lord, so far as it is moral, it put over into the new covenant … yet take the seventh day precisely as the seventh day, and it is an old testament arbitrary institution.[22]

What John Owen seems to be arguing here is that if the fourth commandment identified with specificity which day of the week was the Sabbath, then there might be grounds for believing that it was an ordinance to be confined to the Old Testament period. But, he says, it does not: it comes to us in the form of a moral precept, in which one day out of seven is to be kept holy. The identity of the day is to be established on other grounds.

The Sabbath—Puritan descriptions

It is interesting to note some of the descriptions which the Puritans give of the Sabbath. These designations and titles give us a unique insight into the psychology of Puritan sabbatarianism.

The Sabbath is designated a *crowning of Christ*. So Thomas Brooks:

It is the duty and glory of a Christian to rejoice in the Lord every day, but especially on the Lord's Day … to rejoice in the Lord this day, and to rejoice in all the duties of the day … this is to crown Christ, this is to lift up Christ.[23]

The concept of honouring Christ by honouring his day runs throughout the literature. Matthew Henry says that

It is for the Redeemer's sake that it is called the Lord's Day, an honourable title; and we ought to call it so, that we may show we look upon it as holy of the Lord, and honourable, and so honour it. It bears Christ's image and his superscription; we ought therefore to render to him the things that are his.[24]

Secondly, the Sabbath is described as a *friend of true religion*. Thomas Watson says:

When the falling dust of the world has clogged the wheels of our affections, that they can scarce move towards God, the Sabbath comes, and oils the wheels of our affections and they move swiftly on. God has appointed the Sabbath for this end ... The heart, which all the week was frozen, on the Sabbath melts with the Word. The Sabbath is a friend to religion: it files off the rust of our graces; it is a spiritual jubilee, wherein the soul is set to converse with its Maker.[25]

Similarly, in his epistle to the reader, Owen prefaced his treatise on the Sabbath with the observation that

Amongst all the outward means of conveying to the present generation that religion which was at first taught and delivered unto men by Jesus Christ and his apostles, there hath been none more effectual than the catholic, uninterrupted observations of such a day for the celebration of the religious worship appointed in the gospel.[26]

God, according to the Puritans, gave us the Sabbath in order that pure religion might have a friend in this hostile world. By observing it, the followers of Christ will have respite from the burdens of the week, and will be lifted above the cares of the world to things above.

Thomas Watson also calls the Sabbath a *badge of religion*. 'The primitive Church,' he says, 'had the Lord's Day, which we now celebrate, in high estimation. It was a great badge of their religion to observe this day.'[27] I think we need to recapture this idea of the Sabbath as a badge of religion; although we can too easily content ourselves with the outward appearance of things, nonetheless Christians are called to make a public show of their faith. In some contexts and cultures, publicly observing the Lord's Day will be a very clear indication of our willingness to submit to the Lordship of Christ. On the other hand, if we make no distinction between the Lord's Day and our practices and behaviour on other days of the week, what badge will we wear to show the world what Christ means to us?

One of the favourite Puritan descriptions of the Sabbath also appears in Watson, where he says that 'the Sabbath day is the market-day of the soul'.[28] The same phrase appears in Matthew Henry, who says that 'The Sabbath day is a market-day, a harvest day for the soul; it is an opportunity, it is time fitted for the doing of that which cannot be done at all, or so well done at another time'.[29] Similarly, Lewes Bayly says

The Sabbath day is God's market-day for the week's provision, wherein he will have us to come unto him, and buy of him without silver or money, the bread of angels and water of life, the wine of the sacraments and milk of the word to feed our souls; tried gold to enrich our faith, precious eyesalve to heal our spiritual blindness, and the white raiment of Christ's righteousness to cover our filthy nakedness.'[30]

The use of the biblical metaphor of buying and selling from God is superb. Just as we need to do our weekly shopping for natural provisions, so we need to shop for spiritual provision. Without it, our souls will wither and die. In his wisdom and grace, God has given us such a market day, and he urges us to make full use of it.

Again, Thomas Watson describes the Sabbath as 'the *soul's festival-day*, on which the graces act their part ... on this day holy affections are quickened; the stock of grace is improved; corruptions are weakened; and Satan falls like lightning before the Majesty of the Word'.[31] The Puritans were accustomed to festival days and holy-days, although they did not generally agree with them. Instead, they saw that in the Sabbath, God had made possible a holy-day festival on a weekly basis, and by observing it, provided blessings for his people.

And it is this note of *pleasure* that is the hallmark of the Puritan Sabbath. Nowhere is the day regarded as cumbersome; everywhere it is declared to be a day whose great design is the happiness of God's people. So Timothy Dwight could write to a friend in England:

The Sabbath is observed in New England with a greater degree of sobriety and strictness than in any other part of the world ... By many Christians of this country the strict observation of the Sabbath is esteemed a privilege and not a burden'.[32]

The Sabbath—Puritan directives

What made such a day pleasurable? We ought to remind ourselves that the Puritans made their practice the test of their orthodoxy—everything at last was reducible to practice, and could be subjected to a public test. We will look at two prominent Puritan authors to see what their suggestions are for the keeping of the Sabbath day.

First, Thomas Watson's *Body of Divinity* contains some eighteen closely written and reasoned pages in answer to his question, 'in what manner are we to sanctify the Sabbath?' His answer is, first, negative: 'all secular work must be forborne and suspended, as it is a profanation of the day … it is sacrilege to rob for civil work the time which God has set apart for his worship'.[33] At the same time, Watson argues that there are some things clearly not forbidden; these include 'works of necessity and charity'.

Second, he provides a positive answer. If we are to make the most of the Sabbath day, we must have 'solemn preparation' and 'sacred observance'. How would we prepare our homes, he asks, if a famous prince were to announce his arrival? So Watson says:

When Saturday evening approaches, sound a retreat; call your minds off from the world and summon your thoughts together, to think of the great work of the approaching day. Purge out all unclean affections, which may indispose you for the work of the Sabbath. Evening preparation will be like the tuning of an instrument, it will fit the heart better for the duties of the ensuing Sabbath.[34]

For observing the Sabbath, Watson suggests that we rejoice as it approaches. It should be a day of gladness, and anticipated as such. It would also help us to get up early, he suggests. Did not Christ himself rise early on this day, before the sun was up? Finally, 'having dressed your bodies, you must dress your souls for hearing the word'.[35]

This involves at least four components. *First*, we ought to read the Scriptures privately, seriously and with affection. Otherwise we will not reap the benefit: 'some step out of their bed to hearing. The reason why many get no more good on a Sabbath by the word preached is because they did not breakfast with God in the morning by reading his word'.[36]

Second, we ought to meditate. Watson suggests four things as suitable objects for Sabbath meditation: creation, God's holiness, Christ's love (further explained in nine points), and the glory of heaven.

Third, we ought to pray. On Sabbath morning we should pray for the one who is to preach God's Word to us on that day, so that the Holy Spirit will send the blessing of the gospel on us. 'The tree of mercy,' says Watson, 'will not drop its fruit, unless it be shaken by the hand of prayer'.[37] We should also pray with, and for, our families, with reverence, humility, fervency and hope.

Fourth, we should address ourselves to the hearing of the preached Word. Sitting in church, we ought to send a prayer to heaven for blessing to accompany the Word. We should pay close attention to it, and we ought to beware of *distraction* and *drowsiness*. Regarding the first danger, Watson examines where distractions come from, what they do (seven points here), and how we can get rid of them. We can prevent drowsiness, he suggests, by eating a light diet on the Sabbath. The importance of attending to the Word is further confirmed by five things: first, the fact that it is God who is speaking to us; second, that the issues with which the Gospel deals are serious; third, that it gratifies Satan when we give way to vain thoughts; fourth, that each Sabbath may be our last; and fifth that we will give account for every sermon we hear.

We ought then to guard against the things that make the Sabbath ineffectual to many people. Some go to church out of curiosity, others with prejudice, or covetousness, or partiality, or censoriousness, or disobedience. Our motives should be right, our appetite for spiritual things sharpened, our hearing mixed with faith and meekness of spirit. We ought to aim at remembering what we hear—'be not only attentive but retentive'[38] says Watson.

Next, Watson says that what we hear preached ought to have an effect on the way we live. That is simply to highlight the principle which the apostle James highlights when he says that we should 'be doers of the word and not hearers only' (James 1:23). Or, as Watson puts it, 'the Word preached is not only to inform you but to reform you'.[39] If our Sabbath-keeping is only a matter of taking in information, it is of little value. The real benefit of the Lord's Day comes from the influence the Word has on us over the course of the rest of the week.

One way in which we can assure this, says Watson, is to 'confer with the Word', to use the Lord's Day as a day of exposing ourselves as much as possible to God's Word. Few people do this, he says, 'as if sermons were such secrets that they must not be spoken of again'.[40] But if the Word is to dwell in us richly, then the Lord's Day provides us with the perfect opportunity not only to listen to it, but to consider and meditate upon its meaning.

Watson's final exhortation is:

Close the Sabbath evening with repetition, reading, singing Psalms and prayer. Ask that God would bless the word you have heard. Could we but thus spend a Sabbath, we might be 'in the Spirit on the Lord's Day', our souls would be nourished and comforted; and the Sabbaths we now keep, would be earnests of the everlasting Sabbaths which we shall celebrate in heaven.[41]

In true Puritan style, however, Watson is not exhausted yet! He now moves to his practical application of these points, with three *uses* to which these doctrines may be put. The first is that *it is the Christian's duty to keep the whole of the Sabbath day holy*. It is not a part of the day that is to be sanctified, but the whole: the believer under the new covenant is, in this view, under no less an obligation to consecrate a day to the Lord as was the Jew under the old.

And the whole day is to be *sanctified*, which Watson explains with an exegesis of Isaiah 58:13, in which he has a particularly moving explanation of what it means to 'call the Sabbath a delight':

The Lord's Day on which the Sun of Righteousness shines is both a day of light and delight. This is the day of sweet intercourse between God and the soul. On this day a Christian makes his sallies out to heaven; his soul is lifted above the earth; and can this be without delight? The higher the bird flies, the sweeter it sings. On the Sabbath the soul fixes its love on God, and where love is, there is delight ... Is it not delightful to a queen to be putting on her wedding robes in which she shall meet the king her bridegroom? When we are about Sabbath exercises, we are dressing ourselves and putting on our wedding robes in which we are to meet our heavenly bridegroom the Lord Jesus, and is not this delightful?[42]

The corollary of this is simply this: the Lord's Day is not a day for worldly things. The things of the world are not the things which delight the people of God. Their joy is spiritual, and must be resourced spiritually. And for that purpose, the Sabbath is given to us.

The second use of this doctrine which Watson identifies is that 'they are reproved who, instead of sanctifying the Sabbath, profane it'.[43] With typical Puritan pathos, Watson laments the demise of the Sabbath in his day:

> The people of Israel might not gather manna on the Sabbath, and may we use sports and dancings on this day? ... This is to despise God, to hang out the flag of defiance, to throw down the gauntlet and challenge God himself. Now, how can God endure to be thus saucily confronted by proud dust? Surely he will not suffer this high impudence to go unpunished. God's curse will come upon the Sabbath-breaker; and it will blast where it comes. The law of the land lets Sabbath-breakers alone, but God will not.[44]

Indeed, Watson enumerates the ways God will punish those who profane his day: he will bring 'spiritual plagues' on them, he will give them over to committing other sins, and he will bring visible judgements on them.

In similar vein, Matthew Henry, the prince of Puritan commentators, has an essay entitled *A Serious Address to Those that Profane the Lord's Day*. This is not just an address to men of the world, but to those who profess to be Christians. Henry makes an extremely emotive call to them: 'if you have any regard to the sweet and blessed name of Jesus ... have a conscientious regard to that day which bears this name'.[45] Part of his conviction here is that genuine religion may be judged by the observance of the Christian Sabbath: 'the stream of all religion runs either deep or shallow, according as the banks of the sabbath are kept up or neglected'.[46]

Watson's third use of the Sabbath principle is that 'it exhorts us to Sabbath holiness'.[47] The day is sanctified for the people who are being sanctified. With the weekly reminder of the resurrection of Christ, we are reminded that the will of God is our sanctification, and we will not let this fact slip our mind. Thomas Watson concludes his analysis of the fourth commandment with the thought that 'a conscientious keeping of the Sabbath seasons the heart for God's service all the week after. Christian, the more holy thou art on a Sabbath, the more holy thou wilt be on the week following'.[48] At last, this is one of the most practical and fundamental aspects of Sabbath-keeping for the New Covenant believer, according to the Puritan consciousness and worldview: by observing a holy day of rest, in a rightful spirit and with the right motive, we will be induced and led to live our lives for the rest of the week in a manner consistent with our profession as Christians.

Our second representative Puritan writer is Jonathan Edwards, whose three sermons on *The Perpetuity and Change of the Sabbath* cover much the same ground. It was of Edwards, however, that Martyn Lloyd-Jones said that 'No man is more relevant to the present condition of Christianity than Jonathan Edwards',[49] with his 'ideal combination' of 'the great doctrines with the fire of the Spirit upon them'.[50] A theological and philosophical genius, Edwards' life and work remain a fascinating subject for modern theologians.[51]

Edwards' sermons on the Sabbath[52] are based on 1 Corinthians 16:1–2, and clearly and logically set forth the case for our continuing obligation to observe the fourth commandment. The first sermon highlights the fact that Paul, in spite of his argument against observing 'days and months' (Galatians 4:10), here 'gives the preference to one day of the week, before any other, for the performance of a certain great duty of Christianity'.[53] From this, Edwards proceeds to demonstrate that 'the first day of the week should be distinguished from other days of the week, as a sabbath, to be devoted to religious exercises'[54]. From the biblical data, he deduces the two propositions that God demands one day a week to be devoted to 'rest and religious exercises', and that under the 'gospel dispensation', that day is the first day of the week.

One of the proof texts by which Edwards demonstrates the second of these propositions is Matthew 24:20—'Pray that your flight may not be in winter or on a Sabbath'. The fact that Jesus is speaking about the destruction of Jerusalem, he says, is important, since this was 'after the dissolution of the Jewish constitution and after the Christian dispensation was fully set up.'[55] Yet, it is still the case that Christians were to observe a Sabbath. The meaning of this particular text is disputed by the commentators, but for Edwards it is demonstrable proof that Sabbath-keeping was a principle anticipated by Christ for the duration of the Gospel period.

The second sermon argues for the change of the Sabbath from the last day of the week to the first, with arguments which we have already noted in other contexts. Basic to this is the Puritan understanding of the fourth commandment, which we have already noted, that, while the fourth commandment requires the principle of one day out of seven to be sanctified, it does not identify which day that ought to be. It was the precept governing the manna in Exodus 16 which, according to Edwards, identified the old covenant Sabbath.

But Edwards nuances this in an interesting manner. He refers to Nehemiah 9:14, which says that God visited his people and 'you made known to them your holy Sabbath ...' The reason this was necessary, says Edwards, is that in Egypt the Israelites had lost sight of the seven-day week cycle and the Sabbath principle. Sinai, therefore, was only a reminder of what Egypt had obliterated from their memory.

So the fourth commandment remains in force, its principle intact, but the day changed. The gospel period is called a new creation, says Edwards, so the change of day is fitting, as is the perpetual obligation of Sabbath-keeping. Christ has entered into his rest by virtue of resurrection, just as God entered into rest on the seventh day of creation. Just as the old Sabbath commemorated the ascent of the children of Israel out of the Red Sea, so the new covenant Sabbath commemorates the resurrection. With other arguments based on parallels between creation and redemption, as well as on New Testament texts, Edwards asks whether there is not sufficient evidence to show that 'it is the mind and will of God that the first day of the week should be kept by the Christian church as a Sabbath?'[56]

Having established these points, Edwards turns to application of the doctrine. He exhorts his hearers, first, to be thankful for the Christian Sabbath, and, second, to take care to keep the day holy. He offers five motives towards this latter point. First is the fact that an observation of the Sabbath honours God's name; second, that religion, the business of the Sabbath, is the chief business of our lives; third, that all our time is God's, and when he asks for one day out of seven, he is only asking for what is his own; fourth, that God, by specifically asking for one day in seven to be given to him, offers special blessing on that day; and fifth, that Sabbath-keeping has had a markedly positive effect on religion in general.

So, asks Edwards: 'how ought we to keep the Sabbath?' In answer to this question, Edwards again suggests five propositions.

First, 'we ought to be exceeding careful on this day to abstain from sin'.[57] Of course, Edwards is not saying that we need not be careful on other days;

but he does insist that the sanctity of the Lord's Day increases the guilt and seriousness of any sin committed on it. But the argument has a very practical end in view, for Edwards knows that those who do engage in sinful, worldly practice on the Lord's Day are those who habitually do so on other days, too: 'very commonly those who are used to such things on weekdays have not a conscience to restrain them on the Sabbath'.[58] So it is not a case of engaging in sin for six days and avoiding it on the seventh: it is a case of living holy lives in all our engagements and callings. The sanctifying of the Sabbath ought to have a sanctifying effect in the whole of our lives.

Second, 'we ought to be careful to abstain from all worldly concerns'.[59] Part of the reason for the commandment, says Edwards, is that it is necessary for us, while we are in this world, to concern ourselves with secular matters, and to be engaged in time-bound activities. For that reason, God has given us sacred time, in order that our minds will be elevated to sacred things. The separation of the day serves the interests of the disengaging of our mind from secular activities.

Third, 'we ought to spend the time in religious exercises'.[60] We cannot simply call the Sabbath a day of rest: that would be to take our minds off secular things and fix them on nothing. They will then soon return to the secular things! Just as in heaven's rest the saints are not idle, so the Sabbath-rest that remains for God's people ought to be one of religious activity. It is precisely through meditating on the Scriptures and books according to the Bible, in public and private acts of worship, and in encouraging others to do so also, that we enter into the spiritual blessing signified by the Lord's Day Sabbath.

Fourth, 'we are especially to meditate upon and celebrate the work of redemption'.[61] This, Edwards continues, 'is the day of our deliverance out of Egypt'. Just as Jesus' resurrection was 'the day of the gladness of his heart', so it must be for us. With faith and in obedience, we observe the day as being 'holy to the Lord', and our blessing, as well as that of our family, is increased thereby.

And finally, Edwards suggests, 'works of mercy and charity are very proper and acceptable to Christ on this day'.[62] As Jesus performed miracles of healing and works of charity on the Sabbath day, so too may we; which brings Edwards back to his text, with its charitable collection on the first day of the week for the good of the churches in Corinth.

So, both Thomas Watson and Jonathan Edwards, having established the principle that Sabbath-keeping is a perpetual ordinance, but that it has been modified with the change of day under the gospel, apply the teaching in a very practical way. Some might allege that they head towards the error of the rabbis, who had hedged the old Sabbath about with so many rules and regulations that they were destroying it by their own man-made rules and regulations. But the Puritans were not interested in legalistic Sabbath-keeping which would merit righteousness or favour with God. For them, only the imputed righteousness of Christ could cover guilty sinners. And those who have found acceptance with God have all the more reason to honour the day that keeps the essential truths of redemption before the minds of God's people. It is God's prerogative to command; it is our duty to obey. The fourth commandment has never, in the Puritan view, been annulled or discontinued. It has come to us in a form which mirrors and represents all the spiritual elements of New Covenant salvation. All the more reason to submit, then, to the Lord of the Sabbath, and honour his day.

Let men in whose hearts are the ways of God seriously consider the use that hath been made, under the blessing of God, of the conscientious observation of the Lord's day, in the past and present ages, unto the promotion of holiness, righteousness and religion universally, in the power of it; and if they are not under invincible prejudices, it will be very difficult for them to judge that it is a plant which our heavenly Father hath not planted. For my part, I must not only say, but plead whilst I live in this world, and leave this testimony to the present and future ages, if these papers see the light and do survive, that if I have ever seen anything in the ways and worship of God wherein the power of religion or godliness hath been expressed, anything that hath represented the holiness of the gospel and the Author of it, anything that hath looked like a preludium [prelude] unto the everlasting sabbath and rest with God, which we aim through grace to come unto, it hath been there and with them where and amongst whom the Lord's day hath been had in highest esteem, and a strict observation of it attended unto, as an ordinance of our Lord Jesus Christ.

John Owen, 'Of the Lord's Day', *Works,* Vol. XIX, p. 428

Notes

1 See, for example, **F.N. Lee** on 'The Sabbath in Church History' in *The Covenantal Sabbath*, pp. 239–66 and the historical surveys by **Richard Bauckham** in chapters 9–11 of *From Sabbath to Lord's Day*.

2 **Joey Pipa,** *The Lord's Day* (Fearn, Tain: Christian Focus Publications, 1997), p. 131.

3 **See Pipa,** *Lord's Day,* p. 132 and Bauckham, p. 260.

4 **Pipa,** *Lord's Day,* p. 136.

5 See **Lee,** p. 245.

6 The phrase is **Pipa's** *Lord's Day*, p. 143.

7 It may seem strange to omit any discussion of Calvin and other Reformers, who seem to have argued that the Sabbath is no longer binding on us (see, for example, **Calvin's** discussion on the fourth commandment in the *Institutes*, Book II, Chapter 8). **Geerhardus Vos,** however, warns us that 'some of the continental reformers, out of reaction to the Romish system of holy days … reasoned wrongly' (*Biblical Theology,* p. 157).

8 **J.I. Packer,** *Among God's Giants: The Puritan Vision of the Christian Life* (Eastbourne: Kingsway, 1991), p. 34.

9 **A. Thomson,** *Life of Dr Owen*, in *The Works of John Owen*, Vol 1 (London: Johnstone and Hunter, 1850), p. cxi.

10 **J.I. Packer,** *Among God's Giants*, p. 25.

11 **David Wells,** *No Place for Truth, Or, Whatever Happened to Evangelical Theology?* (Leicester: IVP, 1993), p. 108.

12 **Matthew Henry,** Preface to *Commentary on the Holy Bible* (1706), p. vii.

13 **John Owen,** 'Epistle to the Christian Reader', as an introduction to his 'Treatise on the Sabbath', Vol. 19, *Works,* p. 263.

14 **Thomas Watson,** *A Body of Divinity* (London, 1898), pp. 308–9.

15 *Writings* of **John Owen,** Vol. I, p. xciii.

16 **Benjamin Brook,** *The Lives of the Puritans,* Vol II, 1813 (Morgan, PA: Soli Deo Gloria Publications reprint, 1994), p. 173.

17 **Leland Ryken,** *Worldly Saints: The Puritans as they really were* (Grand Rapids: Zondervan, 1986), p. 129.

18 **Packer,** *Among God's Giants*, p. 314. This is part of his excellent chapter on 'The Puritans and the Lord's Day' in this volume.

19 **Jonathan Edwards,** *Works,* Vol II, p. 95.

20 **Watson,** *A Body of Divinity*, p. 290.

21 **Owen,** *Works,* Vol XIX, p. 396.

22 **Owen,** *Works,* Vol XIX, p. 426.

23 Quoted in **Packer,** *Among God's Giants,* p. 317.

24 **Matthew Henry,** 'A serious address to those that profane the Lord's Day' in *The Complete Works of the Rev. Matthew Henry* (London: Fullarton), Vol I, p. 125.

25 **Watson,** *Body of Divinity,* p. 290.

26 **Owen,** *Works,* Vol XIX, p. 263.

27 **Watson,** *Body of Divinity,* p. 291.

28 **Watson,** *Body of Divinity,* p. 292.

29 **Henry,** *Works,* p. 132.

30 Taken from *The Practice of Piety* and quoted in the *Banner of Truth* magazine, December 1975, p. 6.

31 **Watson,** *Body of Divinity,* p. 292.

32 Quoted in **Iain H. Murray,** *Jonathan Edwards: A New Biography* (Edinburgh: Banner of Truth, 1987), p. 84.

33 **Watson,** *Body of Divinity,* p. 293.

34 **Watson,** *Body of Divinity,* p. 295.

35 **Watson,** *Body of Divinity,* p. 295.

36 **Watson,** *Body of Divinity,* p. 295.

37 **Watson,** *Body of Divinity,* p. 299.

38 **Watson,** *Body of Divinity,* p. 305.

39 **Watson,** *Body of Divinity,* p. 306.

40 **Watson,** *Body of Divinity,* p. 307.

41 **Watson,** *Body of Divinity,* p. 307.

42 **Watson,** *Body of Divinity,* p. 307.

43 **Watson,** *Body of Divinity,* p. 308.

44 **Watson,** *Body of Divinity,* p. 309.

45 **Henry,** 'A Serious Address', p. 125.

46 **Henry,** 'A Serious Address', p. 134.

47 **Watson,** *Body of Divinity,* p. 309.

48 **Watson,** *Body of Divinity,* p. 310.

49 **D.M. Lloyd-Jones,** 'Jonathan Edwards and the Crucial Importance of Revival' in *The Puritans: their origins and successors* (Edinburgh: Banner of Truth Trust, 1987), p. 367.

50 **Lloyd-Jones,** *The Puritans,* p. 368.

51 For more information on Edwards, see **George M. Marsden,** *Jonathan Edwards: A Life* (New Haven: Yale University Press, 2003).

52 In Volume 2 of the Hickman edition of **Edwards'** *Works* (London, 1840), pp. 93–103.

53 J. Edwards, *Works*, Vol II, p. 93.

54 J. Edwards, *Works*, Vol II, p. 94.

55 J. Edwards, *Works*, Vol II, p. 96.

56 J. Edwards, *Works*, Vol II, p. 100.

57 J. Edwards, *Works*, Vol II, p. 102.

58 J. Edwards, *Works*, Vol II, p. 102.

59 J. Edwards, *Works*, Vol II, p. 102.

60 J. Edwards, *Works*, Vol II, p. 103.

61 J. Edwards, *Works*, Vol II, p. 103.

62 J. Edwards, *Works*, Vol II, p. 103.

The Twenty-First Century Christian and the Sabbath

If you keep my commandments, you will abide in my love, just as I have kept my Father's commandments and abide in his love. John 15:10

There can be little doubt that God's people would once again make a dramatic impact on our culture if we were to make a serious attempt to enjoy the weekly rest in preparation for the eternal rest which awaits us.

Alistair Begg[1]

I love Sundays. I love Mondays to Saturdays too, but I especially like Sundays. I always have. I remember as a young boy thinking that the air was different on Sunday morning. Sunday had associations of church, of grandparents calling in for supper, of peace and quiet. There was a noise of traffic in my home town for the half hour before 11am and after 12.15pm. The same pattern was repeated at night, as the only movement on our streets revolved around churchgoing.

I remember listening to a debate in my local school. For some reason, I wasn't allowed to take part. Some of the other Christian pupils were trying to defend the traditional Sabbatarianism of our island. Another team was trying to use every argument to demolish it. I remember one girl on the anti-Sabbath side trying to ridicule the peace and quiet of a typical island Sunday by using the phrase 'suspended animation' to describe our home town on the first day of the week.

She thought it was ridiculous. It was as if you took every life form and froze it for twenty-four hours, during which time things which were OK for the other six days suddenly became sins. She could not understand how anyone in his or her right mind could imagine that a day of rest was good. In her argument, overloaded with prejudice, there was no life in a day of curtailed activity.

How little she knew. Our Sunday *was* life—life in the very best sense.

But I wonder whether today's Christian loves Sunday?

Earlier this year, Channel Four television (a liberal UK TV company) showed a broadcast in which the Ten Commandments were subjected to public scrutiny. The presenter, Jon Snow, introduced the commandments as given to Israel at Sinai to guide them in the desert. Prominent public figures gave their comments on the commandments, on which were relevant to modern life and which were not. The great British public then voted in the new commandments that ought to govern life in this modern age of ours.

The outcome was pretty predictable, with the commandments against worshipping other gods, against graven images, and keeping the Sabbath holy being discarded in favour of the new ethical standards. These included such commandments as 'look after the environment', 'protect children and young people', and the new number one: 'treat others as you would like them to treat you'.

I did not know whether to laugh or cry. The whole business of voting for absolute standards is ludicrous—how can moral absolutes be decided on a show of hands? Is it not possible for the majority to be wrong? Hitler had the backing of hundreds of thousands of supporters in Nazi Germany, but everyone recognizes that his policy of anti-Semitic genocide was wrong.

Apart from that, the business of deciding on popular commandments is unworkable. We don't send footballers out onto the field deciding which rules they'd like to apply to the game today! Nor do we allow people to drive on our roads deciding for themselves which speed limits to adhere to or which side of the road to drive on! If we did, there would be chaos.

Rules are made for a purpose: and it is not to restrict our enjoyment or curtail our behaviour. They are made for our well-being and safety, for our good and for our benefit. The Ten Commandments are the same: they are moral absolutes, given us by our Creator God, in order that we may know fulfilment, purpose and direction in our lives. None of us can keep the commandments perfectly, which is why we need a Saviour. And those of us who trust the Saviour have more reason than most to keep the commandments. The God who gave them at Sinai was none other than Jesus.

We have looked at a variety of passages from the Bible, as well as at different theological perspectives and positions in the previous chapters. As we bring our study to a close, we want to ask: what is the relevance of the fourth commandment to the life of today's Christian? Or, to put it another way, 'What is the relationship of the believer today to the Sabbath commandment?'

We have noted, along the way, that different Christian thinkers supply different answers to that question. Some regard the fourth commandment as of a piece with the other ten, and see no distinction between the Decalogue and the other laws of the Old Testament. They have all been done away in Christ, they say. We are now mandated, so the argument goes, to obey only those commandments which Christ enjoins on us. And nowhere does the New Testament endorse the fourth commandment.

Other believers approach the issue from another angle. They say that under the New Testament, it is not just one day that we keep holy—we keep them all holy. They allege that it is part of the newness and breadth of the fulfilment that has come with Jesus Christ that all of life is sacred to God, and all of our time is holy to him as well.

The burden of this book has been to argue that the fourth commandment is binding on believers still, simply because of the claim of Christ that he is 'Lord of the Sabbath'. Those who confess that 'Jesus is Lord' must reckon with his claim to be 'Lord of the Sabbath'. There must be some abiding principle of Sabbath-keeping for the believer, who is subject to the Lordship of Jesus Christ in every area of life. But how is this to be worked out in practice? What are the principles that ought to govern our lifestyle as believers?

One thing is certainly clear: there has been a dramatic change in the way in which Christians view what is permissible on the Lord's Day. This can be illustrated from the world of professional sports. Eric Liddell famously refused to run on the Lord's Day when the heats for the 100 metres at the Paris Olympics of 1928 where scheduled for Sunday. Interestingly, he then switched to the 400-metre race, and took a gold medal as a result. On the other hand, Jonathan Edwards, the famous triple jumper of our current generation, changed his mind over competing on Sundays. In 1991 he did not compete on a Sunday, but then there was a change:

In 1993, however, he believed that God had told him in a dream that he was to use his ability to its full potential. During those championships he took part in the qualifying round on a Sunday and subsequently took the bronze medal.[2]

How does one assess such a change? In a recent article on the Lord's Day, Rev. Peter Baker of Cardiff expresses his own change of attitude towards strict sabbatarianism:

The second reason I became less uptight about Sundays, particularly in terms of professional, organized sport, was evangelistic. I came to realize that if the gospel and the Christian are to be salt and light, then no section of culture or society could be ignored as a context for the believer to witness to the glory of God and the cross of Christ … If, therefore, a Christian can be called to work and witness as a doctor and that requires a Sunday commitment, does not the same principle apply to the Christian athlete? … It is my observation that we evangelicals have often been selective and eccentric in our application of Sunday observance … I now reckon that a particular approach on these matters, whether sabbatarian or libertarian, like so much else in our glorious cultural heritage in Protestant, Reformed Wales, is a non essential—a non essential that we can spend far too much time arguing about when there are more important battles to fight.[3]

If Peter Baker is correct, then the issue simply becomes a matter of personal conscience and conviction, and each believer can work out what is permissible or not permissible on the Lord's Day. But if, in fact, the commandment governing the Sabbath is now applicable to the Lord's Day, then today's Christian needs to re-visit this particular area of ethics and of morality.

What are our controls?

Perhaps we need to go back to basics here. What are the factors which control and govern the behaviour and lifestyle of the Christian?

First, there is the *Lordship of Jesus Christ.* The early Christian confession—'Jesus is Lord'—was the most subversive statement imaginable in the first century. It was a direct attack on all of Caesar's claims on divinity and sovereignty. For the early believers, their allegiance was first and foremost to 'another king, Jesus' (Acts 17:7). And it is undoubtedly true that Jesus' Lordship extends over all our days, and over all our activities. There is no area of our lives over which he does not claim lordship, or which he does not claim as his own.

Second, there is the *example of Jesus Christ*. Believers want to be like their Lord. He left us an example (1 Peter 2:21), and he calls his servants to be like their Master (Matthew 10:25). We are called to apply in our own lives the standards and the principles that Jesus applied in his. In this way, it is true both that *Jesus* is the light of the world (John 8:12) *and* that his followers are the light of the world (Matthew 5:14). His life in us is what will continue to illuminate a world in the grip of sin's darkness.

And part of what that involves is avoiding the very hypocrisy and self-righteousness of the religious leaders of Jesus' day that brought him into conflict over issues such as the Sabbath. They had one set of values governing Sabbath observance, values which were self-centred and self-righteous. He had another, and he teaches us by his example that there is a right way to observe the fourth commandment, as there is a right way to approach them all.

But it was not without reason that Jesus said to his followers, 'Beware of the leaven of the Pharisees and Sadducees' (Matthew 16:6). His disciples, on that occasion, thought that he was talking about ordinary bread, in which leaven, or yeast, would be one of the main ingredients. When he referred back to incidents which had taken place in their lives, 'then they understood that he did not tell them to beware of the leaven of bread, but of the teaching of the Pharisees and Sadducees' (Matthew 16:12). Like the leaven of the Old Testament which had to be put out of the house at Passover time (Exodus 12:15), there is leaven which has to be put out of our lives too.

So following the example of Christ means being sincere, being without hypocrisy, being without the leaven of self-righteousness. It is possible for Sabbath-keeping to become the basis for self-righteousness and acceptance before God—that was the accusation Jesus made of the Pharisees. But that does not mean that all Sabbath-keeping is legalistic, and it does not mean that all who keep Sabbath do so for that reason. We follow the example of Christ, so our lives should reflect the standards of holiness and purity that characterized his.

Third, there is the *Word of Jesus Christ*. As believers, we live our lives and regulate our behaviour by what Jesus says to us. We take the place that belongs to disciples, at the feet of their Master, and we let his Word sink into our souls. His words are spirit and life (John 6:63), and he teaches that the way of fruit-bearing is the way of obedience (John 15:8–10).

The Sermon on the Mount is a classic illustration of this: in the beatitudes, Jesus describes what kind of people his followers are; in the subsequent parts of the sermon he goes on to show what kind of life they should live. Jesus pronounces his followers to be blessed in all kinds of circumstances. The word 'blessed', as we have seen, is a word applied to the Sabbath in the Old Testament (Genesis 2:3), and talks about the relational aspect of God and the Sabbath—he connects with this day that he has made in a way that is different from his relationship with other days of the week. So it is with his people: they are 'blessed', and they stand in a unique relationship to God.

Such a relationship requires a particular lifestyle. The Sermon on the Mount develops this theme of the kind of life Jesus' followers are to live, and begins with a reference to the commandments. Far from setting them aside, Jesus emphatically says, 'Do not think that I have come to abolish the Law or the Prophets; I have not come to abolish them, but to fulfil them' (Matthew 5:17). Speaking with authority, Jesus does not set the commandments aside; but he does place his own authority over against that of the rabbinical teachers of the Jews, reminding us, his disciples, that 'unless our righteousness exceeds that of the scribes and Pharisees, you will never enter the kingdom of heaven' (Matthew 5:20). For the Pharisees, outward conformity was enough; heart conformity was missing.

Interestingly, that fact was emphasized time and again by the Old Testament prophets.

Joel declares God's call to his people to 'rend your hearts and not your garments' (Joel 2:13), because outward conformity without inward conviction is not pleasing to God. The point is also made with devastating effect in the opening words of Isaiah's prophetic ministry:

What to me is the multitude of your sacrifices? Says the LORD. I have had enough of burnt offerings of rams and the fat of well-fed beasts; I do not delight in the blood of bulls, or of lambs, or of goats …

Bring no more vain offerings; incense is an abomination to me, New moon and Sabbath and the calling of convocations—I cannot endure iniquity and solemn assembly ...

Wash yourselves; make yourselves clean; remove the evil of your deeds from before my eyes; cease to do evil, learn to do good; seek justice, correct oppression; bring justice to the fatherless, plead the widow's cause (Isaiah 1:11, 13, 16, 17).

So Jesus, our great Prophet, is not preaching a new ethic in the Sermon on the Mount; he is simply absolutizing the ethic that was given to the Old Testament believers amid the shadows of that period of redemption history. It is not enough, he says, to say that we have murdered no one; the sixth commandment searches out every murderous thought of the heart. Nor is it enough to say that we have committed no adultery; the seventh commandment condemns every lustful longing and every salacious look. John L. Mackay summarizes it this way:

Jesus illustrates his teaching with six examples in which he contrasts what he says, not with the law as given by Moses, but with the law as presented in a superficial fashion to past and present generations by the religious teachers of the Jews ... Being a citizen of the kingdom of heaven requires inner conformity to the demands of the law.4

That ethical implication of Jesus' words is brought out clearly in the parable with which the Sermon on the Mount concludes. Those who hear his words and put them in to practice are compared to a wise builder who makes sure that his house is built on a solid foundation. Those who hear his words but refuse to do them are compared to a foolish builder, whose house goes up quickly, but is not built on a sure foundation. The test comes with the storm; only one house can withstand the tempest, and that is the house that is firmly grounded on the solid rock.

The effect of such teaching was powerful at the time (Matthew 7:28–9) and still is. Jesus speaks as only God can. Who else could possibly dare to say that the eternal welfare of people depends on their acting on his words? That prerogative belongs alone to God. And Jesus is God.

Because that is so, it is not only the Sermon on the Mount that regulates the lifestyle of the believer. The whole Bible is the manual for citizens of

Jesus' kingdom. To be subject to his lordship means that we view the Scriptures as he viewed them, acknowledging the divinity of both Old and New Testaments. We believe that the whole Scripture is relevant and suited to our needs because that is what Jesus taught. James Montgomery Boice is therefore exactly correct when he says that

Jesus so identified himself with Scripture and so interpreted his ministry in the light of Scripture that it is impossible to weaken the authority of one without at the same time weakening the authority of the other.[5]

So we are *biblical* Christians, not just *New Covenant* believers. We need to take the whole Bible and apply it to the whole of our lives. That means, of course, recognizing the development within Scripture itself. The animal sacrifices of the Old Testament have much to teach us, although we offer none now. Similarly, the wars of the Old Testament teach fundamental spiritual truths, but cannot be used as justification for war today.

Nonetheless the principle is valid: as Christians, we need to recognize that the Bible must be our rule, for the followers of Jesus have no other book to help or guide them. As the Second Answer in the Westminster Shorter Catechism puts it, 'The Word of God, which is contained in the Scriptures of the Old and New Testaments, is the only rule he has given us by which we may glorify and enjoy him'. We dare not detract from Scripture, nor add to Scripture (see Revelation 22:18–19); nor ought we to neglect any part of it.

How ought Scripture to guide my keeping of the Lord's Day?

I have tried to show in the previous chapters that the Sabbath principle runs through the Bible, from beginning to end. God rested on the seventh day to indicate the ultimate design he had in creating the world. His example became the blueprint for human behaviour and the regulation of time. That was reinforced in the precepts governing the gathering of manna in Exodus 16, and was given the supreme sanction of law in the Ten Commandments.

Jesus, while rejecting all hypocritical and self-righteous law-keeping on the part of many in his day, nonetheless declared himself to be Lord of the Sabbath. The day was his to give, and is his to rule. By so naming himself, he was declaring his authority to change the day of rest, which he did by his resurrection on the first day of the week. Thereafter the disciples observed the first day of the week, applying the Sabbath principle to a new day. There is, therefore, such a thing as the New Testament Sabbath, on the first day of the week. Ultimately, heaven is the Sabbath that awaits us, to which each Lord's Day points.

So, on this reading of the Bible, the question of Sabbath observance is inescapable. This is a moral absolute, just as the demand to reverence God's name, to respect one's parents, and to respect life and truth. And the demands of the kingdom of heaven are such that the Sabbath principle is not cast aside; indeed, the requirements for keeping it are more stringent and dig further into the motives of our heart.

Can we, therefore, draw up a list of activities which are permissible or which are not permissible? One church website, which I consulted recently, has a statement about the Sabbath which insists that shaving and polishing shoes are things that ought not to be done on the Sabbath day. But it seems to me that that is getting perilously close to the position against which Jesus argues so often. His polemic is precisely with those who insist that their Sabbath-keeping is valid precisely because they conform to man-made regulations. I do not think it is possible for us to draw up a list of things to do and not to do; but I do think we can ask questions about our Sunday activities which might help us to apply the fourth commandment meaningfully.

IS WHAT I DO ON THE LORD'S DAY CONDUCIVE TO HOLINESS?

The Sabbath principle in the Bible is intimately related to the holiness principle. When God rested on day seven of the creation week, he made the day *holy* (Genesis 2:3; Exodus 20:11). In order to appreciate the nature of the Sabbath, we need to understand the meaning of 'holiness'.

The Hebrew word which means 'holy' comes from a root which means to separate, and comes to be used for anything that is separated from ordinary use. Supremely, God himself is distinct from his creation, and is 'majestic in holiness' (Exodus 15:11). The heavenly beings celebrate his holiness (Isaiah 6:3), and the Bible expresses God's jealousy for his own holiness:

And my holy name I will make known in the midst of my people Israel, and I will not let my holy name be profaned any more. And the nations shall know that I am the Lord, the Holy One in Israel (Ezekiel 39:7).

God is holy—he is both the source and the cause of holiness. 'There is none holy like the LORD' (1 Samuel 2:2). His people are holy people (Exodus 19:6; 1 Peter 2:9). His worship is a holy worship (Psalm 96:9; 1 Timothy 2:8). His prophets were holy prophets (2 Peter 3:2). His temple was a holy temple, both literally and spiritually (1 Kings 8:10–11; Ephesians 2:21). His day, therefore, remains a holy day, to be set apart from a common use (which is what we have six days for), to a Godward, sacred use:

The Sabbath was holy, and the restrictions connected with that day served to maintain its distinctive nature and to guard against its being treated as common.[6]

And this Sabbath was made for man; more fundamental than man's physical need of rest is his spiritual need of holiness, without which no one can see God (Hebrews 12:14). God's provision of a day of rest and worship, with all the glory now of first-day-of-the-week fulfilment and accomplishment, enables us to grow in holiness and to be more and more consecrated to God.

Our activities on the Lord's Day, therefore, should be conducive to holiness; they should foster holiness in our lives and conduct. They should enable us to draw closer to God and to develop a more Christlike mindset, character and worldview. Nothing ought to come in between a believer and that great objective.

The problem with the 'every day a holy day' approach is simply that if everything is holy, nothing is holy. By that I simply mean that if every day is the same, and we are under no moral obligation to observe the Lord's Day as a Christian Sabbath, then there is a whole strand of biblical teaching that we discount to our great loss and disadvantage. There are things common to our lives here—our work, our friendships, our families—in which we must be consecrated to the Lord. But in addition, we have been given one day each week in which we can grow in that consecration.

The Lord's Day is holy, and it speaks of the work of God in the lives of his people, as he makes them holy too. One of my primary concerns, therefore, is that we should ask ourselves regarding all of our activities on the Lord's Day—is this something that will draw me closer to Jesus? That will help me to hate sin? That will deepen my desire to be holy in every aspect of my life and witness?

IS WHAT I DO ON THE LORD'S DAY NECESSARY?

The Puritans identified two categories of work which the Bible sanctions on the Sabbath. First is the category of *necessity*. Jesus illustrates this principle in the cornfields. The pharisees accused him of Sabbath-breaking, because he began to pluck grain and eat the corn. But, citing in his defence the incident of David in the temple, he both asserts his authority over the Sabbath and illustrates the point that some things are necessary on the Sabbath day.

Johannes Vos, in his commentary on the Westminster Larger Catechism, asks the question 'What is meant by 'works of necessity'?' and gives the following lengthy response:

Strictly speaking, works of necessity are works which cannot be avoided, or cannot be postponed until another day. If a house catches fire, the blaze must be extinguished immediately; this is a work of necessity, and does not violate the Sabbath. Domestic animals must be fed and watered; cows must be milked; such tasks are necessary because they cannot be postponed; they do not violate the Sabbath. Even work which might be postponed may properly be performed on the Sabbath, if it results in eliminating other and greater work on the Sabbath day. If fifteen minutes spent repairing an automobile will save two hours of time that would be required to drive to church with a team of horses, or to walk to church, it is legitimate to repair the automobile, because this will result in the least total amount of work on the Sabbath day. There must of course be some allowance for differences of opinion among Christian people about what constitutes a true work of necessity on the Sabbath. Some things are regarded as necessary by conscientious Christians of the present day, which in times past would perhaps not have been considered necessary. The Bible teaches the principle that works of necessity may be done on the Sabbath, and gives some examples of the application of this principle. But the Bible does not provide a ready-made definition of a 'work of necessity', such as could be applied to all cases. By inference from the teachings of the Bible we may say that a work of necessity is (a) that which cannot be postponed; or (b) that work which results in eliminating the greatest possible amount of work on the Sabbath day.[7]

Vos's explanation seems to me to provide a commonsense approach to the whole matter of what constitutes those works which are necessary on the Lord's Day, on the Christian Sabbath. May our activity be easily postponed to some other day? Or may it enable us to reduce the amount of work needing to be done? At the very least, Vos does us the service of highlighting that there is no list of prescribed or proscribed duties: the Sabbath principle of the fourth commandment is a moral one, and must be applied to each situation in turn.

Perhaps it is in this area too that we need to revisit Colossians 2:16, with its prohibition against passing judgement on others regarding a Sabbath. Not everything that is necessary for me to do on the Sabbath day is necessary for my brother Christian to do. It would be quite out of biblical character for anyone—individual, church or organization—to draw up a list of prohibitions. What is 'necessary' may vary from person to person, place to place, or even culture to culture.

But the rule of thumb is still a good one. I remember, as both an undergraduate and a postgraduate, making a conscious decision to do no secular studying on the Lord's Day. I watched other students pour over their course notes and textbooks at all hours, day and night, seven days a week, but I had always been taught the principle that as far as Sunday was concerned—'if it is not necessary, don't'. God honoured that commitment, I believe. What a blessing not to have been under secular pressure, having been liberated into a spiritual reality! Of course, I had Christian friends who did study on Sunday, and I cannot pass judgement on their decision to do so. All I know is that it was not necessary for me, and I lost nothing by spending my Sundays differently.

I mentioned my native Isle of Lewis in my introduction to this book. Sabbatarianism has long been a cherished principle in the island of my youth and now of my work and adult years. In common with other places, people lament the decline of traditional culture, native language and traditional industry. Others push for change, not least in what may or may not be done on a Sunday.

But one thing I observe in all the changes which have taken place from my childhood until now: never was the economy of the island so robust, or its unemployment so low as in the days of evangelical ascendancy, when the vast majority of the people attended church on Sundays, and the harbour was full of fishing boats, moored on Sunday ready to face the demands of a coming working week. There was no talk then of fishing quotas, or of the scarcity of a catch. Do we really think there is no connection between the Creator who owns the fullness of the seas, and the day he claims as his own? Our forefathers here knew the meaning of 'works of necessity', and, though their life was often hard, they grew up with a sense of community and of belonging which the current generation knows nothing of. It is 'the people that know their God' that shall 'stand firm and take action' (Daniel 11:32).

IS WHAT I DO ON THE LORD'S DAY GOING TO BE OF BENEFIT TO OTHERS?

A second category of work which the Puritans identified as permissible on the Sabbath was that of *works of mercy*. Again, Vos is worth quoting in full:

This means work done chiefly without any motive of financial gain, but because of sympathy and compassion for human suffering. Physicians and nurses may properly care for the sick on the Sabbath day, and of course they are entitled to compensation for such work, but what makes such work legitimate on the Sabbath is not the element of profit, but the element of relieving suffering. To visit the sick is certainly proper on the Sabbath, provided it is done with a right motive.[8]

Again, Christ himself provides the supreme endorsement of this position. It is no accident that the Gospel accounts combine Jesus' healing miracles with his witness to the Sabbath, leading to him pose the question on one occasion: 'Is it lawful on the Sabbath day to do good or to do harm, to save life or to kill?' (Mark 3:4). On another, he highlighted the hypocrisy of the Pharisees in their complaint that he had healed on the Sabbath with these words: 'Does not each of you on the Sabbath untie his ox or his donkey from the manger and lead it away to water it? And ought not this woman, a daughter of Abraham whom Satan bound for eighteen years, be loosed from this bond on the Sabbath day?' (Luke 13:15–16).

The principle here is that the Sabbath was always intended to *improve* man's position and condition. In a good world, it was better for man to work. In a good world, it was better for man to have a wife. In a good world, it was better for man to have a Sabbath day. The day was made for man.

And by both precept and example, Jesus himself shows us that benefiting others with charity and mercy is a legitimate application of the Sabbath principle. We can be channels of blessing to others in the way we use our Sabbath, as much as in the way we benefit from it ourselves. We can show hospitality, we can visit the sick, we can engage in things that extend the love and compassion of Jesus Christ into a sinful, fallen world.

Of course there is a sense in which we must be like this all the time. But Jesus does not highlight all time—he highlights Sabbath time. If the Sabbath principle ended with him, then there was no time left for the Pharisees to recover the true meaning of the Sabbath! Here he was teaching them that their prejudices, their hardness and their hypocrisy were together driving a legalistic sabbatarianism which had no place in God's plans. There is a right way to do it, he taught. But according to some current views, the Sabbath was about to end with his work on the cross, so they only had until then to get it right!

It is quite ludicrous to imagine that the principles Jesus taught were merely occasional. They were timeless. And his rules governing the proper interpretation and application of the Sabbath were not intended to be valid only for the remaining few months of his life. They were to be valid until the eternal Sabbath dawns, and the Lord of the Sabbath descends from heaven with a shout.

Then, he will judge the living and the dead. Not the least measure of judgement will be the acts of compassion and the deeds of kindness done in his name (Matthew 25:41–46). If we could imbibe that spirit and follow that example in our lives, it would transform our Sabbath-keeping, and perhaps even the world around us.

IS WHAT I DO ON THE LORD'S DAY GOING TO GIVE CREDIT AND HONOUR TO JESUS CHRIST?

Isn't it ironic that as our society is becoming increasingly multi-faith, it is also becoming increasingly secular? That means that the more religions we have, the less religious we become. We have legitimatized almost every expression of spirituality, yet society, in general, has no interest in the things of God. It is willing to give us religious places like garden allotments—each can do his or her own thing, and sow whatever seed he or she wishes to sow, as long as each one stays on his or her own turf.

Yet the Christian believer is called to make a *public* profession. It is not adequate for the Christian church to retreat to its own corner of the spiritual garden, tending its own soil. We are called to take up a cross and follow Jesus; and you cannot do that without being noticed!

So the question I want to ask here is whether our Sunday activities exalt the name of Jesus Christ? Obviously if we belong to a Christian church, then our worship will give praise to the Saviour. But I am just a little bit concerned that the actual physical act of going to church for many Christians is not a Christ-honouring thing. By that I mean simply this: that the day is long gone in most places where you could recognize the churchgoing public by their appearance. They dressed appropriately for the occasion. For them, going to church was not like going shopping: it was an altogether different form and level of activity. A churchgoing family on the street could readily be identified as such.

Now I realize there is more to Christianity than churchgoing, and more to churchgoing than dressing up. But is dressing down the answer? Do we not have the opportunity, as soon as we step outside our door on a Sunday morning, to show publicly to the whole world where it is we are going? Indeed, in this age of secularization, churchgoing on a Sunday is one of the few habits left to us to demonstrate in a public way what Jesus means to us.

And what about our family lives on a Sunday? Do our private activities give credit to Jesus Christ? Or, to put it another way, does what we do at home on Sunday show that as a family we are devoted to honouring Jesus Christ?

It is important, I think, to note the importance of families in God's purposes of grace and in salvation history. God made a covenant with Abraham *and his children after him*. He had already saved the family of Noah in the ark at the time of the flood. The covenant sign of circumcision (Genesis 17:11) was a clear indicator of God's intention to sanctify the children through the faith of the parents. In Reformed paedobaptism, this principle is the all-important foundation for the practice of infant baptism, on the grounds that 'the promise is for you and for your children' (Acts 2:39).

The family unit was important to God at creation—every bit as important as the Sabbath ordinance. The two are inextricably linked; God gave Adam a wife on day six, and set the example of rest and worship on day seven. It was a family day because it was a holy day. So when we hear Joshua say 'as for me and my house, we will serve the LORD' (Joshua 24:15), we know he means that his household are marked out as covenant members of the covenant community, and they will keep the Sabbath, the day given for the household to rest.

So one test we can apply to our Sabbath observance is this: does the way we spend Sunday in the bosom of our family demonstrate that we are a covenant component of a covenant community? Does it show that in every area of life we are committed to honouring God? And does it show that in the area of God's sacred time, we will not encroach on what is properly his, but will yield to his authority over our lives?

This is how Ligon Duncan and Terry Johnson argue the point:

There is a subtlety to Sabbath observance. Because it excludes secular activity, its 'holy rest' comes to dominate all of life. The family's week must be organized around its inactivity. Consequently, it can function as a plumbline, a litmus test for measuring your commitment to God. Will you submit to the lordship of Christ in this tangible way, this way that forces you to organize your life, to prepare, to complete your secular affairs, and to devote half of 'your' weekend to the things of God?[9]

That is the nature of Sabbath observance under the new covenant. It is not discarded because every day and every activity is sacred. It is the litmus test that in everything we do, we honour Christ above all. If we will not give him this, his day, what will we give him?

IS WHAT I DO ON THE LORD'S DAY GOING TO COMPROMISE MY WITNESS AS A BELIEVER?

In a way this follows on from the last point. If my Sunday activities are secular ones, then they are by definition unnecessary, and they fail to honour Jesus Christ. That is why I cannot agree with the argument from

Peter Baker on the issue of professional sportsmen and women. A profession of faith in Jesus does not necessarily secure a public witness for him through competing on the Lord's Day. This is no polemic against professional sportsmen and women, whose Christian character is demonstrated in many ways through the media. Yet I cannot help feeling that something has been lost when those who profess to honour the Lord do not honour his day.

What could be more uncompromising in our witness, less worldly and self-focused than to devote one day in seven to God as he commanded and as Scripture recommends? We need men and women of God in the world of professional sport. That world requires light and salt too. But we would do well to heed the counsel of President Edwards: 'the first day of the week should be distinguished in the Christian church from other days of the week, as a Sabbath, to be devoted to religious exercises'.[10]

It is part of the tragedy of the professing Christian church at the current time that she is so divided over this issue of observance of the Lord's Day as the Christian Sabbath. If we cannot speak with a unified voice on so fundamental a matter as an issue over which Jesus proclaims his own lordship, then we cannot walk together or win the world. Sadly, there are many Christians in the public eye whose Sabbath observance could be a clear and bright signal of devotion to Jesus Christ were it not for the misguided theology that has taught them that no such requirement now remains in existence.

IS WHAT I DO ON THE LORD'S DAY GOING TO HELP THE TASK OF THE CHURCH?

This brings me to a more fundamental point still. Perhaps what *is* actually lacking in the worldview of today's Christian is a high enough view of the church. Traditionally, Sunday was the day one 'went to church'—the day and the institution went together. It is not surprising to discover now, however, that the one stands or falls with the other. As Christians embrace the view that it does not really matter on which day we worship, so they find that the church in which we worship becomes a matter of personal choice too. And at the same time, as church life in modern Western society erodes and gives way to new, 'seeker friendly' forms of evangelism, times and days of worship must bend to accommodate the needs of those who are actually seeking.

Perhaps the problem is, as David Wells expresses it, that 'Scripture speaks of the church in exalted terms, but what we see of it in the world is often quite disappointing'.[11] Charles Colson suggests that 'the church of fact is always struggling to conform to the church of faith, and the Christian must live in the midst of this tension'.[12] By definition, the church is made up of sinners—sinners saved by grace, but none of them sinless. Such perfection awaits the church in glory; it is not to be experienced here. So if you want to know what's wrong with the church: it's me!

But we need to recover the high ground claimed by the Bible for the people of God. They are the *building* of Christ (Matthew 16:18; Ephesians 2:20), the *body* of Christ (1 Corinthians 12:27) and the *bride* of Christ (Ephesians 5:25, Revelation 19:7). It was for the church that he died and it is the church that he loves. We cannot think of Christ apart from the church, and we cannot think of the church apart from Christ.

And nor must we think of the Lord of the Church as distinct from the Lord of the Sabbath. He has joined together place and time. He did that in the Old Testament when he gave many sabbaths and localized places of worship. And he does it still, in the simplicity of the New Testament structure, where the blessing of the Spirit came on the first day of the week on the infant new testament church, and the followers of Jesus regularly met thereafter on the first day of the week.

Let's be clear about this: neither the gathering of the church nor the holy day of worship was optional for these early Christians. Instinctively, as the Lord poured out his Spirit at Pentecost, the believers 'devoted themselves to the apostles' teaching and fellowship, to the breaking of bread and to prayers' (Acts 2:42). They were solemnly counselled by the writer to the Hebrews in these words:

Let us hold fast the confession of our hope without wavering, for he who promised is faithful. And let us consider how to stir up one another to love and good works, not neglecting to meet together, as is the habit of some, but encouraging one another, and all the more as you see the Day drawing near (Hebrews 10:23–5).

That reference to the 'Day' is interesting: it refers to the coming day of the Lord, the day of the coming of the Lord. It is the day to which the original

Sabbath pointed, and which the New Testament Sabbath anticipates. And in the light of that coming 'Day', the believers are solemnly admonished not to neglect their meeting together.

Nor were they left to decide among themselves which day was their day of worship. 'On the first day of the week' is what Paul wrote in 1 Corinthians 16:2. No introduction, no explanation: it is simply stated as a bald, bland observation. Give your offering at your weekly meeting, on the first day.

Perhaps it is because we are so used to choices in our lives that we find it so easy to opt out of choosing church. Sadly, the choices, which used to be within mainstream evangelicalism, are now in all kinds of spiritualities; in addition to which, 'for the first time in history the church faces powerful, organized, and systematic *secular* competition for the cure of souls'.[13] For many people, church commitment is negotiable in a way that commitment to the secular institutions that govern our lives is not. We easily opt out of church when we would not miss an important social function. We need to reform our priorities if we are to make an impact on our generation.

We need to recover the idea of the church as essential, as a non-negotiable. Consider again Ligon Duncan and Terry Johnson:

If you are not convinced that the whole of Sunday is the Lord's and not yours, you will not be consistent. You will inevitably allow other matters to interfere. Things will come up. But, if you are convinced that Sunday is the market day of the soul, then it changes everything. The question of the Sunday services is settled—you will be there morning and evening. That the issue is dead, so to speak, has a wonderfully therapeutic effect ... Eliminating options help. Because Sunday worship is an inflexible given, everything else has to accommodate it. The fourth commandment tends thereby to cast its influence over the rest of the week.[14]

That is surely what the New Testament church discovered. By meeting together to worship the risen Christ, by making the gathering of the church a priority, they found a key by which to regulate their lives and manage their affairs. Is it not always so? Once we give Jesus his rightful place, everything else will fall into place. Did he not make exactly such a promise? This is his core promise:

Do not be anxious, saying, 'What shall we eat?' or 'What shall we drink?' or 'What shall we wear?' For the Gentiles[15] seek after all these things, and your heavenly Father knows what you need them all. But seek first the kingdom of God and his righteousness and all these things will be added to you (Matthew 6:31–3).

What about ...?

I realize that issues regarding Sabbath observance are not always easy to resolve, particularly for parents. Increasingly, Sunday has become the day for local sports fixtures, friends' birthday parties and employment. It can be difficult to refuse an invitation to an event because it is held on Sunday. And no parents want their children subjected to unnecessary pressures when the time comes for them to seek work. If it is true, as I have argued above, that our Lord's Day observance can be a public badge of our loyalty to Christ, it can also be the issue that will bring scorn, ridicule and contempt. But if the Son of Man is Lord of the Sabbath, we have it on his own authority that 'whoever is ashamed of me and of my words in this adulterous and sinful generation, of him will the Son of Man also be ashamed when he comes in the glory of his Father with the holy angels' (Matthew 8:38).

That means that, whatever the cost for honouring Christ and his day in this world, it is worth it for the honour he will do us in the next. He takes note of every situation, assesses our every motive, and weighs up our every action. He truly does look on the heart.

Still, tricky situations remain. I know of one evangelical minister who conducted a marriage service in his church on a Sunday. That had never been the practice in his church before, and it caused some discussion. Holding weddings on Sundays is perhaps not an issue in other places, but among believers with a high sabbatarian ethic, it upset several people. The minister justified it, however, on the grounds that it is lawful to do good on the Sabbath day. Marriage is both lawful and good, so it must be right. No?

Let's go back to the creation ordinances. Along with the Sabbath, God set the marriage ethic and the work ethic into the pattern of man's life in an unfallen world. Yet the Sabbath commandment effectively modifies one creation ordinance by another: although work is good and beneficial, it is proscribed on the Sabbath.

Can we not argue, therefore, that it is the same for marriage? That the Sabbath principle modifies this too—that although marriage is good for mankind, it is not necessary to conduct a marriage ceremony on the day which God uniquely claims as his own. The Decalogue guards the morality and sanctity both of marriage and the Sabbath, yet it is possible that the conducting of a wedding ceremony on a Sunday will go contrary to the ethos of the very law which guards it.

There is also the fact that the creation ordinance of marriage requires only three elements to constitute a valid marriage union in the eyes of God: a leaving of one's parents, a cleaving to one's partner, and a physical union. Culturally, practices differ from place to place, of course, and perhaps the greatest difficulty is not in the marriage ceremony itself taking place on a Sunday, but the festivities that accompany it encroaching on the sacred time which belongs to God.

In contemporary society, these are not easy issues to deal with, and churches need to be sensitive both to the principles they uphold and the people they represent. At last, however, God's Word is our authority, and increasingly we need to resist the secularizing trends that encroach on our church practice.

This also raises the issue of public protest about issues of Lord's Day observance. What grounds do we have to expect our society to conform to the fourth commandment? And are we encroaching on civil liberties and human rights if we protest against unnecessary travel, or increased shopping opportunities on the Lord's Day?

It seems to me that the issue of civil liberties ('It is my right to travel on a Sunday plane if I so wish …') is a red herring in most cases. By its very nature, law *curtails* liberty, in order to give true liberty room to express itself and to grow. True freedom is not the freedom to do absolutely anything we like—that would lead to chaos and confusion. I have no right to take someone else's money out of the bank, or to drive at 80 miles per hour through a thirty miles per hour speed restriction.

So there are some issues over which the matter of 'human rights' becomes a pretext for lawlessness. We need standards. We need absolute standards. And for that we need a lawgiver. Ravi Zacharias is correct: 'Only a moral system that is logical, meaningful and practical has answers for any society. In hard terms, the morality that atheism teaches, implies or espouses is unlivable'.[16]

That is why we need to recognize that the moral absolutes of the Ten Commandments are, as we have seen, a reflection of the nature of God himself. Life is sacred because he is holy. Marriage is sacred because he is holy. Truth is sacred because he is holy.

Is it right for us to campaign publicly to uphold moral standards in society? Is it right for us to campaign against abortion? Against euthanasia? For marriage? Against same-sex unions? Is it right for Christians to raise a voice in protest against television programmes which publicly and flagrantly defame and blaspheme the name of Jesus Christ? Against licensing laws which would give people unlimited access to alcohol, irrespective of the damage caused to homes, families and communities as a result?

Either we allow a godless, secular, atheistic philosophy to determine what is permissible, or else we raise a voice for the ethics and standards of the bible. And that includes the moral absolute governing our use of the Lord's Day.

Let's also remember that moral absolutes are for our good. They are designed to protect us from harm, to enable us to live the kind of lives God would have us live. It is clearly not good for people to work constantly without a break. Were the great social reformers of the nineteenth century, men like William Wilberforce and Lord Shaftesbury, not driven by their realization that God provided for a day of rest? Will we be silenced from speaking out about immoral employment legislation on the basis of some misguided view of the obsolescence of the fourth commandment?

The tragedy is that everything has been cheapened in our world. Life is cheap. Marriage is cheap. Once you lose sight of the sacred, you cheapen the secular. That is why sensitive, Christlike, gentle protest against the removal of any sacred time from society's calendar is not just desirable. It is essential if we are to prevent our world from slipping deeply into the despair that atheism brings.

Conclusion

This chapter has argued that the biblical principles of Sabbath observance, re-cast in the New Testament in the form of Lord's Day observance, need to be applied by today's Christians in home, school, work and church. It has also argued that there are many areas of difficulty for believers in today's society. But the only alternative to a Sabbath-keeping society is a godless one. And where God is absent, hope is absent too.

Pray—

For Christians in public situations who need to weigh up the matter of what they ought to do or not do on the Lord's Day.

- For today's church, that it will rediscover the blessing of the New Testament Sabbath, and return to wholehearted obedience to the Lord Jesus Christ;
- For agencies and societies which are strenuously resisting secularization at every level, and who are bringing a Christian conscience to bear on public issues;
- For a religious revival, a new Pentecost, and a deep sense of what being in the Spirit on the Lord's Day really means.

The church is the spiritual organism of redemption. The state is the secular, but moral and righteous, organism for safety, justice and welfare in this life. The state is not necessarily Christian. But it is necessarily theistic, because on the atheistic theory its basis, its rights and its healthy existence are lost. Hence, while the church has its use of the Sabbath as the institute of redemption and means of grace, the state has its use of it as the institute of righteousness and the natural knowledge and fear of God. The church accordingly enjoins and seeks to enforce, by her spiritual means, on her members the right spiritual improvement of the day. The state, by its secular power, enjoins and enforces the outward rest of the day, so that the people may, if they will, use it to learn of God and of his righteous law, to cultivate morals and decency, to rest their faculties of body and mind, and to enjoy the ennobling and wholesome moral influences of the family and fireside…

…Theism is essential to the state; the Sabbath is essential to maintain theism. Therefore it is that the state can do no less than maintain an outward Sabbath rest.

Robert L. Dabney, 'The Christian Sabbath', *Discussions,* Vol. II, pp. 549–50

Notes

1 **A. Begg,** *Pathway to Freedom: How God's laws guide our lives* (Chicago: Moody Press), p. 113.

2 Interview with **Jonathan Edwards,** http://www.soon.org.uk/page41.htm, taken from the Internet, March 2005.

3 **Peter Baker,** 'The Lord's Day—an abiding Sabbath?', *The Evangelical Magazine,* July/August 2004, p. 9.

4 **John L. Mackay,** *The Moral Law: Its place in Scripture and its relevance today,* (Newcastle: The Christian Institute, 2004), pp. 42–3.

5 **J.M. Boice,** *Foundations of the Christian Faith* (Leicester: IVP, 1996), p. 43.

6 **J.A. Naude,** שׁדק, New International Dictionary of Old Testament Theology and Exegesis, Volume 3, (Carlisle: Paternoster Press, 1997), p. 880.

7 **J.G. Vos,** *The Westminster Larger Catechism: A Commentary* (Phillipsburg: P&R, 2002), p. 327

8 **Vos,** *Larger Catechism,* p. 328.

9 **J.Ligon Duncan III and Terry L. Johnson,** 'A Call to Family Worship' in **P.G. Ryken, D.W.H. Thomas and J.L. Duncan III** (eds), *Give Praise to God: A Vision for Reforming Worship* (Phillipsburg: P&R, 2003), p. 333.

10 **Edwards,** 'The Perpetuity of the Sabbath', *Works,* Vol. II, p. 94.

11 **David F. Wells,** *Losing our Virtue: Why the Church must recover its moral vision* (Leicester: IVP, 1998), p. 196.

12 **Charles Colson,** *The Body: Being Light in Darkness* (Milton Keynes: Word, 1992), p. 73.

13 **David Powlison,** 'A Flourishing of Fresh Wisdoms: The Call of the Hour in the Ministry of the Word', in **G.L.W. Johnson and R.F. White** (eds), *Whatever Happened to the Reformation?* (Phillipsburg: P&R, 2001), p. 207.

14 **Duncan and Johnson,** 'A Call to Family Worship', p. 333.

15 For 'Gentiles' here, read, 'unbelieving world'.

16 **R. Zacharias,** *A Shattered Visage: The Real Face of Atheism* (Grand Rapids: Baker, 2002), p. 67.

Heaven and the Sabbath

Blessed are the dead who die in the Lord from now on. Blessed indeed, says the Spirit, that they may rest from their labours, for their deeds follow them. Revelation 14:13–14

The worship of the Lord's Day is but a foretaste of the eternal Sabbath yet to come, an emblem of eternal rest.

Cornelis Venema[1]

Island life is never free from tragedy. To live in a place surrounded by water, dependent on the sea, and at the mercy of the weather, inevitably means that sad things happen.

One of the most tragic incidents to happen in the history of my native island of Lewis took place on New Year's Day 1919. Many servicemen were returning from the war, and the sea passage at that time was from Kyle of Lochalsh to Stornoway. Not only were they glad to be going home, but they were also looking forward to celebrating the beginning of a new year with their families.

Some 260 servicemen were assigned to H.M. Yacht *Iolaire*, which carried them safely to the mouth of Stornoway harbour. Within sight of the lights of home, the yacht, which had entered the harbour area at too wide an angle, struck a rock. In the blackness of the night, about three quarters of those on board had perished, lost at sea within yards of land.

Many homes which had eagerly awaited the safe return of their husbands, sons and fathers from the Great World War, now received their bodies for burial. The disaster etched itself deep into the psyche of the Isle of Lewis, affecting every village. Followed by a mass of emigrations to the USA and Canada, it contributed greatly to the decline of a subsequent generation.

The pathos of the story is deeply moving. Home can be so near, yet so far away. How tragic to perish within sight of home! But what a blessing for those who know that their safety is assured, and that they will one day see the King in his beauty, and the land of far distances.

We are going to conclude our look at the Sabbath principle in the Bible and in the lives of God's people by thinking briefly about the Sabbath which is to come. Early on we noted the fact that, by resting on the seventh day of creation, God gave an indication of the point to which he was bringing the world, with the ultimate aim of the world enjoying the fullness of his own presence.

That purpose was never changed or replaced. God still intends to bring a people to glory with him, and to give them a place in his nearer presence. What that first day of rest represented, each Sabbath in Israel's annual calendar also represented. And although the coming of Jesus Christ secured the purposes of redemption to the extent of bringing the old ceremonies to an end and altering the day of rest and worship, still the story awaits its consummation.

Theologians talk about the 'now' and the 'not yet'—and there is a sense in which much that God purposed to do by grace has been achieved. Yet we still anticipate a better future:

What we will be has not yet appeared; but we know that when he appears we shall be like him, because we shall see him as he is (1 John 3:2).

The purpose of God's redemption embraces all the ages: 'those whom he predestined he also called, and those whom he called he also justified, and those whom he justified he also glorified' (Romans 8:30). We have everything in Jesus Christ, if our trust is in him alone. But the final chapter is hidden behind the veil that separates this world from the next.

The Bible has a great deal to say about heaven, about what it is like there, about who is there, about what they do there, and about how to get there. It leaves us in no doubt that Jesus himself, with his execution and death approaching, fully expected that his people would join him in the glory to which he was going (John 17:24). That was the consolation he gave them as the prospect of his suffering and death was weighing on their spirits (John 14:1–2). And it was the prospect that fortified the apostles too. Consider the words of Paul, as he comes near the end of his life:

I have fought the good fight. I have finished the race. I have kept the faith. Henceforth there is laid up for me the crown of righteousness which the Lord, the righteous judge, will award to me on that Day, and not only to me but also to all who have loved his appearing (2 Timothy 4:7–8).

This was what made all the difficulties of the missionary and the evangelistic task worth the while: that 'this slight momentary affliction is preparing us for an eternal weight of glory beyond all comparison' (2 Corinthians 4:17). In the light of heaven, trials and difficulties will be worth it all.

I've already suggested that there is a connection between the Sabbath principle and the hope of heaven. In what sense can we understand that further? How does the Sabbath shed light for us on the kind of place heaven is? How does the Bible's teaching about heaven help us to appreciate the kind of day the Sabbath is? Let's conclude our study by trying to catch a glimpse of home, and by seeing how closely related the twin themes of heaven and the Sabbath really are.

Much could be said, but let me highlight six things the Bible says about heaven.

Heaven is a holy place

How could it be otherwise? It is particularly the abode of the Holy One of Israel. From earliest times he was designated 'The LORD, the God of heaven' (Genesis 24:7), and declared through Moss that 'the LORD is God in heaven above and on the earth beneath; there is no other' (Deuteronomy 4:39). At the dedication of the temple there is an interesting juxtaposition of the idea of God's dwelling-place being in heaven and his special and localized dwelling in the temple:

But will God indeed dwell on the earth? Behold, heaven and the highest heaven cannot contain you; how much less this house that I have built! Yet have regard to the prayer of your servant, and to his plea, O LORD my God, listening to the cry and to the prayer that your servant prays before you this day, that your eyes may be open night and day towards this house, the place of which you have said, 'My name shall be there'... (1 Kings 8:27–29).

With that the glory cloud filled the temple (8:11). David reinforces the connection between heaven and the temple by calling the Ark of the Covenant 'the footstool of our God' (1 Chronicles 28:2). Remember that the Ark contained a copy of the Ten Commandments, highlighting their moral nature and their distinctive characteristics. By thus describing the Ark as the footstool of the God who sits enthroned in heaven, David is reinforcing the connection between the Sabbath law, along with all other laws, and the place of God's splendour.

The imagery is brought to a climax in the book of Revelation, where the temple is identified with the Lamb who is the brightness of the heavenly city. And it is in this context that John tells us that 'nothing unclean will ever enter it, nor anyone who does what is detestable or false, but only those who are written in the Lamb's book of life' (Revelation 21:27). The whole tenor of the Bible's teaching is that while sin mars everything here, nothing will spoil the peace and happiness of God's people in the glory to come.

Heaven is where God sits on the throne of his holiness (Psalm 47:8), and where holy angels sing of the greater holiness of their God (Isaiah 6:3), even as the prophet complains of his own lack of holiness (Isaiah 6:5). The way to heaven is a way of holiness (Isaiah 35:8), and without holiness none of us shall see God (Hebrews 12:14).

How can there not be a connection between the Sabbath, the day that speaks primarily of the holiness of the God of the covenant, and heaven, the place of holiness to which God is bringing his people? Ezekiel pointed out that the Sabbath was not simply a sign of God's own holiness, but a sign that he was *sanctifying* his people, and making them holy (Ezekiel 20:12).

God's people abhor sin. There is a principle of sanctification in their souls: God has set them apart to be holy, and he is perfecting holiness through his work in them, day by day, moment by moment, hour by hour. As we look to Christ now, 'we all, with unveiled face, beholding the glory of the Lord, are being transformed into the same image from one degree of glory to another' (2 Corinthians 3:18). Everything God gives us he gives with this end in view: that we will be better prepared for that place in which he dwells.

And the Sabbath principle is a constant in our lives, a reminder that the God who sanctifies never gives up on his people. He is even now giving them a foretaste of the holiness which they will enjoy when all sin is eradicated from their existence, and they are made like Jesus. A holy Lord's Day, free from the trappings of secularism, free from the pressures of living in a fallen world, focusing on the word, and observed in the presence of God, is the nearest thing we can ever have in this world to what we can expect in the world to come. That's a good reason to keep the Sabbath!

Heaven is a place of rest

Second, heaven is a place where we are freed from the burdens we had to carry in this wilderness world. It is a place into which we enter free of all care. Like the mariners of Psalm 107, we find ourselves here tossed about on the sea of life, but God brings his people home: 'then they were glad that the waters were quiet, and he brought them to their desired haven' (Psalm 107:30).

Heaven was a rest for Christ, after the labours of his earthly ministry. He received the glory promised him by the Father (John 17:5), and was able to promise a thief crucified with him that that very day they would be together in Paradise (Luke 23:43). Jesus entered into Sabbath rest, just as God entered into Sabbath rest. And that is the rest that awaits us.

For Jesus, heaven's rest does not mean that there he does nothing. He is preparing a place for his people (John 14:3), he is interceding for them (Romans 8:34), he equips his church (Ephesians 4:11–12). Perfect rest is not the rest of inactivity; it is the rest of *holy* activity.

So the images which the New Testament uses for heaven combine the ideas of rest and of work. On the one hand, God's people will be brought into the Father's house (John 14:2), with all the implications there of home, security, comfort and peace. They will enjoy a place free from crying and pain (Isaiah 35:11, Revelation 21:4), free from sickness and death, and full of the consolation of God's immediate presence. They will be fully satisfied when they awaken with God's likeness (Psalm 17:15).

On the other hand, they will freely and willingly engage in the activities of heaven, following the Lamb and being fed by him (Revelation 7:17), singing his praise and reigning eternally as kings (Revelation 22:5). There is this remarkable and wonderful combination of metaphors that speak of respite and metaphors that speak of activity.

All of which has its counterpart in our Sabbath observance. There is something quite wrong if our Lord's Day observance simply amounts to a state of 'suspended animation'; it ought to be one of *sacred*, holy animation. One preacher illustrates it graphically this way:

> I find myself regularly falling asleep about three o'clock in the afternoon with chills of gratitude and pleasure for the rest of the Christian Sabbath. Amazingly, even for preachers for whom Sunday is the busiest day of the week, it is also the most restful.[2]

So Eryl Davies is right:

> We should rejoice in anticipating the Sabbath-rest of heaven. There will be no exhausting or dreary work to do there. All God's family will be present and we shall perfectly enjoy the Lord's fellowship and grace. No matter how precious and enjoyable our Sabbath days are here in this world, remember that they are only a shadow of that glorious Sabbath-rest we shall enjoy in heaven.[3]

There are activities appropriate to the Lord's Day now, as there were activities appropriate to the Old Testament Sabbath. And they are the activities that are appropriate to heaven. How can we not enjoy the Lord's Day if we are looking forward to heaven? And how will we enjoy heaven if we do not have a high regard for the Lord's Day Sabbath which we are privileged to enjoy and experience every week of our lives?

Heaven is a place of worship

The supreme activity of heaven is the worship of God in Christ. For all the privileges that are ours in the age of the Holy Spirit, we do everything here through a dim veil; 'we see through a mirror dimly, but then face to face' (1 Corinthians 13:12). The perfect is going to come (1 Corinthians 13:10), and when it does, everything that belonged to the experience of the church here among the shadows of this sinful world will give way to something greater, something more glorious than we have possibly been able to envisage.

As soon as John catches a glimpse of heaven in Revelation 4:2, he sees a throne. The throne is the dominant motif. Everything in heaven speaks about the crowning glory and the majestic supremacy of the Lord Jesus

Christ. And where he is, he is worshipped. The living creatures sing of his holiness and bless him for his having made all things (Revelation 4:8–11). A 'new song' is sung in which the Lamb is praised for his work of redemption (Revelation 5:9). And those who surround the throne serve him in his temple (Revelation 7:10). The vision John saw was the vision of a glorified church at worship.

Worship is what we are made for. God redeems his people, gives them a sacred place, and leads them into worship. That pattern recurs throughout Scripture, and will be consummated when the people of God are victorious over their enemies, including death, the 'last enemy' (1 Corinthians 15:26). They will then have a place of worship, around the throne of God and of the Lamb.

Worship was a dominant theme of Old Testament Sabbath observance. The day was to be 'sanctified', and given to God, lived in a remarkable way in his presence and before his face. The New Testament Sabbath, the Lord's Day, was the day of worship for the early church. And the activity of worship further connects the Sabbath here with the heaven that is to come.

One of the Old Testament Psalms is given the heading 'A Song for the Sabbath'. It says that 'it is good to give thanks to the LORD, to sing praises to your name, O Most High' (Psalm 92:1). It goes on to talk about God's work being the source of our joy (v 4), it contrasts the eternality of God with the temporality of man (vv 7–9), it rejoices in a personal knowledge of God's work in human life (vv 10–11), and it concludes with the beautiful image of God's people planted like the cedars of Lebanon in God's house, bearing fruit and demonstrating the faithfulness of God (vv 12–15).

These are the themes of the worship of God's people still, and will be their song throughout the ages of eternity. They will sing of the mercy of the Lord for ever, as Psalm 89:1 puts it. The song of heaven is 'the song of Moses, the servant of God, and the song of the Lamb' (Revelation 15:3), a song that embraces the whole sweep of redemptive history from the first climactic moments of Israel's release from Egypt to the consummate redemption of God's people from the grave.

And these ought to be our themes each Lord's Day, as we take up the Word of God anew, submit to its authority, learn its meaning, apply its precepts, sing its praises, proclaim its gospel and exalt its Christ. We worship God week by week because heaven-bound pilgrims love to do so, and will do so throughout all eternity.

Heaven is for family

Heaven will be the gathering together of the family of God. Already we know that we have much in common with glorified saints. We are 'fellow citizens with the saints and members of the household of God' (Ephesians 2:19). We have been asked to come, not to Mount Sinai, with its thunderings and threatenings, but

To Mount Zion and to the city of the living God, the heavenly Jerusalem, and to innumerable angels in festal gathering and to the assembly of the firstborn who are enrolled in heaven, and to God, the judge of all, and to the spirits of the righteous made perfect, and to Jesus, the mediator of a new covenant, and to the sprinkled blood that speaks a better word than the blood of Abel (Hebrews 12:22–4).

Our present life is lived on earth, yet 'our citizenship is in heaven' (Philippians 3:20). This much we have in common with all of God's children.

Hebrews 2 describes the work of Jesus as our priest. It talks of how Jesus was made lower than the angels, and was made like his people. Those whom he was to save were partakers of 'flesh and blood', so he too became like them:

For it was fitting that he, for whom and by whom all things exist, in bringing many sons to glory, should make the founder of their salvation perfect through suffering. For he who sanctifies and those who are sanctified all have one origin. That is why he is not ashamed to call them brothers, saying, 'I will tell of your name to my brothers; in the midst of the congregation I will sing your praise' (Hebrews 2:10–12).

The reason the eternal Son of God partook of flesh and blood, coming down to earth and living and dying among men, was so that he would take 'many sons' back to heaven with him. Here is something that all his people have in common: he is Saviour, brother, friend to them all, and they are all one in him (Galatians 3:28). When the work of redemption is consummated, Jesus will be resplendent in the glory of heaven and will be able to say, 'Behold, I and the children whom the LORD has given me are signs and portents in Israel from the LORD of hosts who dwells on Mount Zion' (Isaiah 8:18).

Time and again Jesus expresses the conviction that ultimately, all his people will be together in glory. He teaches that the Son of Man will gather all his elect people to one place, from every corner of the universe (Matthew 24:31). When he institutes the Lord's Supper, Jesus anticipates a heavenly banquet with all his disciples in a better place (Matthew 26:29). To those who stayed with him in his trials, Jesus promises a kingdom, and offers the prospect of eating and drinking with him in the glory of heaven (Luke 22:28–30). He promises to prepare a place for his people in heaven 'that where I am you may be also' (John 14:3). And ultimately he expresses his desire in this way: 'Father, I desire that they also, whom you have given me, may be with me where I am, to see my glory that you have given me because you loved me before the foundation of the world' (John 17:24).

The apostles carry the same hope forward in their letters. To the Thessalonian believers, mourning their beloved Christian dead, Paul urges consideration of the great doctrine of Christ's return at which, he says, 'the dead in Christ will rise first. Then we who are alive, who are left, will be caught up together with them in the clouds to meet the Lord in the air, and so we will always be with the Lord' (1 Thessalonians 4:16–17). And John, in the Book of Revelation, describes the gathering of heaven like the assembling of a marriage feast; the combined voices of glory sing 'Hallelujah! For the Lord our God the Almighty reigns. Let us rejoice and exult and give him the glory, for the marriage of the Lamb has come, and his Bride has made herself ready; it was granted her to clothe herself with fine linen, bright and pure—for the fine linen is the righteous deeds of the saints' (Revelation 19:6–8).

When God gave the Sabbath to man, it was never to man in isolation. The rest of the seventh day of creation, as we saw, imposed a pattern of behaviour on both Adam and Eve. Together, as the core of the nuclear family, they were to get the benefit of the ordinance of rest, worship and holiness by observing the day of God's rest with him, and with each other. Similarly, the law of the manna in Exodus 16 set apart the seventh day of the week as the day when the whole camp would rest from work and enjoy God's blessing. The fourth commandment stipulated a day of rest, and, in distinction from all the other commandments, addressed a plurality of people ('you, or your son, or your daughter ...'). This was a day for *corporate* rest and worship.

Similarly in the New Testament, the Lord's Day was observed universally by the people of God. They came together on that day. The risen Lord visited the disciples on the day of the resurrection when they were gathered together (John 20:19); similarly the day of Pentecost realized its blessing on the disciples when 'they were all together in one place' (Acts 2:1). To be sure, John kept a Sabbath rest on the Lord's Day even when he was banished to Patmos (Revelation 1:10). His physical isolation did not prevent him from expressing his solidarity with the church which was observing the Lord's Day throughout Asia Minor.

The clear, unmistakable fact of Scripture is that the Sabbath, like heaven, is for all of God's people. It is a family day for us, both literally and spiritually. One of the primary social benefits of the Lord's Day is that it enables families to be together. As I have watched my children grow from youngsters into teenagers, asserting their independence, learning to drive and keeping late hours through the week, I am glad that we start each week together. Modern life means that we see so little of our families in the normal course of things. It's good to have a day when the family unit can be together as such.

But it is also good spiritually: the Lord's Day enables the Lord's people to assemble together as the spiritual family they are. They need to gather, to assemble, and to congregate. From different backgrounds, under different circumstances, with different pressures and concerns, all of God's people have a day, a desire and a duty to meet up for praise and worship. In our Highland Presbyterian tradition, communion times highlight this even more. As I write this, our communion services are about to begin. We can expect to have visitors with us from other congregations on that particular Sunday. They will come from north, south, east and west, and will worship the Lamb. There will be an enlarged family gathering in our church that day.

And that is precisely where the Sabbath principle and the hope of heaven converge. Do we love the gathered assembly of the saints on the Lord's Day? If so, heaven is for us. If not, we are not for heaven. It is surely one of the benchmarks of our real hope of glory that what we expect to do then, in joining with all of God's people to sing his praises for all eternity, we will want to do now, in our weekly anticipation of heaven's promised homecoming.

Heaven is for resurrected saints

Fifth, there is a clear relation between the doctrine of heaven and the doctrine of the resurrection, and this again is a fundamental point at which the Sabbath principle relates clearly to the future hope of the church. Paul deals thoroughly with the doctrine of resurrection in 1 Corinthians 15. Against the philosophical arguments of those who argued that there can be no such thing as a resurrection from the dead, Paul argues that 'if Christ has not been raised, then our preaching is in vain, and your faith is in vain' (v14). More devastating still, he argues, 'those also who have fallen asleep in Christ have perished. If in this life only we have hoped in Christ we are of all people most to be pitied' (vv18–19).

But in fact, Paul argues, the resurrection of Christ was only the beginning: he was 'the firstfruits of those who have fallen asleep' (v 20); 'each in his own order: Christ the firstfruits, then at his coming those who belong to Christ. Then comes the end, when he delivers the kingdom to God the Father after destroying every rule and every authority and power' (vv 23–4).

The doctrine of a future hope goes hand in hand with the doctrine of the resurrection; furthermore, the doctrine of general resurrection goes hand in hand with the doctrine of the personal resurrection of Jesus Christ. Because he triumphed over death, his people will share in that victory and in that conquest.

This is not a specifically New Testament doctrine. Its earliest expression is probably in Job 19:25–27:

For I know that my Redeemer lives, and at the last he will stand upon the earth. And after my skin has been thus destroyed, yet in my flesh I shall see God, whom I shall see for myself, and my eyes shall behold, and not another.

It is celebrated in the Psalms (16:10–11; 17:15; 23:6). It is expressed by Daniel in the memorable words that 'many of those who sleep in the dust of the earth shall awake, some to everlasting life, and some to shame and everlasting contempt' (Daniel 12:3). It becomes the bedrock, foundation doctrine of all New Testament hope and living. The fact that death will give up its dead (Revelation 20:13) means that we have every reason to persevere in the Christian life and walk.

Indeed, it is difficult to find a New Testament passage dealing with the resurrection that does not turn it into the most useful and practical of doctrines. Paul's treatise in 1 Corinthians 15 ends with the great 'therefore, my beloved brothers, be steadfast, immovable, always abounding in the work of the Lord, knowing that in the Lord your labour is not in vain' (v52). Similarly, as Paul reflects that 'we await a Saviour, the Lord Jesus Christ, who will transform our lowly body to be like his glorious body, by the power that enables him even to subject all things to himself', he again draws the implication: 'therefore, my brothers, whom I love and long for, my joy and crown, stand firm thus in the Lord, my beloved' (Philippians 3:21–4:1).

Peter does the same thing. The world will reach its omega point he says, just as the original world was destroyed by a universal flood. God's patience will reach its limit, and he will judge the world in righteousness. Because of that, Peter asks,

what sort of people ought you to be in lives of holiness and godliness, waiting for and hastening the coming of the day of God, because of which the heavens will be set on fire and dissolved, and the heavenly bodies will melt as they burn. But according to his promise we are waiting for new heavens and a new earth in which righteousness dwells. Therefore, beloved, since you are waiting for these, be diligent to be found by him without spot or blemish' (2 Peter 3:11–14).

John, too, brings out the ethical implications of the great doctrine that 'when he appears we shall be like him, because we shall see him as he is'— 'everyone who thus hopes in him purifies himself as he is pure' (1 John 3:2–3).

The glory of heaven is not simply the glory of passing immediately into the presence of Jesus Christ on death. That is certainly taught in Scripture.

To be 'away from the body' is to be 'at home with the Lord' (2 Corinthians 5:8). Paul says to the Philippian believers, 'My desire is to depart and be with Christ, for that is far better' (Philippians 1:23).

Yet what saints experience at death is only intermediate: it is the prelude to something greater, when their bodies, having lain in the dust of the earth, will experience victory over death, resurrection power through Jesus Christ, and will arise, with glorified, spiritually enhanced qualities which will enable them to experience heaven in a way that disembodied souls alone could not. As Joni Eareckson Tada puts it, 'One day, the Resurrection. And then, heaven. Then, rest.'[4]

Is it not interesting that Paul moves from his colossal treatment of resurrection in 1 Corinthians 15 to his statement about collections:

Now concerning the collection for the saints: as I directed the churches of Galatia, so you also are to do. On the first day of every week, each of you is to put something aside and store it up, as he may prosper, so that there will be no collecting when I come (1 Corinthians 16:1–2).

For, as we have seen, it was nothing other than (and could have been nothing *less than*) the resurrection of Jesus Christ that effected the change of day for the church of God in the world, so that the Sabbath principle was to be applied to the first day of the week rather than to the last. With all its overtones of new creation, of fulfilment, of conquest and achievement, the resurrection of Jesus was alone sufficient to re-cast the weekly pattern of worship and work for God's people. It is perfectly natural, therefore, that, having dealt with the major issue of the resurrection, the mind of Paul should turn to the new Sabbath which the resurrection had given the church. Something spectacular had taken place with Christ's resurrection, as a result of which something spectacular will take place for all of God's people. So Paul says 'in the light of this, you do something special when you meet on the first day of the week'. That is the day that speaks of resurrection victory, of the risen Christ, of the reason why heaven is assured.

We believe in the resurrection of the dead. We believe in supernaturalisms, in things that defy natural, rationalistic explanations;

things that are above reason, though not contrary to reason; things that defy explanations on our part, which are mysterious to us. But we believe because Jesus is alive. That is why we keep the Lord's Day Sabbath. And that is why we look forward to heaven too.

Heaven is the place of the King

Finally, heaven is the city of the great King. Everything about the Bible's picture of the future glory of heaven speaks royalty, majesty and sovereignty, from the image of the throne in the centre of heaven (Revelation 4:2), to the concept of 'the new Jerusalem' (Revelation 21). Jerusalem was the city of David, the city of Israel's king, and therefore 'the city of the great King' (Psalm 48:1). It represented God's rule over his people, through his divinely appointed Davidic monarch (Psalm 2:6–8).

The messianic, kingly strands of Old Testament revelation culminate in Jesus Christ. He is King of kings and Lord of lords (Revelation 19:16), 'the root and descendant of David' (Revelation 22:16). Heaven is where God reigns, and it is the place to which the ascended Christ has been exalted; as a consequence of his total obedience to death, 'God has highly exalted him and bestowed on him the name that is above every name' (Philippians 2:9). In the case of the Saviour, resurrection was followed by ascension, and by glorification. He had had glory with the Father before the world existed (John 17:5), but now he was to experience that glorious existence not just as the divine Son, but as the Son who is the God-man. Jesus comes to us as Prophet, Priest and King, and he returns to God as Prophet, Priest and King, having accomplished his work on earth, continuing his work in heaven, and awaiting the promise that he will put 'all his enemies under his feet' (1 Corinthians 15:25).

To be in heaven, therefore, is to 'enter the palace of the king' (Psalm 45:15). Those who have crowned him here as their own Lord and Saviour have the prospect of being with, and honouring, their king, throughout the endless ages of eternity. As kings and priests, they reign with him, sharing in his royal privileges and prerogatives. What Balaam observed in Israel long ago will be realized in its fullness in the glory of heaven: 'The LORD their God is with them, and the shout of a king is among them' (Numbers 23:21).

And, again, that is precisely what the experience of God's people ought to be Sabbath by Sabbath, Lord's Day by Lord's Day. They ought to experience the presence of the Lord and the shout of the king. *Their* Sabbath is *His* Day! It is the King's day, and it is the day on which they gather to the King's house, with the King's people, to hear the King's voice speaking to them in the King's word. There they sing the King's praise, dedicate themselves to the King's service, and receive encouragement in the King's presence. The first day of the week ought to be a day of royal blessing, royal presence and royal pardon.

Ultimately, that is what our study is all about. Is the Lord of the Sabbath the Lord of our lives? Is the King who fills heaven, yet dwells with men on the earth, our Lord and Saviour? Do we have any personal knowledge of the King who conquered death, and by his resurrection transformed the very landscape of redemptive history? Who took us out of the realm of shadows, types and symbols in to the fullness and light of the New Testament? If so, then the prospect before us is that we will dwell in his house for ever, resting, worshipping, praising him in the holy, clean air of the celestial city.

And if that is our hope, then it is our privilege to anticipate it week by week in the observing of a holy day to the Lord 'on the first day of the week'. Let us quicken our step to glory, and quicken our resolve to spend our Sundays in anticipation of the greatest Sabbath of all!

Now in this worthy man there was a concentrating and joining together of the parts of nature and the parts of industry, and likewise of the parts of grace. And that which did steer his conversation, and rule all aright, was indeed the true fear of God, which caused him to set the stamp of religion on all his courses in his whole conversation.

For the Lord's day, it may a little be discerned by that. He had a wonderful care to keep it holy. He was as eminent as any in his profession for that. He would not intermeddle with the businesses of his calling on that day. He did not think it enough to hear the sermon and divine service, and then to go to the works of his calling. And in this he is to be commended. For whose good hath God appointed the Lord's day? Is it not for our own? Should not we grow base and earthly-minded, if one day in seven we should not be heavenly-minded, and think upon our everlasting condition in another world? Shall we think much then of that which God appoints for us?

Richard Sibbes, 'The Bride's Longing': Sermon on Revelation 22:20, preached at the funeral of Sir Thomas Crew and first published 1638, *The Works of Richard Sibbes* (Edinburgh, 1863), Vol. VI, p. 557

Notes

1 C.P. **Venema,** *The Promise of the Future*, (Edinburgh: Banner of Truth, 2000), p. 476.
2 **J.L. Duncan III and T.L. Johnson,** 'A Call to Family Worship', in **P.G. Ryken, D.W.H. Thomas and J.L.Duncan III** (eds), *Give Praise to God*, (Phillipsburg: P&R, 2003), p. 333.
3 **E. Davies,** Heaven *is a far better place: What the Bible teaches about heaven* (Evangelical Press, 1999), p. 139.
4 **Joni Eareckson Tada,** *Heaven: Your Real Home* (Grand Rapids: Zondervan, 1996), p. 200.

There are other resources available for further study on this theme.

Among good discussions of the Lord's Day are Glen Knecht, *The Day God Made* (Edinburgh: Banner of Truth, 2003), Joseph A. Pipa, *The Lord's Day* (Fearn, Tain: Christian Focus Publications, 1997) and Walter Chantry *Call the Sabbath a Delight* (Edinburgh: Banner of Truth, 1991).

Among recommend treatments of the Ten Commandments as a whole are Brian H. Edwards, *The Ten Commandments for Today* (Epsom: Day One Publications, 1996) and Alistair Begg, *Pathway to Freedom* (Chicago: Moody Publishers, 2003).

The following discussions are also very helpful:

New Horizons (the magazine of the Orthodox Presbyterian Church), March 2003, entitled 'Call the Sabbath a Delight'

Discussion of the Lord's Day in the Reports to the General Assembly of the Free Church of Scotland 2005 (available online at http://www.freechurch.org/assembly/reports2005.pdf)

James Packer, 'The Puritans and the Lord's Day', in *Among God's Giants: The Puritan Vision of the Christian Life* (Eastbourne: Kingsway, 1991)

R.L. Dabney, 'The Christian Sabbath: its nature, design and proper observance', in *Discussions of Robert Lewis Dabney*, Vol. 1, (Edinburgh: Banner of Truth, 1982)

B.B. Warfield, 'The Foundations of the Sabbath in the Word of God', in *Selected Shorter Writings Vol. 1*, J. Meeter, ed. (Presbyterian and Reformed, 1980)

P.G. Ryken, D.W.H. Thomas and J. Ligon Duncan III (eds.), *Give Praise to God: A Vision for Reforming Worship* (Presbyterian and Reformed, 2003)

J.L. Mackay, *Exodus: A Mentor Commentary* (Fearn, Tain: Mentor, 2001)

Index

Index